LATIN AMERICAN IDENTITY AND
CONSTRUCTIONS OF DIFFERENCE

Hispanic Issues

HISPANIC ISSUES
VOLUME 10

LATIN AMERICAN IDENTITY AND CONSTRUCTIONS OF DIFFERENCE

AMARYLL CHANADY
◆
EDITOR

UNIVERSITY OF MINNESOTA PRESS
MINNEAPOLIS   LONDON

Grateful acknowledgment is made for permission to reprint from the following: León Portilla, "La filosofía náhuatl," copyright 1957 by León Portilla, reprinted by permission of the Universidad National Autónoma de México; Derek Walcott, *Omeros*, copyright 1990 by Derek Walcott, reprinted by permission of Farrar, Straus & Giroux, Inc.

The publishers ask copyright holders to contact them if permission has inadvertently not been sought or if proper acknowledgment has not been made.

Published by the University of Minnesota Press
2037 University Avenue Southeast, Minneapolis, MN 55455-3092
Printed in the United States of America on acid-free paper

Library of Congress Cataloging-in-Publication Data

Latin American identity and construction of difference / Amaryll Chanady, editor.
    p.   cm. — (Hispanic issues ; v. 10)
    Includes bibliographical references and index.
    ISBN 0-8166-2408-9 (alk. paper). — ISBN 0-8166-2409-7 (pbk. : alk. paper)
    1. Latin American literature—History and criticism. 2. Identity (Psychology) in literature. 3. Literature and society—Latin America.
    4. Latin America—Civilization. I. Chanady, Amaryll Beatrice, 1954-
  II. Series: Hispanic issues ; 10.
    PQ7081.L357   1994
    860.9'98—dc20   93-25437
                                                 CIP

Hispanic Issues

Nicholas Spadaccini
Editor in Chief

Gwendolyn Barnes-Karol
Antonio Ramos-Gascón
Jenaro Talens
General Editors

Jennifer M. Lang
Donna Buhl LeGrand
Associate Editors

Kathy Schmidt
Assistant Editor

Contents

◆ Introduction

Latin American Imagined Communities and the Postmodern Challenge

Amaryll Chanady

I will begin with a question posed by one of the contributors to this volume, Blanca de Arancibia: "We must ask ourselves, however, how it is possible to investigate literature from the perspective of the problematic we propose [identity], at a time when the affirmation of identity in contemporary texts can be considered as a belated 'modernist nostalgia' or an 'invitation to exclusion' and 'closure.' " Projects such as the present one, in fact, find themselves in a particular predicament. At a symposium held at Johns Hopkins University in 1966, Jacques Derrida presented a paper entitled "Structure, Sign, and Play in the Discourse of the Human Sciences," which has often been considered as one of the primary texts of deconstruction. In his remarks on the innovative nature of the work of Claude Lévi-Strauss, one of the founders of French structuralism, Derrida demonstrates that the anthropologist and ethnographer not only consolidated the foundations of structuralism as it was to be practiced for many years, but also conceptualized (although in an incomplete manner) the possibility of going beyond structuralism. According to Derrida, this important development consists in thinking about the "structurality of structure" (249) and the infinite freeplay of signs, rather than searching nostalgically for an inexistent center or origin. Any investigation of collective identity today, if it is not to become an essentialist quest for a national spirit or soul, must necessarily bear in mind that knowledge is constructed, and that this construction is endlessly renewed. Not only is there no such thing as cultural essence, but our very conceptualization of collective identity is subject to interpretation, renewal, and criticism.

In his article on the nation as "dissemiNation," Homi Bhabha distinguishes between the *pedagogical*, or the constitution of identity based on historical origins, and the *performative*, or

> process of signification that must erase any prior or
> originary presence of the nation-people to demonstrate the
> prodigious, living principle of the people as that continual
> process by which the national life is redeemed and
> signified as a repeating and reproductive process. (297)

At the same time that the nation is constructed, it is deconstructed by the successive, and always complementary and substitutive, interpretations whose incompleteness and constant succession and mutual contradictions demonstrate the inexistence of any originary center: its space is "*internally* marked by cultural difference and the heterogeneous histories of contending peoples, antagonistic authorities, and tense cultural locations" (299; emphasis in the original). Bhabha criticizes Benedict Anderson's conceptualization of the collective identification of the people, and of the community created by language, for missing "the alienating and iterative time of the sign" (309). Just as Derrida had pointed out that the understanding of structure necessarily involves at least an incomplete awareness of structurality (which is not pursued by the structuralists, on account of the continuing nostalgia for an absent center), Bhabha, twenty-four years later, argues that Anderson's study of the construction of nationhood did not quite take into account the complexity of the functioning of the sign in its incessant and always-renewed structuring of meaning.

This problematization of meaning must be situated within the delegitimization of discourse characteristic of so-called postmodernity, which goes back at least to Nietzsche's "interpretation of interpretation," to use Derrida's expression (265), and is itself frequently considered an inevitable result of the self-questioning of modernity carried to its extreme.[1] Whereas nation building can be seen as a project of modernity in its desire for self-affirmation, self-understanding, and construction of a workable paradigm, the radical postmodern delegitimization of paradigms erodes the basis of the imagined community. It is not only postmodern questionings, however, that challenge the conception of the nation, but also certain postcolonial voices. The relationship between postmodernity and postcolonialism is complex, and one could engage in endless arguments about whether postcolonial challenges to Western hegemony contributed significantly to the West's problematization of its own paradigms, or whether it was the West's questioning of the legitimacy of its values and authority that enabled postcolonial voices to be heard. What is significant is that some of the most recent challenges to the Western concept of nation have come from postcolonial societies, and are formulated with the terminology and on the basis of insights derived from poststructuralist thought, and in particular, as in the case of Bhabha, from deconstructive criticism in the Derridean vein. Bhabha's description of the large city as a heterogeneous space of "emergent identifications and new social movements" and of "transnational dissemination" ("DissemiNation" 320) situates the postcolonial challenge within the center, which is now home to an increasing number of migrants from the "periphery," many of whom have mastered the discourse of the dominant Western institutions. And it is not only the conception of identity in the center that is criticized, but also that of emergent and oppositional identities of marginalized ethnic groups. R. Radhakrishnan, for example, establishes a connection between poststructuralist thought and "radical ethnicity": "The politics of the 'post-' may now enable the generous production of non-authoritarian and non-territorial realities/ knowledges whereby boundaries would be recognized and transcended, limitations accepted and transformed" (218). The very model of identity is questioned, and the term itself placed within quotation marks, as R. Radhakrishnan proposes the following objectives: "empowerment and enfranchisement of contingent 'identities,' the overthrow of the general hegemony of Identity, and the prevention of the essentialization/hypostasis and the fetishization of 'difference' " (211).

In the case of Latin America, monolithic conceptions of identity have also been criticized recently by intellectuals who are well versed in postmodern thought and various postmodern concepts, and who advocate heterogeneity both in theoretical constructions and in the conceptualization of identity. In a book entitled *Crítica de la identidad*, Julio Ortega affirms what several critics have pointed out, namely, that "ours is a conflictive and hierarchized identity" ("la nuestra es una identidad conflictiva y jerarquizada"), while criticizing the monolithic conception of identity and the "incessant production" of an "official-national identity" by the "ideological state apparatuses" (217). He also questions the concept of identity:

> No podemos pretender una identidad generalizada y
> niveladora, ni mucho menos conciliadora. Sólo podemos
> pensar en una identidad consciente de su peculiaridad y
> su pluralidad, enraizada en la historia común y en el
> proyecto colectivo. Una identidad crítica empezaría, por
> lo tanto, criticando las preconcepciones de la idea misma
> de identidad, su etnocentrismo latente . . . (216)
> We cannot aspire to a generalized and "leveling"
> identity, and certainly not one that is conciliative. We
> can only think of an identity that is conscious of its
> peculiarity and plurality, rooted in a common history
> and collective project. A critical identity would thus
> begin by criticizing the preconceptions of the very idea
> of identity, its latent ethnocentrism . . . [2]

Other scholars challenge the monological discourse and strategies of nation building in Latin America from a particular position. Not all of them explicitly situate their arguments with respect to a postmodern problematization of the concept of identity, but all do revendicate a reconceptualization of Latin America as plural, hybrid, and heterogeneous, which contrasts with the monologic discourse of *Hispanidad*. Josaphat Kubayanda, for instance, discusses the marginalization of "Black Latin

America," and analyzes examples of a "Black minority counter-discourse" (119). With respect to Aimé Césaire's project, he explains that the

> desire and the quest for a genuinely plural reality are at
> the heart of minority discourse. The African presence in
> the New World, according to Césaire, not only
> undermines mainstream monolithism but makes
> possible, theoretically at least, a unique multifacetedness
> which admits to collective or multiple existence in
> America. (120)

José Piedra, in "Literary Whiteness and the Afro-Hispanic Difference," criticizes the concept of Hispanic "race" as "the unifying principle for the dissemination of *Hispanidad*" (285) and the "illusion of one pure, constant, and splendorous whiteness for all Hispanics" (310). He discusses the texts of some oppositional Afro-Hispanic voices, such as José Ventura and Baltasar Esquivel in the eighteenth century, whose difference was not entirely erased by "the campaign of the imperial language against difference" (291) and its imposition of "rhetorical whiteness" as "a symbolic acceptance of the system" (292), and thus draws our attention to the discursive marginalization of minority writers who refuse to eradicate all traces of their cultural difference and blend into the hegemonic practices of institutionalized discourse. Such studies increasingly problematize the literary canon, based on a select number of texts considered representative of an "authentic" Latin American expression conforming to the criteria of the dominant sectors of society that situate themselves within the Hispanic heritage. According to Ian Isodore Smart in his essay on *The Afro-Hispanic Review* (a journal first published at Howard University in 1982, before moving to the University of Missouri-Columbia), "Africa, Europe, and native America are the three pillars on which rest the civilization and culture that is peculiar to all of the Americas. . . . Any program of Latin American studies that undervalues the African factor would be irreparably truncated and necessarily imperfect" (194).

This questioning of institutionalized Latin American studies may eventually lead to the publication of less monolithic literary histories, as has recently occurred in the area of American literature, where several critics of the North American literary canon have published more comprehensive literary histories that take into account the production of noncanonic authors (see Bercovitch's *Reconstructing American Literary History*, and Ruoff's *Redefining American Literary History*). The European Asociación de Estudios de Literaturas y Sociedades de América Latina (AELSAL) has embarked on a long-term project of rewriting Latin American literary history called "Hacia una historia social de la literatura latinoamericana," in which the notion of Great Literature, and even literature, is problematized. In his introduction to the third volume of the project, entitled *Literaturas más allá de la marginalidad*, Julio Peñate Rivero explains that the contributors to the project are interested in

> manifestaciones culturales que desbordan ampliamente los límites de la letra impresa, como es el caso, entre otros muchos, de la tradición oral y de la música popular. (9)
> cultural manifestations that largely exceed the limits of the printed word, as is the case, among many others, with oral tradition and popular music.

Another essay in that volume, Gina Canepa's "Representatividad y marginalidad literarias y la historiografía de la literatura latinoamericana," criticizes the "androcratic discourse" of Latin American literary history, and Jean-Paul Borel's text entitled "¿Una historia más?" questions not only geographic boundaries by advocating the inclusion of American Hispanic writers, but also linguistic boundaries:

> ¿No son "latinoamericanos" los diez millones . . . de habitantes de USA cuya lengua materna es el castellano, y los francohablantes de Canadá? ¿Y qué hacemos con otros muchos millones de personas de lengua "amerindia" (o africana) y que no saben una palabra de español o de portugués, en la mayor parte de los países concernidos? . . . Bastará con justificar, cuando se presente la necesidad, la inclusión de textos en guaraní o en neerlandés. (32-33)
> Are not the ten million . . . Spanish-speaking inhabitants of the United States "Latin American," and the

Francophones of Canada? And what do we do with the many millions of people speaking "Amerindian" (or African) languages and who do not speak a word of Spanish or Portuguese, in the majority of the countries concerned? . . . We will simply have to justify, when necessary, the inclusion of texts in Guarani or Dutch.

Borel's discussion of the meaning of the term Latin American suggests a particularly shifting and "fuzzy" notion; he bases his inclusion of Chicanos on linguistic criteria (excluding any consideration of geographical boundaries), and his inclusion of Dutch speakers (presumably from Suriname) on geographical (but definitely not linguistic) ones. The resulting "category" includes all those ethnic groups who have previously been marginalized by hegemonic cultural institutions south of the Rio Grande, as well as Spanish-speaking citizens (but not others) of the United States. Of course the debate concerning the extension of the term Latin America is not new (does it include French or Creole speakers in the Caribbean, and if so, should one exclude or include French-speaking Canadians?), but the AELSAL project deliberately conceptualizes Latin American culture as heterogeneous, hybrid, constantly changing, disseminated in space, and ultimately very difficult to define.

José David Saldívar effects a similar explosion of traditional categories by discussing texts written by Chicano writers such as Rolando Hinojosa and African American authors such as Ntozake Shange, in a book whose title, *The Dialectics of Our America*, is an obvious reference to José Martí's expression "Nuestra América": "Our [mestizo and Hispanic] America," as opposed to the "Other" America—the United States. Saldívar's reappropriation and recontextualization of Martí's term (whose introduction and propagation since the end of the nineteenth century must be situated within a strategy of resistance to U.S. hegemony, and related to the desire to constitute a specific Latin American identity as opposed to that of the United States, as well as to that of Spain), can be interpreted as a subversion of a politics of identity based on a simplistic differentiation with respect to an external Other. In his discussion of the German translation of Hinojosa's *Klail City y sus alrededores*, Saldívar points out that the German publisher had difficulty deciding whether to market the novel as Latin American or U.S. literature, which illustrates "Chicano literature's profound intertextual and crosscultural footing in both U.S. and Latin American literatures" (63). He quotes Hinojosa's translator, Yolanda Julia Broyles, who sees the author's work as "a prime example of the type of Chicano literature which is *sin fronteras* [without borders]. It is born at the spiritual, political, and economic intersection of the Anglo and Mexican worlds" (63). With respect to Hinojosa's *Claros Varones de Belken*, Saldívar refers to the author's "plural poesis" and cultural poetics as "an interplay of oppositional histories, economies, voices, songs, and inflected utterances" (76).

Thus it is not merely a question of rewriting literary history and expanding the canon in order to include difference, but also one of conceptualizing a particular literary manifestation as culturally hybrid in a specific sense. This hybridity goes beyond Bakhtinian polyphony or heteroglossia, and certainly beyond the appropriation or assimilation of various intranational Others in a strategy of textualizing the multifaceted culture of a country as a means of colonizing it symbolically and homogenizing difference in an institutional practice that consolidates dominant forms of identity construction. Many Latin American discourses of identity emphasizing the mestizo nature of the continent's culture merely subscribe to another form of monolithic ideology in which the problem of the marginalized Other can be solved by simple integration within dominant cultural, political, economic, and discursive practices, and not by a willingness to listen to the Other's "voice" as truly oppositional and capable of modifying hegemonic concepts of the nation and strategies of nation building.[3] Neither is the new concept of hybridity equivalent to Brazilian *modernismo*'s "cannibalization" of foreign influences in order to construct a specific form of cultural expression.

Guillermo Gómez-Peña's remark, quoted by Saldívar, that "the border is not an abyss that will save us from threatening otherness, but a place where . . . otherness yields, becomes us, and therefore [becomes] comprehensible," and that the Border should be a "cardinal intersection of many realities" (150), as well as Renato Rosaldo's conception of the Border as "the site of the implosion of the Third World into the first" (Saldívar 150) and Homi Bhabha's description of the city as the site of "transnational dissemination," implies the deconstruction of the traditional categories of Self and Other, Sameness and Difference, National and Foreign culture. The imaginary constitution of the nation with respect to an external Other, which characterized the nation-building strategies at the end of the eighteenth and the beginning of the nineteenth centuries, is being replaced by a radical questioning of the very concept of distinction between identity and alterity.

The criticism of monolithic conceptions of nationhood is not new. In a lecture delivered at the Sorbonne in 1882 entitled "Qu'est-ce qu'une nation?" ("What Is a Nation?"), Ernest Renan rejects several interpretations of what constitutes a nation. It is not a dynasty established by an earlier conquest. Neither is it a particular "race" (in the older and more general sense of the term, that is, as a specific cultural group), because the "ethnographic principle" is based on erroneous assumptions and the "primordial right of races" is "narrow" and "perilous for genuine progress" (13). Renan's comments on "race" are relevant to conceptions of identity in Latin America:

> The truth is that there is no pure race and that to make politics depend upon ethnographic analysis is to surrender it to a chimera. . . . A Frenchman is neither a Gaul, nor a Frank, nor a Burgundian. Rather, he is what has emerged out of the cauldron in which, presided over by the King of France, the most diverse elements have together been simmering. . . . Race, as we historians understand it, is therefore something which is made and unmade. . . . The leading nations of Europe are nations of essentially mixed blood. . . . In ethnography, as in all forms of study, systems change; this is the condition of progress. (14-16)

Renan also rejects the sharing of a common language as an absolute criterion for the existence of the nation, arguing that an "exclusive concern with language, like an excessive preoccupation with race, . . . enclose[s] one within a specific culture, con-

sidered as national," and that "nothing could be worse for the
mind; nothing could be more disturbing for civilization" (17).
Religion is hardly more satisfactory as a basis of nationhood, according to Renan, because it has become "an individual matter." As for a "community of interest," it lacks the "sentimental" implications of nationhood, and geography furnishes only
arbitrary criteria (18).

Ernesto Sábato's short journalistic text entitled "Qu'est-ce que
l'identité d'une nation?" (What is the identity of a nation?),
which unconsciously echoes Renan's conference, introduces the
term "identity" and formulates analogous objections to the conceptualization of the nation in monolithic terms. The Argentine
author asks *which* identity one is referring to when one discusses
Latin American identity (European, indigenous, African?) and
points out that even these supposed founding "identities" were
rapidly dissolved in a complex process of intermingling and
transculturation: "nothing pertaining to humans is essentially
pure, everything invariably presents itself as mixed, complex,
impure. Purity only exists in the Platonic realm of ideal objects"
(32). Not only does Sábato emphasize the cultural plurality and
hybridity of the continent today, but he also problematizes the
"Spanish" identity of the colonizers, reminding us of the importance of the Jewish element in Spain, as well as the Arabic presence, through which Hellenic thought was introduced to the
country in the Middle Ages. The philosophy of Aristotle, which
has always been considered as the essence of Western (European) rationality, was in fact filtered through the Arab thinker
Averroës, who in turn transmitted it to the Jewish philosopher
Maimonides. Sábato concludes his short article with the following plea:

> Let us accept history as it is, always dirty and entangled,
> and not run after supposed identities. Even the gods of
> Olympus, who appear as archetypes of Greek identity,
> were far from being pure, contaminated as they were by
> Egyptian and Asiatic divinities. (32)

These comments discredit the frequent elucubrations on
Spanish American identity as the permanence of an idealized

and homogenized Hispanic culture, which is supposedly perpetuated in an uncontaminated form in mythologized places such as the Argentine interior (the land of the gauchos), or on Latin American identity as the quintessential example of mestizo culture, in which several ethnic groups and cultures are intermingled in a crucible that distills the best qualities of each component and will eventually produce a superior "fifth race" imbued with all the attributes of a chosen people (see José Vasconcelos, *La raza cósmica*).

Accepting genealogical hybridity, however, does not entail a truly heterogeneous conception of identity. If we return to Renan's final criterion for establishing and identifying a nation, we realize that homogeneity returns in a different form. The double criterion of nationhood, as Renan perceives it, is the "possession in common of a rich legacy of memories" or "common glories in the past," on the one hand, and "present-day consent," a "common will," "large-scale solidarity," and a "daily plebiscite," on the other (19). Bhabha rightly points out the inconsistency of the latter category when he asks whether the "iterative plebiscite" does not decenter the "totalizing pedagogy of the will" ("DissemiNation" 310). Renan's emphasis on the importance of forgetting the past in the construction of nationhood (the example he gives is the massacre of Saint Bartholomew in France in 1572) leads Bhabha to make the following comment: "To be obliged to forget—in the construction of the national present—is not a question of historical memory; it is the construction of a discourse on society that *performs* the problematic totalization of the national will" ("DissemiNation" 311; emphasis in the original).

Because of the "impossible unity of the nation as a symbolic force" (Bhabha, "Introduction" 1), any construction of a coherent view of the nation, or sustained strategy of nation building, necessarily leads to homogenization. As Renan writes, "unity is always effected by means of brutality" (11). What this means is not only that the nonhegemonic sectors of society are "obliged to forget," and concomitantly obliged to adopt dominant cultural paradigms in several spheres, but that this "forgetting" is the result of marginalization and silencing, if not literal annihilation. If progress in historical studies "often constitutes a danger for [the principle of] nationality" (Renan 11), it also permits the revendication of an alternative past by these marginalized groups. To quote Bhabha, "Being obliged to forget becomes the basis for remembering the nation, peopling it anew, imagining the possibility of other contending and liberating forms of cultural identification" ("DissemiNation" 311).

Whereas no French citizen remembers, as Renan points out, "whether he is a Burgundian, an Alan, a Taifale, or a Visigoth" (11), partly because the cultural and symbolic homogenization occurred more than ten centuries ago, and partly because the Germanic invaders adopted Christianity and the language of the colonized to the point of forgetting their own, the situation is quite different in Latin America. This is why we must problematize the transfer of a European paradigm—the modern construction of the nation and poststructuralist challenges to monolithic "imagined communities," to use Benedict Anderson's term—to a postcolonial society (or group of societies, as the differences between Latin American nations preclude a homogenizing model of Latin American Society) that has constituted itself as a challenge to metropolitan domination and monolithic paradigms of the colonizers. Latin American postcolonial societies were "born in difference," as the nations struggled for independence against an imperial center. Furthermore, the homogenization characteristic of modern nation building never acquired the same dimensions—or rather, the same "success"—as in most Western European nations, for several reasons: the persistent political, economic, and cultural disjunctions between various ethnic-racial groups (European and Amerindian); the widespread institution of de facto or de jure slavery, which maintained the internal Other in a marginalized position; and the pre-Columbian presence of highly developed centers of civilization (Maya, Inca) and indigenous imperial structures (Aztec, Inca). Also, the paradigm of anthropophagy can be applied to all Latin American nations, because they constituted their plural identities largely by integrating and adapting paradigms that were often consciously perceived as originating elsewhere and elaborated by other societies.

Difference, in other words, is constitutive of Latin America, right from its post-Columbian beginnings, and even though no society is a homogeneous whole, in spite of strategies of nation building and homogenization, difference in the "New World" has been extensively symbolized, constantly thematized, and frequently held up as one of the foundations of an "authentic Latin American identity." The "modern" process of nation building is thus not yet completed when "postmodern" challenges already question the paradigm of the nation. What Alejo Carpentier considered as one of the main characteristics of Latin American marvelous reality, namely, the coexistence of radically different styles of architecture, cultural formations, worldviews, and especially historical stages (as in *Los pasos perdidos*, for example, in which the protagonist travels not only through different geographical regions, but also through different periods of time, and reaches the realm of prehistoric society), is equally applicable to the present symbolization of identity: while Latin America is still frequently considered in terms of the "modern" constitution of imagined communities, it is also increasingly seen in terms of a postmodern hybrid and constantly renewed structuring of nationhood (or other forms of collective identity), which encompasses but also goes beyond the perception of Latin America as a postcolonial, and therefore multicultural and hybrid, society. These different views and approaches are of course often incompatible.

An interesting example of a rather problematic conceptualization of Latin America as hybrid is Roberto Fernández Retamar's widely read "Caliban: Notes Toward a Discussion of Culture in Our America" (first published in 1971), in which the Cuban essayist describes his indignation at the question asked by a European journalist as to whether there is such a thing as Latin American culture, when the very act of conceiving of such a question demonstrates a "visible colonialist nostalgia" and a belief that Latin American culture is "but a distorted echo of what occurs elsewhere" (3). Fernández Retamar revalorizes the Shakespearean motif of Caliban, the barbarian enslaved by Prospero, who represents civilization. In a significant act of "forgetting" ("forgetting" had been identified by Renan as one of the most important prerequisites for the constitution of the modern nation), Fernández Retamar explains that

> Prospero invaded the islands, killed our ancestors, enslaved Caliban, and taught him his language to make himself understood. What else can Caliban do but use that same language—today he has no other—to curse him . . . I know no other metaphor more expressive of our cultural situation, of our reality. (14)

Not only is Caliban the colonized barbarian "obliged to forget" his own history and culture, as Amerindian languages have all but disappeared from the Caribbean, but, even more interesting, the mestizos and Creole descendants of the colonizer have forgotten their origins as metropolitan Prosperos, as they identify with Caliban in a strategy of self-affirmation with respect to the neocolonial Prospero, identified both with North America (with respect to economic and political hegemony) and with Europe (with respect to dominant cultural paradigms). The passage following the previous quotation from Fernández Retamar's text illustrates the deliberate forgetting of origins and differences in a unifying strategy of solidarity and resistance, which of course is not identical to totalizing nation building in nineteenth-century Europe, but which nevertheless manifests a similar process of establishing analogies between entirely different entities:

> From Túpac Amaru, *Tiradentes*, Toussaint-Louverture, Simón Bolívar, Father Hidalgo, José Artigas, Bernardo O'Higgins, Benito Juárez, Antonio Macio, and José Martí, to Emiliano Zapata, Augusto César Sandino, Julio Antonio Mella, Pedro Albizu Campos, Lázaro Cárdenas, Fidel Castro, and Ernesto Che Guevara, from the Inca Garcilaso de la Vega, the *Aleijadinho*, the popular music of the Antilles, José Hernández, Eugenio María de Hostos, Manuel González Prada, Rubén Darío (yes, when all is said and done), Baldomero Lillo, and Horacio Quiroga, to Mexican muralism, Heitor Villa-Lobos, César Vallejo, José Carlos Mariátegui, Ezequiel Martínez Estrada, Carlos Gardel, Pablo Neruda, Alejo Carpentier, Nicolás Guillén, Aimé Césaire, José María Arguedas,

Violeta Parra, and Frantz Fanon—what is our history, what is our culture, if not the history and culture of Caliban? (14)

It seems surprising that such heterogeneous figures are all subsumed by the same symbol. What, in fact, does Túpac Amaru, the indigenous leader of a revolt against the colonial regime, have in common with Pablo Neruda, a widely acclaimed poet who acceded to the ultimate Western canonization with the rewarding of the Nobel Prize, and who also fulfilled official functions in his own country as consul, thus becoming firmly entrenched within certain dominant institutions? Furthermore, how adequate is the metaphor of Caliban when applied to figures canonized in Europe and Latin America, and extremely cultured in the most traditional and "metropolitan" sense of the term, as in the case of Carpentier, who is frequently considered hermetic and hyperintellectual, and whose work is read mainly by a highly educated minority? What all these figures have in common is their contribution to the collective imaginary of Latin America, to its cultural heritage as preserved in written texts— historical, political, and literary—and especially to the way in which its reality is explicitly symbolized as specific, and thus different from that of other societies. They are definitely not all Calibanic figures (in a sense more consonant with the usual interpretation of the motif) who rebel against their masters, but most of them are Calibanic in that they have learned to adapt the metropolitan "languages" and develop an original form of expression. This is the situation of all Creole societies, which emerge from settler colonies (in which the original colonizer remained in the colonized territories and created a society significantly different from the metropolis), as well as that of previously colonized societies that have expelled the colonizers but preserved the metropolitan culture to a large extent, as opposed to formerly colonized societies that expelled the colonizers, rejected the latter's culture, and recuperated their own "original" (autochthonous) culture (or rather, "invented" new traditions, in the sense of Hobsbawm's "invention of tradition"). Fernández Retamar's juxtaposition of diverse writers and historical figures xxiv ◆ AMARYLL CHANADY

also serves as a demonstration of the richness of Latin American culture, and thus as a reply to the European journalist's question, which was interpreted by the essayist as an expression of the metropolitan conviction of superiority with respect to the periphery.

What is mainly operating in this kind of discourse is the creation of what Bhabha calls a "dimension of depth" in his discussion of John Locke's conceptualization of the "continuity of consciousness ensuring the sameness of a rational being," or, in other words, personhood or identity:

> For the consciousness of the past . . . is precisely that unifying third dimension, that agency of *depth*, that brings together in an analogical relation (dismissive of the differences that construct temporality and signification), "that same consciousness uniting those distant actions into the same person, *whatever substances contributed to their production.*" ("Interrogating Identity" 192; Bhabha's emphasis)

This consciousness of depth based on the analogical consciousness, which is deconstructed by poststructuralist critics such as Bhabha, who advocates a more hybrid and changing conception of nation as "dissemiNation," implies a vertical unification of elements and events from different time periods, reminding us of Ernst Bloch's explanation of what constitutes a successful nationalist strategy: one that is based on the reactualization of elements from diverse historical contexts (as opposed to Fredric Jameson's postmodern evacuation of history in a hybrid construction of reality that eliminates any historical depth or meaningfulness; see Moser). In the case of Fernández Retamar's essay, the creation of depth also entails a horizontal unification of heterogeneous sectors of society with widely divergent interests. Social conflict, resistance to dominant paradigms, subversions of canonical discourse, the questioning of political, economic, and cultural institutions, all of which characterize any given society, are dichotomized in several ways—but always between "Us" (Latin Americans) and "Them" (Europeans and North Americans): geographically between the periphery and the center, metaphorically between Caliban and Prospero, and politically between Marxists and capitalists.

Fernández Retamar's text is thus an illuminating example of the transformation of "modern" (as applied to nineteenth-century Europe) strategies of collective identity construction in the "periphery," and from a postcolonial perspective. It is simultaneously a discourse of resistance, a problematization of metropolitan paradigms, and a criticism of neocolonial power structures; and a discourse of unification, continental solidarity, and homogenization. Contrary to a postcolonial text that revendicates an "original" and "authentic" identity, nostalgically searching for its largely obliterated cultural and religious roots in an ethnic past, "Caliban" ostensibly integrates internal difference (between ethnic groups, for example) within a relatively homogeneous postcolonial identity, without emphasizing the actual internal conflicts that this form of totalization conceals. On the one hand, then, the author of "Caliban" appropriates the "analogizing" strategies of modern nation construction; on the other, he criticizes monolithic metropolitan paradigms and revalorizes the negative Other (Caliban) of European civilization. His strategy, which does not integrate the poststructuralist insights concerning oppositional identity construction (such as that of Radhakrishnan, for example), although internal difference is apparently valorized, illustrates one of the inevitable contradictions of postcolonial society.

The Colonized Other

Renan's brief discussion of the Germanic invaders' adoption of the culture of the colonized indicates a very different attitude on the part of the colonizer toward the "cultural Other" than in the case of the European colonization of non-European territories. The Germanic "cultural Other" was a population that had been "civilized" by one of the most "advanced" cultures at that time in Europe, whereas the Spanish discoverers came upon indigenous inhabitants in the New World who seemed to live in a state of almost absolute primitivism, lacking (according to Columbus, for example) religion and social institutions. Throughout the five hundred years since the "discovery," the Amerindian has remained the "Other" for a large number of Latin Americans, in spite of widespread miscegenation and the recurring efforts to "appropriate" the indigenous Other in the construction of a cultural identity contrasting with that of the European metropolis or North America. In a situation where the cultural values of the colonizer were clearly dominant and considered superior, "forgetting" the indigenous heritage was a widely adopted strategy on the part of the mestizos in their desire to leave behind their marginalized condition. The twentieth-century "indigenist" novels present numerous examples of mestizos who ally themselves with their white overseers to oppress and exploit the Amerindians (see, for example, Jorge Icaza's *Huasipungo*), or who try to imitate those of European descent by accumulating material goods (as in the case of the newly rich mestizos in Gustavo Alfredo Jácome's *Porqué se fueron las garzas*).

At the same time that many mestizos were actively "forgetting" their heritage (and, of course, were also forced to forget), others, such as the Inca Garcilaso de la Vega and Huamán Poma de Ayala, were reconstructing the pre-Columbian past in a conscious act of remembering, resistance, and criticism of the conquest. As Hernán Vidal has pointed out, oppositional discourses as well as the official legitimizing discourses of the conquest have always existed, and this was particularly true in the case of mestizo writers. Many of these oppositional texts were censured for several centuries, and their rediscovery led to a greater knowledge of alternative subjectivities (for an analysis of "alternative historiography" in Garcilaso, for example, see Rabasa's essay in this volume). The enormous interest suscitated during the past decade by colonial writing, especially that of mestizo and indigenous authors, has had important consequences for the "remembering" of the internal Other as different. Also significant for the perpetuation of the concept of the indigenous population as "Other" was the rise of European ethnography following the "discovery" of the New World, and the collection of detailed information on native culture, which partly counteracted the obliteration of the cultural manifestations of the colonized during the initial period of the conquest. While some missionaries were destroying idols and burning codices, others, such as Bernardino de Sahagún, Juan de Torquemada, and Motolinía, were collecting and organizing knowledge on Indian cultures. The situation is thus entirely different from that of the invading Germanic tribes many centuries earlier, because the cultural institutions of the latter were not as "advanced" as those that had previously been adopted by (and imposed on) the colonized. Those invaders could not assume the "superior gaze" of the eighteenth-century representatives of modern civilization who were able to systematize the knowledge of those who were supposedly incapable of doing so. As Michel de Certeau pointed out in *L'écriture de l'histoire* (The writing of history), modern ethnography was based on the disjunction between the European subject, capable of self-conscious introspection and historical understanding, and the indigenous Other, a mere object of study, because European scholars believed that "Indians" possessed neither history nor the means of understanding their own culture.

This "difference," which was consolidated by ethnographic and archaeological studies, and revendicated (in a different way, of course) by certain oppositional mestizo writers, became one of the most important symbols of specificity for the constitution of cultural identity by nonindigenous intellectuals, as I have pointed out elsewhere ("Latin American Discourses of Identity"). But the "difference" constructed by the Europeans and Latin Americans of European descent in their representation of Indian culture as something static, in an essentializing and frequently idealizing strategy, is not the same as that revendicated by the native inhabitants of Latin America. The "remembering" of the Amerindians is not that of a José Martí in his essay "Nuestra América," or of a Fernández Retamar in "Caliban." As de Certeau remarks in "The Politics of Silence":

> In their villages, the Indians preserve a painful
> recognition of four and a half centuries of colonization.
> Dominated but not vanquished, they keep alive the
> memory of what the Europeans have "forgotten"—a
> continuous series of uprisings and awakenings which

have left hardly a trace in the occupiers' historiographical literature. (226-27)

According to de Certeau, the increasingly visible leaders of indigenous groups do not revendicate an essentialized Difference, a "cultural identity frozen by the ethnologist (when he does not bring it into being!), isolated from society as a whole, withdrawn from history, and doomed to repeat itself in a quasi-mechanical way," but a "style of action" (228), a particular way of demanding better political and economic conditions. What is interesting in the most recent declarations of spokesmen and spokeswomen of Amerindian organizations, is that they explicitly reject even the "positive" European construction of the "Other" (although this may be accompanied by the best of intentions) as an idealizing and restrictive valorization. Asunción Ontiveros Yulquila, the general coordinator of the Consejo Indio de Sud América (Indian Council of South America), criticizes the widespread depiction of Indians as Rousseauistic noble savages who desire nothing else but to live in simple communion with nature, uncontaminated by the vices of modern civilization:

> Bajo ningún punto de vista, la Indianidad pretendió ni pretende marginarse de la evolución de la humanidad; menos aún refugiarse en un *conservadorismo* cultural, cuidando *solamente* nuestros monumentos históricos o parques nacionales . . . La Indianidad jamás estuvo ni está contra las ciencias de Occidente o de Oriente . . . (128)

> From no point of view did the Indian community (*Indianidad*) want to set itself apart from the evolution of humanity, nor does it want to today; and even less does it want to take refuge in a cultural *conservatism, only* preserving our historical monuments or national parks . . . The Indian community was never, and is not, against the sciences of the West or the East . . . (Emphasis in the original)

What it wants is a "democracy of cultures," "self-determination," and "integral liberation" (130-31).

To return to my discussion of "forgetting," I conclude this section on Indian culture as "different" by pointing out that one of the most publicized acts of "remembering" since the "discovery" of 1492, namely, the celebration by official Spanish and Latin American organizations of the five-hundredth anniversary of Columbus's voyage, is vehemently criticized by native groups, who are giving voice to their own act of remembering: the genocide, ethnocide, and exploitation of which the first inhabitants of the Americas and their descendants have been the victims. The reactualization of the past (as appropriation, invention, fictionalization, and institutionalization), which has always been an essential element of the constitution of cultural identity, is thus radically split between different perspectives.

The Colonizer as Other

The second way in which explicitly recognized difference is constitutive of identity construction in Latin America has to do with the process of differentiation with respect to the colonizer immediately preceding the independence movements, and the rejection of the colonial past after independence. Several literary works of the preindependence period present the Creoles as living in a new Edenic paradise that they must name and give shape to by hard work, while rejecting the deleterious influence of the "dead traditions" and decadence of the metropolis (see Vidal, especially the chapter entitled "Literatura prerrevolucionaria y revolucionaria"). In the nineteenth century, as Edmundo O'Gorman has pointed out, many Latin Americans considered Spain to be

> un país atrasado, un país dominado por la ignorancia,
> un país que carece de fábricas y de industrias. España es
> un pesadísimo lastre para América; un país que sólo ha
> podido vivir a costa de sus colonias. (Quoted in Martínez
> 87)

> a backward country, dominated by ignorance, a country
> that lacks factories and industries. Spain is a dead
> weight for America; a country that was only able to
> survive by living off its colonies.

Latin American identity is thus conceptualized in terms of opposition to the ex-colonizer. Although the concept of cultural or national identity nearly always implies differentiation with respect to a collectivity considered as Other (for example, the construction of contrasting identities by France and Germany: Rationalist and Cartesian versus sentimental and militaristic), and is never merely a construction of historical continuity uniting different elements in the nation's past, the Latin American construction of identity was based to a very large extent on its differentiation with respect to the colonizer, and subsequently with respect to neocolonial powers. Fernández Retamar's list of Calibans demonstrates a strategy of identity construction analogous to Locke's schema of personal identity construction, but what is particularly significant is that the Cuban essayist designates the Latin American figures worthy of mention as *Caliban*—as the Other of Prospero. Caliban cannot exist by himself, for the very concept indicates the perspective of an Other who considers him inferior. This is in fact the predicament of all postcolonial societies. Whereas the European nations in the nineteenth century constructed their identity around national heroes and a "glorious past," to use Renan's term, and only secondarily in opposition to a national and cultural Other (this statement is somewhat simplistic, because the conceptualization of German identity was often explicitly based on a rejection of French culture around the turn of the eighteenth century), postcolonial identity is primarily affirmed through a subversive act of rejecting colonial domination and the cultural impositions of the external Other.

An interesting discussion of the construction of Latin American identity as difference with respect to Europe is found in Roberto Schwarz's article "Nacional por subtração" (National by subtraction), in which the Brazilian literary critic emphasizes a frequently treated theme in Latin American essays and a fundamental component of the "continental" imaginary: the "artificial, inauthentic, imitated" character of cultural life (29). This imitation of the metropolis leads to the "inadequacy" of certain cultural manifestations, such as Santa Claus's appearing in winter clothes in the middle of summer. It also leads to the rapid succession of literary currents and methodologies that are in vogue abroad, without any single one of them being sufficiently developed before it is replaced by another. Each generation is more interested in the recent theoretical production of the "advanced countries" than in that of the generations that preceded it in its own country, so intellectual life is characterized by considerable discontinuity. Conscious of this "inadequacy" of imported models, many intellectuals went to the opposite extreme of believing that "it was sufficient not to reproduce the metropolitan tendency in order to attain a more substantive intellectual life" (32). They saw the recovery of "genuine national culture" as a "reconquest," an "expulsion of the invaders," and an "elimination of what was not indigenous": "the residue, in this operation of subtracting, would be the authentic substance of the country" (32-33). Schwarz points out that the same "illusion" had existed in the nineteenth century, when the renewal of Brazilian culture was to be attributed far less to the "exclusion" of the Portuguese model than to the "diversification" of European models (33). More conservative thinkers, however, rejected French and English models in order to recuperate an "authentic country," without realizing that this only entailed a return to the colonial system. One extreme example of this search for authenticity is Policarpo Quaresma's decision to express himself in Tupi, although this was a foreign language for him. The examples given by Schwarz indicate that Latin American identity has frequently been conceptualized on the basis of comparisons with metropolitan models, in which the "positive pole" is constituted by those models and Latin American identity is constructed as the negative pole, or vice versa.

I will rapidly give some other examples of identity construction as a negation of the "center," although not all of these are as extreme as those described by Schwarz. José Martí's expression "Our America" ("Nuestra América") constitutes a reappropriation of the name America, which had been "appropriated" by the United States. "Our America" is then conceptualized partly in contrast with the north, and two of the "markers of difference" (I am borrowing this term from Ashcroft et al. 144) are miscegenation and the Hispanic heritage in Latin America. Alejo Carpentier's notion of *lo real maravilloso* (marvelous realism, or marvelous reality: a type of narrative in which reality is described as marvelous, or the consideration of reality as marvelous) was developed as a response to several factors, including the intertext of chronicles of the discovery, in which the New World was perceived as miraculous; the presence of large numbers of indigenous (and Afro-Caribbean) communities in which people believed in the supernatural; the desire to valorize Latin America and its "authentic mode of expression," which would be introduced to readers of the metropolis; the influence of the French surrealists, who criticized many facets of modern European civilization (including the domination of rational paradigms) and tried to create a more adequate perception of reality through dreams, hypnosis, and automatic writing, and also looked for a more "authentic" way of life among "primitive" societies; and the desire to construct a social imaginary that would constitute a specific Latin American identity. Many of these factors are related to the conception of the New World as different with respect to Europe: not only because of its "marvelous reality," miscegenation, and juxtaposition of heterogeneous styles, but also because of its form of writing (*lo real maravilloso*), which Carpentier considered as genuine and authentic in comparison with the European surrealists' artificial re-creation of the marvelous and the reactualization of traditional fantastic motifs. The notion of marvelous realism is thus partially a response to surrealism in which the latter is "negated": Carpentier claims that marvelous realism is not surrealism and that, contrary to surrealism, it is not based on artificial literary devices.

Latin American Identity as Hybrid

The third way in which difference is constitutive of Latin American models of identity construction is related to the hybrid nature of the newly developing societies in the New World and the heterogeneous influences they received. In this way of conceptualizing Latin American identity, "difference" is not represented by the indigenous population (the first and most obvious localization of alterity); neither is it represented by the European or North American Other, or Latin America as different from metropolitan societies (the second form of alterity, particularly prevalent before and after the independence movements). In the third model, difference is located irremediably within Latin American society, and considered as constitutive of its identity. Terms such as Martí's "mestizo America," José María Arguedas's "Indo-America," Angel Rama's "transculture," and Ventura García Calderón's "Indo-Afro-Sino-Ibero-America" (Ortega 86) indicate an attempt to conceive of Latin American culture as hybrid (whether this recognized internal "difference" was sometimes only a pretext for differentiating between Latin America and Europe is another matter).

In his study of the formation of the Peruvian literary tradition, Antonio Cornejo Polar points out that the "veritable abysses of instability and polymorphism" (1989: 14) produced by the complex mixture of social classes and ethnic groups in Peru, in which several contending national projects coexist at any given time, has led to a particularly heterogeneous tradition riven by numerous internal contradictions:

> La conflictiva multiplicidad de nuestras tradiciones literarias es parte de la densidad heteróclita de la literatura peruana en su conjunto, de la índole quebrada de una cultura sin centro propio, o con varios ejes incompatibles, y de una sociedad hecha pedazos por una conquista que no cesa desde hace cinco siglos. (19)
> The conflictual multiplicity of our literary traditions is part of the heteroclite density of Peruvian literature as a whole, of the broken nature of a culture without its own center, or with several incompatible axes, and of a society that was smashed into fragments by a conquest that has not ceased for five centuries.

Even the hegemonic literary system is characterized by "contradictory simultaneities" (14). In "La literatura latinoamericana y sus literaturas regionales y nacionales como totalidades contradictorias," Cornejo Polar explicitly problematizes the application of the European paradigm of "national literatures," with its emphasis on unity and homogeneity, to the hybrid reality of Latin America (124). He criticizes the restriction of the concept of

"Latin American literature" to cultural productions written in European languages and subject to Western aesthetic norms, which necessarily entails the marginalization of autochthonous and popular literary traditions (125), and argues that "modern bourgeois rationality" did not impregnate the totality of Latin American society, as was the case in Europe, with the result that "no system can be representative of Latin America or include within itself alone the vast and heteroclite field of Latin American literatures" (126). Cornejo Polar rejects the concept of plurality, however, because it designates a "neutral space" of independent systems and does not address the fact that these multiple literary systems "are immersed in a single historical course" (127). He therefore adopts the paradigm of "contradictory totality," in which a "single historical process" affects diverse regional groups in different ways (128). In spite of his insistence on the "heteroclite" nature of Latin American literature, he explicitly affirms its "specifically Latin American character" (129); thus his redefined concept of plurality does not explicitly problematize the notion of identity itself, as is the case with critics such as Saldívar or Bhabha.

Cornejo Polar makes an especially interesting observation when he points out that the classical concept of the nation is applicable to practically no Latin American country (1987: 130), and that regional models for studying literature are just as useful as national ones. Jean Franco has effected a similar critique of the transfer of European paradigms pertaining to the concept of the nation in her rejection of Fredric Jameson's (1986) theory of "Third World" literature as national allegory. Whereas she agrees that there was a strong "link between national formation and the novel" in Latin America in the past, she states that not only is "the nation" a contested term today, but also that it is "no longer the inevitable framework for either political or cultural projects" (204). Latin Americans such as Carlos Monsiváis, for example, have extensively analyzed social movements that "spring up on the margins of the hegemonic national project" (1988: 212). Many Latin American novels of the twentieth century have contested this project, which was linked not only to modernity, but also to repression, and the terms of their problematization of the nation, as Franco goes on to say, are "far too complex to be labeled 'national allegory' ": "In place of an identifiable microcosm of the nation, such novels offer a motley space in which different historical developments and different cultures overlap. What they enact is the unfinished and impossible project of the modernizing state" (205). Although it is debatable whether Jameson's concept of national allegory is restricted to a "modern" conceptualization of a monolithic national project, or applicable to narratives in general (and not only novels) that allegorize the "public" or political while ostensibly describing the "private" or personal (Jameson explicitly suggests this), his claim that all "Third World" literature is allegorical in this sense is a generalization and a homogenization of literature written in the postcolonial world, as Aijaz Ahmad has pointed out.

Many critics have recently studied various forms of popular literature and have argued for its inclusion in the literary canon, which they believe should become more representative of the hybrid nature of the continent. Rafael Gutiérrez Girardot, for example, emphasizes the importance of popular literature ("literatura trivial") in the nineteenth century, and advocates the inclusion of parliamentary and religious discourse in literary studies (95-96). Carlos Monsiváis problematizes the concept of "national culture" in Mexico, for it excludes indigenous culture as well as that of mestizos, "urban pariahs," and women (1985: 39). Numerous scholars have been insisting for the past few decades that Latin American culture is hybrid, and that any monolithic conception of it entails a simplification of the complex reality of the continent, as well as the marginalization of many social and ethnic groups. As I have already mentioned, canonicity and what is considered as Latin American literature is subject to increasing critical scrutiny, as "silenced voices" are demanding to be heard.

In many recent models of hybrid identity, Latin America is conceptualized not as a transplanted European culture that blends to a certain extent with an internal indigenous Other, but as a constantly changing crucible of heterogeneous influences. For an increasing number of intellectuals, there is no such thing

xxxvi ◆ AMARYLL CHANADY

as an "authentic" Latin American culture, not even a mestizo synthesis. In his criticism of the conception of Latin Americans as "monkeys and parrots," imitating exogenous models, Bernardo Subercaseaux advocates the concept of "appropriation," which he defines in the following way:

> El concepto de "apropiación," más que a una idea de dependencia y de dominación exógena apunta a una fertilidad, a un proceso creativo a través del cual se convierten en "propios" o "apropiados" elementos ajenos. (130)
>
> The concept of "appropriation," more than an idea of dependency and external domination, points to a fertility, a creative process through which foreign elements are converted into "one's own" or "appropriated" ones.

Insisting on the active nature of the adaptation and transformation of external elements, Subercaseaux considers concepts such as "influence" inadequate. His model also

> niega la existencia de un núcleo cultural endógeno incontaminado, rechaza el mito del purismo cultural y los esencialismos de cualquier tipo, puesto que lo latinoamericano no sería algo hecho o acabado, sino algo que estaría constantemente haciéndose. (132)
>
> denies the existence of an uncontaminated endogenous cultural nucleus, and rejects the myth of cultural purism and essentialism of any kind, because what is Latin American (*lo latinoamericano*) is not something completed or finished, but something that is constantly in the process of being constructed.

He emphasizes the importance of considering Latin American identity as "a construction and an intellectual representation" (135), which precludes a static conception of immutable essences. Subercaseaux's valorization of the appropriation of foreign influences is analogous to the Brazilian Anthropophagist Movement's reversal of the pejorative term "cannibal" in order to valorize the selective "devouring" of cultural influences and the transformation of these in the creation of a national culture.

One of the most important studies of the hybrid and changing nature of Latin American culture is still Angel Rama's *Transculturación narrativa en América Latina* (1982), in which he stresses the complexity of the changes brought about by cultural interrelations.

Maybe it is this hybridity of cultural interchange, as the Spanish colonial presence was replaced by the influence of the British, the propagation of French thought, the penetration of North American cultural and economic paradigms, and the numerous cultural contributions of Asian immigrants and newcomers from other European countries besides Spain, as well as the cultural revival of Afro-Caribbean and Afro-Brazilian groups, that has kept alive the quest motif that originated in the first voyages of the discoverers of the "New World." As the Venezuelan philosopher Ernesto Mayz Vallenilla wrote in 1955:

> ¿No es entonces, señores, una cierta "expectativa" lo más crucial de nuestra conciencia cultural? . . . ¿Pero es que *no somos todavía*? O será, al contrario, que ya somos y nuestro ser más íntimo consiste en un eterno "no ser siempre todavía." (140; see also Mayz Vallenilla 1969)

> Is not, Gentlemen, a certain "expectation" the most crucial part of our cultural conscience? . . . But does that mean that we *are not yet*? Or is it, on the contrary, that we already are, and that our most intimate being consists of an eternal "always not yet being." (Emphasis in the original.)

The Postmodern Challenge

At this point I would like to return to the subject of the "postmodern challenge." How does this affect a conception of national/cultural/continental identity that is already conceived in terms of difference? An interesting illustration of precisely this problem is Julio Cortázar's *Rayuela* (*Hopscotch*), published right at the beginning of the period of "postmodern consciousness," that is, in 1963, three years before Derrida "deconstructed structuralism" at the conference at Johns Hopkins in 1966. Horacio Oliveira's unrelenting search for a "center" or a "kibbutz of desire" is continued in spite of the fact that the protagonist suspects that no center exists. It is not gratuitous that Heisenberg is mentioned in this novel; his "uncertainty principle" is considered by many postmodern theoreticians as a significant landmark in the development of the postmodern delegitimization of discourses, knowledge, and values. Although this search for a "center" can be interpreted as the general search for new certainties and meanings at a time when Western society is becoming increasingly aware of the lack of absolute foundations and the erosion of values and previously held beliefs (and of course this is one of the reasons for *Rayuela's* popularity in European and North American intellectual circles), Cortázar's novel must also be situated with respect to Argentinean, and to a certain extent Latin American in general, identity quests. Oliveira first tries to find his "center" in Paris, and then, disillusioned, returns to Buenos Aires (which does not constitute a genuine "homecoming," however, because he continues his search). As the fictional author Morelli suggests, maybe the "center" can only be approached by endlessly renewed experiments in writing, which we can also interpret as a never-ending process of symbolizing and textualizing collective identity; his insistence on the active participation of the reader in the cocreation of the narrative indicates infinite possibilities of (re)writing, and infinite opportunities for the affirmation of difference. Nevertheless, the nostalgic desire for certainty, for a center, for a palpable collective identity, will always remain, and not just because of the general human need for certainties, but also because of the particular nature of Latin American identity construction within difference, which has never led to the creation of the kind of "imagined community" that characterized the European nation-states in the nineteenth century. This difference is also not that of the European and North American poststructuralist intellectuals. As Kumkum Sangari writes in "The Politics of the Possible":

> The problems of meaning and representation that beset the "Third World" are very different from the slippage of meaning and of the "real" which currently confronts

academic discourses of Europe and America. . . . It is
useful to maintain a distinction between the realized
difficulty of knowing and the preasserted or a priori
difficulty of knowing. And if we agree, then surely the
problem of meaning for the "Third World" is also at
bottom entangled in the problems of social and political
aspiration and reconstitution. (161; emphasis in the
original)

In this volume, all essays are either directly or indirectly concerned with this kind of conjunctural and historical difference,
which is not that of Derridean poststructuralist difference, but
one that requires the realization of "the notion of knowledge as
provisional and of truth as historically circumscribed" in order
to "work from positions of engagement within the local and
contemporary" (Sangari 161), even though some of the contributors resort to concepts and terms of poststructuralist theory.
Poststructuralist difference can be a challenge in several ways: it
provides the conceptual tools for problematizing the dominant
paradigms of the "center" [in fact, it has enabled some Latin
American intellectuals to claim a superiority, as Schwarz suggests in "Nacional por subtração," where he ironically remarks
that the contemporary European philosophical deconstruction
of concepts such as "original" and "copy" has increased Latin
American self-esteem by conceptually transforming its inhabitants from "backward to advanced, . . . from inferior to superior,
. . . and that is because those countries that live the humiliation
of the explicit and inevitable copy are more prepared than the
metropolis to let go of the illusions of the primary origin" (35)],
but it also questions the very process of identity construction,
even though Latin America has not yet produced the same kind
of "modern" imagined communities as Europe has.

The question of hybridity inevitably brings me back to the
problematic relationship between postmodernism and postcolonialism that I mentioned at the beginning of this introduction.
Hybridity is a central concept in most contemporary studies of
postcolonial societies, as the process of colonization necessarily
entails cultural intermingling. Ashcroft et al. point out that
"much innovative philosophical and theoretical debate in post-

colonial areas centres on the relationships between pure ancestry and cultural and racial hybridization" (154). Although poststructuralism has also deconstructed notions such as purity,
essence, and origins, the postcolonial emphasis on hybridity has
a much older history in Latin America. Ashcroft et al. are correct
in stressing that while postmodernism and poststructuralism
"intersect" with postcolonial writing and theory, and while the
former "offer perspectives which illuminate some of the crucial
issues addressed by the post-colonial text . . . post-colonial discourse itself is constituted in texts prior to and independent of
them" (155). These authors go on to discuss the danger of appropriating recent European theories, which may lead to the re-
incorporation of postcolonial culture

> into a new internationalist and universalist paradigm.
> This incorporative practice is shared by both the
> apparently apolitical and ahistorical theories of
> poststructuralism and the socio-cultural and determinist
> theories based in contemporary Marxist thought. (155-56)

Linda Hutcheon has also warned us about the problematic
conflation of postmodernism and postcolonialism, and indicated an essential distinction between the two, which corresponds to Sangari's differentiation between various types of
"difference":

> While I want to argue here that the links between the
> post-colonial and the postmodern are strong and clear
> ones, I also want to underline from the start the major
> difference, a difference post-colonial art and criticism
> share with various forms of feminism. Both have distinct
> political agendas and often a theory of agency that allow
> them to go beyond the postmodern limits of
> deconstructing existing orthodoxies into the realisms of
> social and political action. While it is true that post-
> colonial literature, for example, is also inevitably
> implicated and, in Helen Tiffin's words, "informed by
> the imperial vision," it still possesses a strong political
> motivation that is intrinsic to its oppositionality. (150)

Although postmodern theories provide useful grounds for

postcolonial challenges to metropolitan paradigms and hegemony (for an example, see Zea 266-84), as well as for the problematization of monolithic and exclusionary nationalist models in Latin America, they are also increasingly criticized as apolitical and thus destructive of the very foundations for constructing oppositional subjectivities. The precarious balance between the postmodern delegitimization of discourses and values in general and the desire for self-affirmation within an unequal power relationship in a postcolonial context is thus not likely to be resolved in the near future.

Most essays in this volume reflect these aporias to a certain degree. In "The Antinomies of Latin American Discourses of Identity and Their Fictional Representation," Fernando Aínsa illustrates what I presented as the third way in which difference can be considered as a constituent component of Latin American identity construction. Not only does he describe the constant dichotomization of reality in discourses that successively emphasize one pole of a series of opposites (such as center-periphery, city-country, civilization-barbarism), but he emphasizes Latin America's "capacity to receive and assimilate all kinds of influences and reflect, in complex textual structures, the varied expressions of a world that considers itself diverse." Enrique Dussel illustrates the second conceptualization of difference as he discusses Zea's contribution to a Latin American philosophy that is explicitly constituted as different with respect to Europe, enabling us to problematize "Eurocentrism and the fallacy of development, so characteristic of contemporary Euro-North American philosophy."

Several essays deal with the subject of identity and difference in literature. In "Modernity, Postmodernity, and Novelistic Form in Latin America," Françoise Perus combines the two perspectives on difference (as internal hybridization and as differentiation with respect to an external Other) in her discussion of the textualization of "profound internal sociocultural divisions" and the periphery's development of a form of novelistic writing that can be distinguished from the European novel by its subversion of metropolitan notions of time and a hybridization very different from the Bakhtinian "polyphony" characterizing the work of such authors as Dostoyevski. Blanca de Arancibia integrates poststructuralist notions such as the delegitimization of History and "original discourse" with an acute awareness of the ubiquitous "intercultural dynamic" of the postmodern age, in order to demonstrate the aporias of contemporary identity construction in Argentine narrative. The novels she studies (Abel Posse's rewriting of the "discovery") and her concluding quotation (" . . . we can see things differently . . . ") situate her work not only within the postmodern problematic of difference, but also with respect to historically determined conflicts of interpretation in a heterogeneous society, where formerly dominant conceptions of history are questioned. With Zilá Bernd's "The Construction and Deconstruction of Identity in Brazilian Literature" we move to a different linguistic area, and a different perspective on Otherness. Here the Other is not Europe or North America, but the internal Other (the first type of difference I had noted in Latin American identity construction): first, the native inhabitant of Brazil, who was marginalized, idealized, and always misrepresented in the emergent national literature; and second, the Afro-Brazilian, who was completely "concealed," until modern authors such as João Ubaldo Ribeiro tried to give voice to this silenced Other and re-create an alternative conceptualization of reality.

Enrique Dussel's second essay returns us to the discipline of philosophy, but applied to the indigenous Other. In "A Nahuatl Interpretation of the Conquest: From the 'Parousia' of the Gods to the 'Invasion,' " traditional European (and Eurocentric) interpretations of Moctezuma's "irrational" vacillation when faced with the arrival of Cortés and his men are questioned; Dussel provides a minutely documented argument to demonstrate the "rationality" of Moctezuma's behavior as seen from a non-Eurocentric perspective. Dussel's extensive knowledge of European philosophical traditions and academic discourse makes his reinterpretation of Aztec thought *as philosophy* particularly significant as a denial of the European ethnographers' representation of the indigenous Other as incapable of systematic thought. José Rabasa's "On Writing Back: Alternative Historiography in *La Florida del Inca*" examines Garcilaso de la Vega's text as an illustration and revendication of a discourse differing from those produced by official institutions. The contemporary Mexican Indian is the focus of Pierre Beaucage's essay, "The Opossum and the Coyote: Ethnic Identity and Ethnohistory in the Sierra Norte de Puebla (Mexico)," which treats the subject from an anthropological perspective and discusses the conceptualization of ethnic identity in that discipline. Beaucage's demonstration of changing identity construction (based on several years of fieldwork in indigenous communities) problematizes many traditional "inventions" of the Indian Other founded on an erroneous belief in immutable essences.

Finally, Iris M. Zavala's contribution, "A Caribbean Social Imaginary: Redoubled Notes on Critical-Fiction against the Gaze of Ulysses," deconstructs hegemonic paradigms and criticizes unequal power structures from a specific, assumed situation within the "periphery." This essay's form also constitutes a subversion of the traditional paradigms of academic discourse, as the writer and critic integrates passages from her novelistic writing, concepts from the most recent poststructuralist approaches, and an explicit politically committed stance.

Notes

1. Although a considerable amount of terminological confusion surrounds these concepts, I propose to use the term postmodernity to refer not only to the past three decades marked by an unequaled information explosion, technological innovation, and the loss of values in the so-called developed world (corresponding to Lyotard's "postmodern condition"), but also to the general questioning of all certainties, the "delegitimization of discourse" initiated by Nietzsche, and the implications of Heisenberg's "uncertainty principle." As for the term postmodernism, I prefer to apply it to a particular artistic style characterized by the integration of heterogeneous forms, rejection of traditional aesthetic canons, narrative fragmentation, emphasis on literature as production, and extreme self-consciousness. I use the term poststructuralism to refer to the vast body of heterogeneous literary and cultural theory produced in the past twenty-five years that integrates the insights of modern European thinkers such as Foucault and Derrida. This working definition is of course simplistic and open to debate, as is the distinction I establish between postmodernity and postmodernism, for there are obvious connections between the two.

2. Throughout this volume, English translations of texts are my own translations, unless citation is given to a published English source.

3. I have discussed what I call the "appropriation of the Amerindian Other" in the context of identity construction and differentiation with respect to the European ex-colonizer and North America in Chanady, "Latin American Discourses of Identity."

Works Cited

Ahmad, Aijaz. "Jameson's Rhetoric of Otherness and the 'National Allegory.' " *Social Text* 17 (Fall 1987): 3-25.

Anderson, Benedict. *Imagined Communities: Reflections on the Origin and Spread of Nationalism*. London: Verso, 1983.

Arguedas, José María. *Formación de una cultura nacional indoamericana*. Mexico City: Siglo veintiuno, 1975.

Ashcroft, Bill, Gareth Griffiths, and Helen Tiffin. *The Empire Writes Back: Theory and Practice in Post-Colonial Literatures*. London and New York: Routledge, 1989.

Bercovitch, Sacvan. *Reconstructing American Literary History*. Cambridge: Harvard Univ. Press, 1986.

Bhabha, Homi. "DissemiNation: Time, Narrative, and the Margins of the Modern Nation." Bhabha, *Nation and Narration*. 291-322.

———. "Interrogating Identity: The Postcolonial Prerogative." *Anatomy of Racism*. Ed. David Theo Goldberg. Minneapolis: Univ. of Minnesota Press, 1990. 183-209.

———. "Introduction: Narrating the Nation." Bhabha, *Nation and Narration*. 1-7.

———, ed. *Nation and Narration*. London and New York: Routledge, 1990.

Bloch, Ernst. *Erbschaft dieser Zeit*. Frankfurt am Main: Suhrkamp, 1969.

Borel, Jean-Paul. "¿Una historia más?" Bremer and Peñate Rivero. 17-37.

Bremer, Thomas, and Julio Peñate Rivero, eds. *Literaturas más allá de la marginalidad. Hacia una historia social de la literatura latinoamericana*. Vol. 3. Giessen and Neuchâtel: AELSAL, 1988.

Canepa, Gina. "Representatividad y marginalidad literarias y la historiografía de la literatura latinoamericana." Bremer and Peñate Rivero. 114-129.

Carpentier, Alejo. *Los pasos perdidos*. Caracas: R. MUS, 1953.

Certeau, Michel de. *L'écriture de l'histoire*. Paris: Gallimard, 1975.

———. "The Politics of Silence: The Long March of the Indians." In de Certeau, *Heterologies: Discourse on the Other*. Trans. Brian Massumi and Wlad Godzich. Minneapolis: Univ. of Minnesota Press, 1986. 225-233.

Chanady, Amaryll. "Latin American Discourses of Identity and the Appropriation of the Amerindian Other." *Sociocriticism* 6, 1-2 (1990): 33-48.

Contreras, Jesús, ed. *La cara india, la cruz del 92. Identidad étnica y movimientos indios*. Madrid: Editorial Revolución, 1988.

Cornejo Polar, Antonio. "La literatura latinoamericana y sus literaturas regionales y nacionales como totalidades contradictorias." *Hacia una historia de la literatura latinoamericana*. Ed. Ana Pizarro. Mexico City: El Colegio de México, 1987. 123-136.

———. *La formación de la tradición literaria en el Perú*. Lima: Centro de estudios y publicaciones, 1989.

Cortázar, Julio. *Rayuela*. Ed. Andrés Amorós. Madrid: Cátedra, 1984. First published 1963.

Derrida, Jacques. "Structure, Sign, and Play in the Discourse of the Human Sciences." *The Structuralist Controversy: The Languages of Criticism and the Sciences of Man*. Ed. Richard Macksey and Eugene Donato. Baltimore and London: The Johns Hopkins Univ. Press, 1970. 247-265.

Fernández Retamar, Roberto. *Caliban and Other Essays*. Trans. Edward Baker. Minneapolis: Univ. of Minnesota Press, 1989.

Franco, Jean. "The Nation as Imagined Community." *The New Historicism*. Ed. H. Aram Veeser. New York: Routledge, 1989. 204-212.

Gutiérrez Girardot, Rafael. "Revisión de la historiografía literaria latinoamericana." *Hacia una historia de la literatura latinoamericana*. Ed. Ana Pizarro. Mexico City: El Colegio de México, 1987. 79-100.

Hobsbawm, Eric, and Terence Rangers, eds. *The Invention of Tradition*. Cambridge: Cambridge Univ. Press, 1983.

Hutcheon, Linda. " 'Circling the Downspout of Empire': Post-Colonialism and Postmodernism." *Ariel* 20, 1 (1989): 149-175.

Icaza, Jorge. *Huasipungo*. Buenos Aires: Losada, 1975. First published 1934.

Jácome, Gustavo Alfredo. *Porqué se fueron las garzas*. Barcelona: Seix Barral, 1980.

Jameson, Fredric. "Postmodernism; or, The Cultural Logic of Late Capitalism." *New Left Review* 146 (1984): 53-92.

———. "Third-World Literature in the Era of Multinational Capitalism." *Social Text* 15 (Fall 1986): 65-88.

Kubayanda, Josaphat B. "Minority Discourse and the African Collective: Some Examples from Latin American and Caribbean Literature." *Cultural Critique* 6 (1987): 113-130.

Martí, José. "Nuestra América." *Antología mínima*. Vol. 1. Havana: Instituto Cubano del Libro, 1972. 307-317.

Martínez, José Luis. *Unidad y diversidad de la literatura latinoamericana*. Mexico City: Joaquín Mortiz, 1979.

Mayz Vallenilla, Ernesto. "Examen de Nuestra Conciencia Cultural." *Revista Nacional de Cultura* (Caracas) 17, 3 (1955): 121-140.

———. "El problema de América." *El problema de América*. Caracas: Dirección de Cultura, Univ. Central de Venezuela, 1969. 55-112. First published 1957.

Monsiváis, Carlos. "De algunos problemas del término 'Cultura Nacional' en México." *Revista occidental. Estudios latinoamericanos* 2, 1 (1985): 37-48.

———. *Entrada libre, crónicas de la sociedad que se organiza*. Mexico City: Era, 1988.

Moser, Walter. "Le travail du non-contemporain. Historiophagie ou historiographie?" *Etudes Littéraires* 22, 2 (1989): 25-41.

Ontiveros Yulquila, Asunción. "Identidad y movimientos indios." Contreras. 113-132.

Ortega, Julio. *Crítica de la identidad. La pregunta por el Perú en su literatura*. Mexico City: Fondo de Cultura Económica, 1988.

Peñate Rivero, Julio. "Introducción: La marginalidad al centro." Bremer and Peñate Rivero. 9-15.

Piedra, José. "Literary Whiteness and the Afro-Hispanic Difference." *The Bounds of Race: Perspectives on Hegemony and Resistance*. Ed. Dominick LaCapra. Ithaca and London: Cornell Univ. Press, 1991. 278-310.

Radhakrishnan, R. "Ethnic Identity and Post-Structuralist Difference." *Cultural Critique* 6 (1987): 199-220.

Rama, Angel. *Transculturación narrativa en América Latina*. Mexico City: Siglo veintiuno, 1982.

Renan, Ernest. "What Is a Nation?" Bhabha, *Nation and Narration*. 8-22.

Ruoff, A. LaVonne Brown, and Jerry W. Ward, Jr., eds. *Redefining American Literary History*. New York: MLA, 1990.

Sábato, Ernesto. "Qu'est-ce que l'identité d'une nation?" *Le Monde Diplomatique* (November 1991): 32.

Saldívar, José David. *The Dialectics of Our America: Genealogy, Cultural Critique, and Literary History*. Durham and London: Duke Univ. Press, 1991.

Sangari, Kumkum. "The Politics of the Possible." *Cultural Critique* 7 (1987): 157-185.

Schwarz, Roberto. "Nacional por subtração." *Que horas são? Ensaios*. São Paolo: Editora Schwarcz, 1987. 29-48.

Smart, Ian Isodore. "*The Afro-Hispanic Review*." *Philosophy and Literature in Latin America: A Critical Assessment of the Current Situation*. Ed. Jorge J. E. Gracia and Mireya Camurati. Albany: SUNY Press, 1989. 194-200.

Subercaseaux, Bernardo. "La apropiación cultural en el pensamiento y la cultura de América latina." *Estudios públicos* (Chile) 30 (1988): 125-135.

Tiffin, Helen. "Post-Colonial Literatures and Counter-Discourse." *Kunapipi* 9, 3 (1987): 17-34.

Vasconcelos, José. *La raza cósmica. Misión de la raza iberoamericana*. Madrid: Aguilar, 1966. First published 1925.

Vidal, Hernán. *Socio-historia de la literatura colonial hispanoamericana: tres lecturas orgánicas*. Towards a Social History of Hispanic and Luso-Brazilian Literature. Minneapolis: Institute for the Study of Ideologies and Literature, 1985.

Zea, Leopoldo. *Discurso desde la marginación y la barbarie*. Barcelona: Anthropos, 1988.

◆ Chapter 1

The Antinomies of Latin American Discourses of Identity and Their Fictional Representation

Fernando Aínsa

(translated by Amaryll Chanady)

From Christopher Columbus's letters and the first chronicles and accounts of the New World to the essayists and writers of our day, America has defined itself as a continent of extremes and excesses, of realities polarized by irreducible antinomies, with a history composed of tensions, clashes, and discontinuities and with a society built upon inequalities and asymmetries. A world without nuances or intermediate terms, in which contradictions are superimposed and not resolved, and where every project that is enthusiastically undertaken appears to be frustrated before completion, America reflects in the pages of its best literature its traumatic and fragmentary experiences, far removed from any gradual and smooth historical evolution.

Projects meant to be *models* of "other worlds" simply turned out to be "bad copies": first as an imitation of Spain, and then as liberating and civilizing forces, although they were merely "imports" from England, France, and the United States. Finally, in the twentieth century, these projects resurfaced as irreducible extremes of an ideological spectrum reaching from the openly revolutionary to the conservative, and even reactionary and dictatorial. These different models, with their variants and variables, appear as frustrated attempts and scattered efforts nourishing the "cemetery of ideologies" with which the history of ideas in Latin America is metaphorized in a somewhat hasty judgment. Summarizing this antinomic constant within which America must accept and pay for "models foreign to these fatherlands," the philosopher Leopoldo Zea asks:

> ¿Cristianismo o paganismo? ¿Civilización o barbarie?;
> otros dirán ¿socialismo o barbarie? Cristianismo,
> civilización, socialismo, como lo que no se es y se debe
> ser; paganismo, barbarie, como lo que se es y se debe
> dejar de ser. Cristianismo, civilización, socialismo, frutos
> de la historia de pueblos que los hicieron surgir de sus
> propias y peculiares experiencias históricas y culturales,
> que no fueron frutos de experiencias extrañas a sí
> mismos, sino soluciones históricas que partieron de la
> propia existencia. Todo esto es lo que ha faltado a
> nuestra región una y otra vez encubierta. (1990: 20)

> Christianity or paganism? Civilization or barbarism? Others
> would say, Socialism or barbarism? Christianity, civili-
> zation, socialism, or that which one is not and should be;
> paganism, barbarism, or that which one is and should stop
> being. Christianity, civilization, socialism, products of the
> history of societies that brought them forth from their own
> specific historical and cultural experiences, not products of
> experiences that were strange in themselves, but historical
> solutions that arose from genuine existence. All this has
> been lacking in our region, which has been prey to
> repeated concealment.

The images and representations of *lo americano* in essays and literary texts are therefore created on the basis of dichotomies arising from the opposition of essential characteristics that are presented as antithetical and mutually neutralizing: the rural and the urban, the native and the foreign, rootedness and escape, barbarism and civilization, bucolic Arcadia and chaotic violence, extreme poverty and ostentatious wealth, obtuse conservatism and voluntaristic revolution. In the name of these unresolved antinomies, America jealously defends its particularities as well as its constantly more interdependent international relations; it preaches continental unity, while it exalts nationalist claims or becomes involved in local quarrels.

In this context, artistic expression oscillates between tradition and modernity, between ruralism or indigenist and "New Worldist" (*mundonovista*) origins, and open and cosmopolitan urbanism; and runs the gamut of naturalism, social realism, and the fantastic, not excluding "magical realism" and "marvelous realism" (*real maravilloso*). Literary history that illustrates this and comments on it is characterized by passionate polemics and polarized dichotomies between exalted forms of political engagement and invitations to escapism and alienation, between what Cedomil Goic calls the "contradictory aspirations of the search for identity and national affirmation on the one hand, and simultaneous Europeanization and modernization on the other" (23).

America, a continent without "intermediate terms," without moderation or ambiguity, is the stage par excellence of the baroque and the hyperbolic grotesque, in whose name—as is enthusiastically claimed—everything is possible: from the absurd to the delirious, from Hell to Paradise, and where one bets simultaneously on a nostalgically relived past and a future that is vehemently projected after every daily failure. It is a continent that has been the ideal stage for utopia from Thomas More until the present day, and that has had at its disposal the two dimensions necessary to every "principle of hope": time and space.

The antinomies expressed by these extremes structure a large proportion of contemporary Latin American discourses of identity. This essay is written from this perspective, although some preliminary remarks are necessary before developing the main argument. The reason for the region's constant preoccupation with defining its cultural identity and the continent's way of conceptualizing identity in terms of polarized expressions must first be elucidated.

The Fictional Components of the Configuration of Identity

The past few years have seen a proliferation of all kinds of references to Latin American identity in articles, essays, books, and discourses. It is brandished even in political platforms and programs. Literary works do not escape the magical resonance

4 ◆ FERNANDO AINSA

of implicit or direct allusions, which are present in all genres, from poetry to narrative fiction and from theater to the essay. The emphasis placed by criticism on the configuration of identity in fictional discourse proves this from the most diverse angles: colloquia, seminars, conferences, and collective and individual volumes dedicated to the subject, in which the foundations have been built for an authentic critical methodology for the reading of narrative from the perspective of the identity problematic.

It does not seem exaggerated, therefore, to begin by claiming that much of what is understood today as Latin American cultural identity owes its definition to narrative. The short story and the novel—solemnly baptized by José Angel Valente "the genre of emancipation" (Amorós 15)—effectively complete the work of scholars in other genres or disciplines, such as essayists and philosophers, by actively contributing to the search for and definition of the peculiar and specific signs of what is understood by "American identity." In fiction, archetypes, symbols, and signs of the specificity of the continent are condensed and crystallized in a greater variety of ways and with more polysemy than in other types of discourse such as the political (especially when the latter is reductive or Manichaean) or the sociological and anthropological, which are generally more dependent on "imported" theoretical or ideological models.

The signs and characteristics of what is understood by the term "America" arise with singular force from many literary pages, expressing and condensing better than a political statement the reality of oppressed or marginalized groups. Authors, characters, and readers can identify with this form of authenticity. Owing to the vigor of imaginative "condensation" provided by fiction, some novels can even end up appearing as the essence of a culture, defining and categorizing what can be an individual, local, regional, national, or continental "integral vision" of *lo americano*. In these cases, the statistical data and scientific and objective information seem secondary beside the evocative power of an image or the suggestiveness of a metaphor.

Books That Make Societies

Literature's function of constructing reality explains the indissoluble union that seems to link societies and literary works. It is "books that make societies" ("los libros que hacen los pueblos"), as Ezequiel Martínez Estrada liked to say (160) in order to refer to "inverse paternity": the book creates the society that wrote it, of which the paradigmatic example is the Bible. The identity of societies is crystallized in representative texts such as the *Iliad*, the *Aeneid*, the *Kalevala*, the *Cantar del Mio Cid*, or *As Lusiadas*, in a process that continues in the historical fiction of romanticism and the great realist and naturalist cycles of the nineteenth century. That is the case in Europe with Balzac's *Comédie humaine*, many of Zola's novels, and Russian fiction by Gogol, Tolstoy, and Dostoyevski. Many examples also exist in the great national epics of Asia, whose identifying characteristics lay the foundations of a national identity and even a regional identity, as with the epic poem *Ramayana*.

An analogous situation occurs in America. If we think, for example, about the representation of Paraguayan identity, we can observe how its "fictional reading," starting from the work of an author such as Augusto Roa Bastos, has provided a previously unexpressed thickness and cultural density to Paraguay, although this richness already existed in reality. It seems as if cultural identity had been enriched through narrative, although the author of *Hijo de hombre* and *Yo el Supremo* only *revealed* myths that were symbols of a cultural diversity not perceived in its rich complexity by anthropological, sociological, or political discourse.

It is difficult to imagine Andean identity in Peru without the literary representation created by Ciro Alegría's *El mundo es ancho y ajeno* or José María Arguedas's *Los ríos profundos*. Brazil expresses its identity through Graciliano Ramos and João Guimaraes Rosa; indigenous Guatemala through Miguel Angel Asturias; the Missions region between Argentina and Paraguay through the short stories of Horacio Quiroga; and Venezuela through the novelistic production of Rómulo Gallegos. In the same way, the world of the gauchos is inevitably represented by the archetype created by José Hernández's poem *Martín Fierro* and Ricardo Güiraldes's *Don Segundo Sombra*, and a particular view of traditional Cuba is expressed by Cirilo Villaverde's *Cecilia Valdés*.

All these authors provide a sensitive and far-reaching knowledge of peoples and nations, in rural as well as urban areas. With respect to the latter, we need only think of the foundational character of the urban identity of Mexico City, Buenos Aires, and Lima in such novels as Carlos Fuentes's *La región más transparente* or Leopoldo Marechal's *Adán Buenosayres* and in the *limeño* fiction of Julio Ramón Ribeyro. The same applies to the historical novels that, in the nineteenth century and at the beginning of the twentieth, depict the modalities of national formation in Spanish America better than any historiographical study. An investigation of the independent and constitutive origins of the modern state appears in the cycle of historical novels written by the Uruguayan author Eduardo Acevedo Díaz and the Argentinean Manuel Gálvez, and in the partly epic, partly testimonial novels of the Mexican revolution, whose contribution to the consciousness of contemporary "Mexicanness" (*mexicanidad*) is indisputable.

This identity that fiction "condenses" and reflects, however, is not single or unified. Speaking about Latin American identity does not imply referring to a uniform or homogeneous character, because the continent is essentially diverse and open to influences and exchange. When they are not antagonistic, minorities and various alternative voices also make up an identity that is composed as much of a certain unity shown in opposition to other cultures, as of an internal diversity that it is capable of maintaining. As the philosopher Mario Sambarino has stated: "That Latin America is unique, because there exists no other Latin America except this one, does not mean that it is *one*, in the sense that there is unity. Disunion does not exclude identity. Neither does diversity" (65; emphasis in the original).

Latin American identity is under no circumstances an identity "with respect to itself" ("consigo misma"), as in the case of an inanimate object in relation to its own nature. Neither is *identity* the same as *identical*, or as one, single, same, or uniform. Identity, oneness, and unity are notions that belong to another sphere. Sambarino adds:

> América Latina no es por ahora un Estado, ni una Federación ni una Confederación de Estados; no es un país, ni una nacionalidad jurídicamente; y es por lo menos discutible o dudoso que pueda pensarse en una nacionalidad moral común, de la que sólo tendría conciencia una ínfima minoría de su población; no posee unidad territorial; comprende varias culturas muy diversas, que a su vez admiten diferenciaciones internas considerables; a veces hay más de una nacionalidad cultural dentro de una misma nacionalidad jurídica, y a veces una misma nacionalidad cultural se presenta en territorios que corresponden a nacionalidades jurídicas diferentes; así los guajiros en Colombia y Venezuela, los grupos aymaras y quechuas en Bolivia y Perú. (67)

> Latin America is not at the moment a State, or a Federation or Confederation of States; it is not a country, or a nationality from the legal point of view; and it is at the very least disputable or doubtful whether one can think of a common moral nationality, of which only a small minority of the population is aware. It does not have territorial unity; it comprises several very different cultures, which themselves have considerable internal differentiations. Sometimes there is more than one cultural nationality within a single juridical nationality, and sometimes a single cultural nationality appears in territories belonging to different juridical nationalities, as with the Guajiros in Colombia and Venezuela, or the Aymara and Quechua groups in Bolivia and Peru.

The concept of cultural identity thus encompasses a great diversity of expression, which poses the problem of cultural regionalisms and the necessary balance—generally expressed in internal tensions—between unity and diversity, particularity and universality.

Models of the World and Changing Signs of Identity

In the name of this diversity, different models of the world have been proposed, and these become veritable formative principles that determine the "point of view" of Latin Americans in relation to the objects of their surroundings. As Tatiana Grigorieva has said, "each society, as it accumulates historical experience, becomes used to focalizing the world from its own point of view" (*Tradición artística japonesa*; quoted in Kuzmischev 15). These points of view change throughout history and are frequently openly antagonistic, because reality is polarized and characterized by many contrasts.

The models of the world or the signs of Latin American identity have not always been the same throughout time. In literature, the neoclassical movements, the baroque, romanticism, *costumbrismo*, realism, Spanish American *modernismo*, and the avant-gardes of the twentieth century have all generated successive models that have defined *lo americano* and, as a result, the traits of what is claimed to be the continent's cultural identity. In each case, the aesthetic or ideological platforms of the predominant movement have condensed a particular and different view of the world. If the baroque stresses the diversity and the possibilities of Latin American cultural miscegenation, romanticism helps consolidate the idea of nation, "idiosyncrasy," and the return to the past (*pasatismo*) that inspired Indianism (*indianismo*) and whose literary manifestations proliferate from Mexico to Uruguay, including Ecuador, Peru, and Brazil.

Each period has thus had its own ideas about how the world is, how it has been, and how it should be, and this is represented archetypically through local, national, or macrostructural regional models such as Spanish America, Iberoamerica, or Latin America. These models are not unique, but above all they differ among themselves to the extent that they express and represent the extremes of the very antinomies they bring into play. Through dialectic confrontations, they are better capable of expressing the complex Latin American reality.

The attempts at defining Iberoamerican identity, or what others have called the "idiosyncrasy," *being* (*ser*) or *idea* of America, traverse the options that these antinomies provide—those of the extreme sign that participates and is sustained by its opposite— and polarize all discourse in an unavoidable manner. All signs (or signals) of identity are sustained by their opposites, forming pairs of antinomies that ostensibly fashion the constant problematic of Latin American fictional discourse.

The Dialectic of Antinomies

The characteristics that make Latin American cultural identity single and diverse belong to a history of creativity that founds cultures that are new, different, in a state of permanent transformation, but above all marked by antinomies structured around two pairs of opposites: that of the center and the periphery (constructed in space), and that of tradition and modernity (elaborated in time). The two axes of *space* and *time* constitute the points of departure of a series of dichotomies, dialectically related to each other and to historical (time) and geographical (space) referents, and easily identifiable in the best pages of fiction.

The Centripetal and Centrifugal Movements

The axes of the spatial antinomy (center/periphery) and those of time (tradition/modernity) cross each other in a double movement: the centripetal one of withdrawal and isolationism, and the centrifugal one of receptivity to outside influences, a veritable diastole and systole of a history composed of revendications of the past and open wagers on the future.

According to the centripetal movement, authenticity and the genuine roots of identity are preserved in the hidden interior of America and in the archaic past that is remembered with nostalgia, as in the case of the retroactive idealization of pre-Hispanic indigenous civilizations. Simple ways of life and autarkic, exogenous, and well-differentiated forms of expression, in the ethical as well as the cultural sphere, are advocated as valid in a world threatened by acculturation and homogenization.

Visions of the future in this centripetal movement are inevitably conditioned by values of the past, creating the impression that Latin America has difficulty with imagining a future that is not a reactualization of a past that probably never existed as it is imagined. It is obvious that many critical expositions of the present situation—especially of the rural or indigenous world—harbor an unresolved contradiction between projects concerning what Latin America *should be* in the future (these often embrace radical alternatives) and the commemorative idealization of the past.

The centripetal movement takes the form of exalting ethnic roots, tradition, the rural and "primitive" world, the autochthonous element, autarky and self-sufficient life-styles. In narrative it gives rise to Indianism, indigenism, *criollismo*, New Worldism (*mundonovismo*), regionalist exclusivism, and expressions of literary nationalism and aesthetic Americanism.

From this perspective of the centripetal movement, the study of the history of ideas and of artistic and literary movements enables us to identify a terminology that has insisted on "recuperating our past," "promoting our own values," "searching for authenticity," "combating foreign ideas," "avoiding alienation," "being faithful to ourselves," and, more recently, denouncing deculturation and even cultural imperialism. These terms all express a preoccupation with an identity threatened by homogenizing tendencies of the external world.

This context has given rise to a succession of expositions and theories about "American being" (*el ser americano*), the "idea of America," "Americanness" (*americanidad*), "national consciousness," "American expression and originality," and notions such as "idiosyncrasy," "nativism," "the autochthonous," and "specificity." These conceptualizations express the perceived problems on the local, national, or regional level.

According to the centrifugal movement, Latin American identity is the result of an inevitable interplay of reflections between the Old World (or, so-called Western culture) and the New, mirrors that repeatedly send each other signs, images, symbols, and myths of every kind. America is the result of migratory floods, a varied and large-scale miscegenation and a transculturation open to external influences. Accepting modernization originating abroad is the only way of establishing the necessary intercultural dialogue between Europe and America. This explains America's insertion within the world, or the *universal* condition of *lo americano*.

Latin America, as Leopoldo Zea has pointed out, has a twofold past, and thus a twofold heritage: its own and that of Europe, and that is why it cannot reject either one or the other. This is precisely what gives the continent its specificity and a significant number of its antinomies. Alienated, or even ex-centric with respect to its own interior reality, the identity resulting from the centrifugal movement is plural, and its diversity is the most adequate expression and summary of the world's ethnic and cultural mosaic, in short, of its universality. Mestizo, majority, and pluralistic America best defines this identity shaped from day to day in a process of permanent creation and re-creation. This movement privileges Latin American incorporation and enrichment over simple discontinuity, and prefers examples of creative, variegated, and "multiversal" encounters and mixtures, intercultural relations punctuated by confrontations, clashes, resistances, assimilations, learning experiences, appropriations, or exchanges that are sufficiently positive, without being less conflictual, to be able to indicate a fascinating outcome. Thus Zea asks the following question:

¿Qué somos? ¿Americanos? ¿Europeos? ¿Indios? ¿Españoles? Y con ello, la inútil lucha del mestizo por semejarse al padre negando a la madre, y del criollo añorando el mundo de su padre. Una identidad que se quiere resolver por la negación de una de las partes, mediante el doloroso esfuerzo de amputar lo que no podía serlo. El querer ser como otro para dejar de ser como otro para dejar de ser sí mismo, en un innatural esfuerzo por anular la propia e ineludible identidad. (1990: 10)

What are we? Americans? Europeans? Indians? Spaniards? And on top of all that, we have the useless struggle of the mestizo to resemble the father and negate the mother, and of the Creole longing for the world of the father. An identity that one tries to solve by negating one of its parts, through the painful effort of amputating that which could not be that world. Wanting to be like someone else in order to stop being like someone else in order to stop being oneself, in an unnatural effort to annul one's own unavoidable identity.

This largely explains the exacerbated identity problem that the denial of mestizo reality implies, as one tries to eradicate an ambivalent duality by the simple elimination of one of its antagonistic components (indigenous and European), denying miscegenation its primordial virtue and reducing it to its bastard character, seen as shameful in its illegitimacy.[1]

The centripetal and centrifugal movements that have marked the cultural history of the continent appear far from being overcome and still nourish debates on identity. Integration, or even synthesis and syncretism, which have been given a favorable impetus by notions such as transculturation or cultural miscegenation, are too recent to have eliminated completely the antinomic dialectic in which Latin America has carried on dramatic debates throughout its history. Literary paradigms are Carpentier's novel *Los pasos perdidos* for the centripetal movement and Julio Cortázar's *Rayuela* for the centrifugal.

Geographic Antinomy and Its Literary Signification

These movements can also be recognized in the terms of American geography, whose social and cultural (if not political) realities confront each other far beyond the distance, measurable in kilometers, that separates a large modern city from fields, deserts, or rain forests. Cultural distance can be larger than the geographic and always expresses an intense, even if not violent, opposition. The geographic antinomy is structured around two pairs of basic oppositions: the opposition center/periphery, intimately related to the dualistic sociophilosophical conception of dependency/liberation; and the opposition of tradition and modernity, which gives rise to the conception of traditional culture as an antithesis of contemporary life. These are the poles of time and space that constitute the points of departure of a series of dialectically related antinomies whose geographic forms of expression have vast axiological connotations.

The best-known expressions oppose the countryside to the city, and the interior to the port. In this schematic model a rural cultural identity, which claims to be realistic and close to the society's roots, but at the same time "barbarous," is defined in opposition to an urban identity that is escapist and prey to all kinds of "foreign," "escapist," "exoticist," and aestheticist influences, but representative of the newly emerging urban sectors, which are thus considered bearers of what one understands by civilization (according to some) or pernicious "foreign ideas" (according to others).

The paradigmatic dualism of Latin American narrative is rightly based on the geographic antinomy: countryside (rural world) versus the city (urban world). In this model, the inherent values of rural society are opposed to those of urban society, and the interior (the "invisible country" of which Eduardo Mallea spoke) to the port city (the "visible country"), open to the rest of the world and its influences.

The geographic antinomy that is simplified in the opposition between countryside and city, or rural life and urbanism, translates the more general antinomy of nationalism opposed to internationalism, and idolatry of the past (tradition) opposed to modernity (innovation), pairs that are synthesized in another antinomy: autochthonous character versus universal character.

Thus, a major sector of literary and essayistic discourse advocates an identity based on the quest of an image of itself that begins in its own origins (the autochthonous). The latter, it is claimed, is the only way of preventing alienation, acculturation of what is authentic, and the threat to what one considers as one's genuine identity. At the same time, however, this invocation of the past implies the rejection of foreign cultures and new contacts, as well as the fear of inevitable miscegenation that characterizes Latin America, and this can open the doors to nationalist chauvinism. The desire for specificity is therefore an anachronism, besides being simplistic (if not openly conservative) in its idealization of the "primitive world."

Regionalism versus Cosmopolitanism

Because of this dualistic construction, which generates so many contradictions, it is not surprising that in literature every avant-garde has identified itself as an urban phenomenon and that regionalism has acquired importance and maintained its relevance to the extent that rural underdevelopment persisted, or as a nostalgic manner of providing art with a telluric base.

These mythologized referents of rootedness and communion with nature are directly related to the degree of ruralization or urbanization in each cultural area, and it is through this connection that the relationship between central and ex-centric cultures is conceived and the tension-ridden penetration of peripheral cultures by metropolitan ones is translated. This assimilation of rootedness and rurality, which appears desirable and necessary in some cases, ends up being excessively tributary and dependent in others. As Saúl Yurkievich has pointed out:

> El pasatismo y el futurismo en América Latina están íntimamente vinculados con la flagrante diferencia entre sociedades agrarias, arcaicas, duales o feudales, de escasa diferenciación productiva y estructuralmente inmóviles, y sociedades de relativo desarrollo industrial, alto grado de urbanización y escolarización, considerable diversificación y movilidad de clases. La cultura rural, más estable y con más neta identidad étnica, es conservadora, se repliega sobre sí misma para preservar su singularidad del embate homogenizador de la civilización urbana. Al margen de la revolución tecnológica y de la era de las comunicaciones, no vive la aceleración histórica, el culto al cambio o al intercambio ni las trasformaciones tan vertiginosas como radicales de las grandes ciudades, las del revoltijo contrastante, las del aluvión inmigratorio, las de la mezcolanza multitudinaria, las removedoras masivas, las provocadoras de los encuentros y los desequilibrios mayores. (7-8)

> Idolatry of the past and of the future in Latin America is intimately related to the flagrant difference between agrarian, archaic, dual, or feudal societies, characterized by little productive differentiation and structurally immobile, and societies that are industrially relatively developed, and enjoy a high degree of urbanization and schooling, as well as considerable diversification and class mobility. Rural culture, with its greater stability and more clearly defined ethnic identity, is conservative and withdrawn in order to preserve its singularity from the homogenizing thrust of urban civilization. On the margins of the technological revolution and the era of communication, it does not experience historical acceleration, the cult of change or exchange, or the dizzying as well as radical transformations of the large cities caused by contrasting jumbles, migratory floods, multitudinous mixing, and massive upheavals, which produce major clashes and instabilities.

For Yurkievich, as I have already mentioned, regionalism and cosmopolitanism are directly related to the degree of ruralization or urbanization of each cultural area. Celebrating the past and looking toward the future thus appear to be intimately related to the differences existing between agrarian societies, characterized by an immobile structure, underdevelopment, and the absence of a "cult of change," and urban societies, which are ethnically and socially more diversified, relatively or highly industrialized, and open to interchange, "fashions," and influences.

As I have already mentioned, those who define themselves as cosmopolitan claim that accepting modernization from abroad is the only way of establishing the necessary intercultural dialogue between Europe and America. The options, according to Carlos Fuentes in *La nueva novela hispanoamericana*, are posited in terms of "provincial content and anachronistic form" (23) for some, and the imitation of avant-garde styles and themes for others.

Creative writers, and intellectuals in general, must struggle between these two conflicting perspectives, and the debates in essays and criticism have revolved around subjects such as tradition and novelty, continuity and rupture, integration and change, evolution and revolution, escape and closeness to one's roots, receptivity toward "other" cultures, and isolationist and defensive withdrawal into oneself. In a simplistic approach to the problem, conceptual associations of this kind posit that what is authentically American in the cultural sphere is inherent in the indigenous, native element, and in forms of radical and intransigent nationalism. By contrast, what is foreign and assimilated to universalism is at the base of uprootedness and escapism, alienation, or the nostalgia for Europe ("el mal de Europa") referred to by Manuel Gálvez.

This tension-ridden relation opposes central cultures to peripheral (ex-centric) ones, because each antinomic term gives rise to positive or negative reactions according to the political, aesthetic, or ideological point of view and according to the particular historical moment, which is frequently seen as isochronous with respect to Europe or within Latin America. Its periodization has been reflected in a changing dichotomy, sometimes concentrated in one capital city and unknown in another, and is characterized by a pendular rhythm that has varied in intensity or has combined various traits and types of valorization in epochs that do not correspond to those in Europe, and that even diverge among the various Latin American countries, as well as within each one of these.

This phenomenon first occurred in the colonial debate between Creoles and people of Peninsular origin, and was followed by the polarization of the eighteenth century and the period of independence, after which the debate became even more dichotomized, throughout the nineteenth century, between the notions of civilization and barbarism, conservatism and liberalism, regionalism and cosmopolitanism, and, more recently, in the debate that opposes the concepts of dependency and liberation. We need only recall the antinomies generated by the baroque, romanticism, positivism, existentialism, and, much later, Marxism.

Some Antinomies That Characterize Latin American Fictional Discourse

Examples of antinomic pairs follow, grouped in a particular category based on their cultural, geographical, philosophical, literary, or political significations. Positive and negative connotations are juxtaposed according to the aesthetic, ideological, or political points of view involved. The borders between the two are often ambiguous and oscillating, because a dialectical interaction operates between the various conceptualizations, depending on the historical period and the countries considered.

Centripetal movement	Centrifugal movement
I	
Unity	Diversity
	Pluralism
One	Multiple
Microcultural	Macrocultural
Endogenous culture	Exogenous culture
	Transculturation
	Intercultural relations
Ex-centric culture	Central culture

Peripheral culture	Metropolitan culture
Marginal culture	
Autochthonous	Exotic
Authentic	Foreign
Autarky	Interdependence
Isolationism	Participation

II

Interior	Port
Countryside	City
Tellurism	Urban
Barbarism	Civilization
Masses	Elite
Creole	Hispanic
Native	Immigrant
Indigenous	European

III

Tradition	Modernity
Anachronism	Novelty
Nostalgia	Renewal
Immobilism	Innovation
Withdrawal	Openness
Continuity	Rupture
Closeness to one's roots	Escapism
Identity	Alienation
Resistance	Submission
Caliban	Ariel
Nationalism	Universalism

IV

Romanticism	Neoclassicism
Costumbrismo (*Afrancesamiento*)	French influence
Indianism	Hispanism
Indigenism	
Criollismo (*Modernismo*)	Latin American modernism
Americanism	Avant-garde
Regionalism	Cosmopolitanism
Realism	Magic realism
	Marvelous realism
	(*lo real maravilloso*)
	Fantastic literature

V

Independence	Dependency
Conservative	Liberal
Right	Left
Backwardness	Development
Oppression	Liberation
Dictatorship	Democracy
	Revolution
Religious	Secular
Anti-imperialism	Depéndency
Nationalism	Internationalism
Neocolonial	Metropolitan

The first impression produced by this list of characteristics is one of confusion and heterogeneity, which, analyzed in detail, appears to be the result of a contrasting superposition rather than a periodized succession. Yet these concepts constitute a typological and conceptual grid to which must be added other antinomies based on historical categories or aesthetic-literary movements on the subregional, national, or local scale. Thus, in Argentine historiography, the Unitarians are opposed to the Federalists, *porteños* (inhabitants of the capital) to provincials, and the city of Córdoba to Buenos Aires; in Uruguayan history the oppositions involve *blancos* and *colorados*, chieftains (*caudillos*) and educated men (*doctores*), and Montevideo and Buenos Aires. In the casuistical precision of the aesthetic movements, the Boedo group has been opposed to the Florida in a binary dialectic that is repeated in most of the Latin American continent, and which includes geographic parallels, such as the opposition between the Guayaquil (port) group to that of Quito (capital-interior) in Ecuador.

Typological Series of Antinomic Representations of Identity

Any attempt at defining a typology of identity as a function of antinomies implies the association of pairs of opposites whose extremes appear as constituents of representations of identity, giving rise in turn to connected typological series. For example, if we posit the series countryside-interior-closeness to one's roots-authentic-tradition-conservative-nationalist, we can construct the opposite series as follows: port-city-uprootedness-foreign-novelty-liberal-internationalist. In these systems of equivalences we can identify the positive and negative aspects of each category, according to the (ideological) system taken into account. For example, elements such as authenticity and closeness to one's roots, considered positive by some, coexist in the same series with political conservatism, considered negative by others.

Transposed to an ideological frame of reference, this model implies an opposition between *progressive* and *cosmopolitan* on the one hand, and *reactionary* and *nationalist* on the other. It is based on the supposition that if dictatorship is opposed to democracy, the progressive internationalists (the *doctores*) are the champions of the latter, and the traditionalist nationalists (the *caudillos*) represent the former. The models can easily be inverted, however, if we characterize them typologically according to the antinomy dependency/independence, and associate their extremes to the sociophilosophical concepts of imperialism /submission on the one hand and revolution/liberation on the other, or backwardness versus development. We thus obtain a result that appears contradictory with respect to the former paradigm, so that dependent-alienated-cosmopolitan is now opposed to independent-isolationist-traditional. According to this model, dictatorships appear to be allied with international dependency, and authentic democracy is associated with zealous nationalism, while modernity is seen as alienating, to the extent that it is foreign and turned toward the outside world. Closeness to one's roots and tradition are transformed into virtues that can be juxtaposed in typological series identified with liberation.

Identifications of this kind suppose on a cultural level—and in a simplistic approach to the problem—that what is *authentically* American is inherent in the indigenous and native element, and in radical and intransigent forms of nationalism. The *foreign* dimension, assimilated to universalism, is considered to be at the base of uprootedness, escapism, alienation, and "longing for Europe" (Gálvez's "mal de Europa").

The "American Problems"

The oppositions and divisions represented by these antinomies explain the invention of a large number of the so-called American problems on the basis of which the region's identity is dichotomized. In general, the partisans of each of these antagonistic positions have attributed the negative aspects of Latin American culture (or what they consider to be negative aspects) to the champions of the opposing group. In fact, as Angel Rama and other critics have explained,

> la cosmovisión realista y la fantástica, la atención referencial a la historia y su negación, el manejo de la lengua culta y la recuperación del habla popular, la expresividad existencial y la imposibilidad objetivante, esos opuestos convivirán dentro del movimiento en variadísimas dosificaciones, por lo cual singularizan parcialidades. (Rama 295)

> the realistic and fantastic worldview, the referential attention to history and its negation, the use of cultivated language and the recuperation of popular speech, existential expressivity and objectifying impassivity, these opposites supposedly coexist within the movement in a large variety of doses, and this is why they singularize prejudices.

Some writers have elaborated a list of "problems" on the basis of the oppositions and divisions that fragment identity. As Abelardo Villegas reminds us,

> muchos autores han señalado que en la sociedad latinoamericana conviven grupos sociales correspondientes a todos los grados de la evolución humana. Difícilmente puede señalarse con precisión en qué etapa de la civilización occidental se encuentra la sociedad latinoamericana. En Latinoamérica lo que se ha acumulado son las puras contradicciones irresolutas, contradicciones anacrónicas por presentarse en un tiempo que no es el suyo. (16)

> many authors have pointed out that social groups corresponding to every stage of human evolution coexist in Latin American society. It is difficult to determine precisely at which stage of Western civilization Latin

American society is situated. In Latin America, what has accumulated consists of pure unresolved contradictions, which are anachronistic because they occur in a period that is not their own.

The "American invariables," whose failings are enumerated by Ezequiel Martínez Estrada, are the colonial, the indigenous, the *gauchesco*, the "alluvial," and the "unassimilated clots that one tries to hide" (Real de Azúa 87). With the importation of elements from other cultural systems, propagated through schools, immigration, foreign capital, economic development, and new arts and techniques, one tries to "exorcize these malignant weights" (ibid.). Because these imported systems lack "spirit," new problems are created: "a barbarism corrupted by culture; a clinging and bastard culture." This demonstrates an obvious lack of understanding of the intense process of "transculturation" and "acculturation" created in America, especially since the waves of immigration inundated the continent between 1880 and 1920 (ibid.).

Three problems in particular have been widely discussed. First, *racial obstacles*, stemming from the heterogeneity of ethnic origins and the conflicts resulting from the coexistence of blacks, Amerindians, and mestizos, as well as from the diversity subsequent to immigration, which was generally composed of the poorest and least educated Europeans coming from southern Italy, Spain, or the Near East. The bibliography in this field is extensive, and includes Alcides Arguedas's *Pueblo enfermo* (1903), César Zumeta's collection of essays entitled *Continente enfermo* (1899), Francisco Bulnes's *El porvenir de los pueblos latinoamericanos* (1899), and Carlos Octavio Bunge's well-known *Nuestra América* (1903). The debate was already present in the essays of Domingo Faustino Sarmiento and Juan Bautista Alberdi, and in the reflections of those who were initially in favor of immigration but later became worried about its effects. Narrative fiction also reacted to massive immigration in a polarized manner; some authors welcomed the resulting acculturation, while others were afraid of the curse of the Tower of Babel, as we see in Eugenio Cambaceres's fiction.

The second problem concerns the *difficulty of communication*

and human settlement. This is inevitable in a continent considered inhospitable and largely isolated because of its inaccessible
rain forests, deserts, swamps, and mountains, in contrast to the
prairies of North America or the "domesticated" geography of
Europe with its harmonious and culturally "signified" land-
scapes that have existed from classical times until today.

Finally, the third problem of *social contradictions* is evident in
such issues as native barbarism struggling against European civilization; the church allied with feudal backwardness and indigenous superstition; and the Spanish Catholic heritage as a definite obstacle in an America preoccupied with positivism,
evolutionism, and scientistic rationalism.

The "Conspiracy Vision" of History

The historical dialectic of Latin American identity is informed by
this polarized movement. In fact, the intense external influences
have given rise to a "conspiracy vision" of history: from the
Black Legend to cultural imperialism, from colonialism to neo-
colonialism, from alienation to consumerism, the list of faults of
the Others (from the Spaniards of the conquest to the *Yanquis* of
our time) is long and fraught with mutual reproaches.

Latin America, some critics claim, was the victim of a conspiracy. The acculturation it has undergone is interpreted as a form
of dependency whose direct culprits are not only people from
abroad, but also collaborationist agents within the continent.
The traditional anti-imperialist discourse in Latin America denounces the phenomenon that appeared in Mexico with the so-
called *malinchismo*, and equates it with the attitude of the local
oligarchies and the middle classes allied with international capital. The latter are seen as traitors to their country (*vendepatrias*),
Sepoys and worms (*gusanos*) by some, as "useful cretins" by
others, and in the case of the educated class given to cultural
imitation, as flashy adventurers (*rastacueros*), "transplanted
people," and a crowd of American "aborigines" traveling
through Europe and the United States with openmouthed admiration. Examples of this attitude are presented in the novels *Los
transplantados* by Alberto Blest Gana and *Criollos en París* by
Joaquín Edwards Bello, and in the fauna of travelers in the

works of Eugenio Cambaceres, Manuel Gálvez, Ricardo Güiraldes, Enrique Larreta, Mateo Magariños Solsona, Carlos Reyles, Augusto D'Halmar, and the contemporary authors Carlos Martínez Moreno, Fernando Alegría, Alfredo Bryce Echenique, José Donoso, and many others.

"We will know history in order to be able to condemn it," wrote Francisco Bilbao in *Evangelio americano*, in which he enumerated the "evils imported by Hispanic culture": fanaticism, despotism, and ignorance (38). To these are added, after the publication of José Enrique Rodó's *Ariel*, the "evils" of the materialist and pragmatic Anglo-Saxon world, which create the irreconcilable antinomy between Ariel and Caliban.

Although the inculpation of the Other has changed its object throughout the years, it has continued to feed the conspiracy theory, which represents Latin America as the center of a conspiracy directed against its integrity, beginning with the unforeseen "stumbling" of Christopher Columbus over a continent intercepting his path toward the "real" Indies.

Toward a Fictional Synthesis of Antinomies

When we consider Latin American literary creation and essayistic writing, we may wonder whether expressions of contradictory antinomies are not actually expressions of polarities, in which each extreme participates in its opposite. From this perspective, the opposing positions would disappear in the absence of their contrary, as if the literary creation in which they appear requires a permanent tension between opposing terms; this aspect seems to be a key element in narrative. It is evident that concepts such as integration, and even synthesis or syncretism, which are popularized by notions such as transculturation, are too recent to have eliminated completely this dialectic of opposites within which Latin America has always situated its debates.

The Latin American Nationalization of Universal Symbols

It is important to point out that contemporary fiction is enriched by these very antinomies structuring reality. The fact that literature was able to renew itself as was the case in Latin America in the past few years is precisely the result of its capacity to receive and assimilate all kinds of influences and reflect, in complex textual structures, the varied expressions of a world that considers itself diverse.

The universal receptivity toward influences is manifest in texts that at the same time revalorize indigenous sources of American culture. Forgotten traditions and deep-rooted myths have been recuperated, and in this process it was easy to identify the signs that unite the cultural history of the continent with the Judeo-Christian, Latin, and Greek sources of Western literature.

This nationalization and Americanization of myths, symbols, leitmotivs, and images that seem to be exclusive to European culture probably constitute one of the most interesting characteristics of contemporary artistic expression. The inventory of myths and symbols, and the recognition of a common cultural ethos can contribute to this task of definition, whose most explicit paradigms arise from the best pages of contemporary fiction. In this context we can recognize the opposing images of *historical* and *essential* humanity, moving closer to each other within a neohumanism of renewed contents.

This narrative fiction that integrates opposites within a single text seems to overcome the traditional opposition between Hispanists and indigenists, between formalists and politically committed artists, and between realists and the writers of fantastic literature. The content/form antinomy is reduced to a field of succedaneous positions creating the illusion of a debate. In this context, the notions of modernity and tradition are no longer as mutually exclusive as was once thought. The elements of traditional order, no matter how archaic they are, are regrouped and combined with innovative signs or elements in order to produce a new order, in which a form of tradition is perpetuated with the variants that indicate the adjustments necessary for survival and continuity and whose signs can be identified in any traditional society.

We thus discover, and not without a certain amount of surprise, that from this perspective a universal vision of what it is to be Latin American is not necessarily based on the so-called

Western culture. Without explicitly revendicating this or converting it into a programmatic platform, Latin America can finally feel in charge of its own identity, that is to say, of its long-awaited historical maturity, beyond the antinomies with which the vicissitudes of history are characterized.

Notes

1. In this context, Zea writes: "The miscegenation of peoples and cultures as it occurs within a relation of dependency creates an aborted monster rejected by the dominator as well as the dominated. Making a child of it, as another expression of humankind and therefore legitimate, has been the preoccupation of Latin Americans persistently searching for a definition of their own identity" (1970: 129).

Works Cited

Aínsa, Fernando. *Los buscadores de la utopía*. Caracas: Monte Avila, 1977.

_____. *Identidad cultural de Iberoamérica en su narrativa*. Madrid: Gredos, 1986.

Amorós, Andrés. *Introducción a la novela hispanoamericana actual*. Madrid: Anaya, 1971.

Bilbao, Francisco. *Evangelio americano*. Buenos Aires: Edición de Manuel Bilbao, 1864.

Fuentes, Carlos. *La nueva novela hispanoamericana*. Mexico City: Joaquín Mortiz, 1969.

Goic, Cedomil. *Historia crítica de la literatura hispanoamericana*. Vol. 2. Madrid: Editorial crítica, 1991.

Kuzmischev, Vladimir. "Identidad y cultura latinoamericana." *Nuestra América* (Mexico) 8 (1981): 11-107.

Martínez Estrada, Ezequiel. *En torno a Kafka y otros ensayos*. Barcelona: Seix Barral, 1967.

Ortega, Julio. *La contemplación y la fiesta*. Caracas: Monte Avila, 1969.

Rama, Angel. *La novela latinoamericana, 1920-1980*. Bogotá: Procultura, 1982.

Real de Azúa, Carlos. *Historia visible e historia esotérica*. Montevideo: Cañicanto, 1975.

Sambarino, Mario. *Identidad, tradición, autenticidad (Tres problemas de América Latina)*. Caracas: Centro de Estudios Latinoamericanos "Rómulo Gallegos," 1980.

Villegas, Abelardo. *Reformismo en el pensamiento latinoamericano*. Mexico City: Siglo veintiuno, 1972.

Yurkievich, Saúl. *A través de la trama*. Barcelona: Muchnik Editores, 1984.

Zea, Leopoldo. *Nuestra América*. Madrid: Revista de Occidente, 1970.

_____. *Descubrimiento e identidad latinoamericana*. Mexico City: UNAM, 1990.

◆ **Chapter 2**

Leopoldo Zea's Project of a Philosophy of Latin American History

Enrique Dussel

In honor of Leopoldo Zea's eightieth year (1992), more than fifty years after the beginning of his philosophical project (1941), in appreciation.

(translated by Amaryll Chanady)

Filosofía como compromiso . . . pero no como lo entienden algunos profesores de filosofía, . . . sino compromiso inevitable que todo hombre, filósofo o no, tiene con sus *circunstancias*, realidad o mundo. (Zea 1952a: 11)

Philosophy as compromise . . . not as some professors of philosophy understand it, . . . but as the inevitable compromise that every person, whether a philosopher or not, has with individual *circumstances*, reality or world. (Emphasis in the original)

El no haber querido tomar conciencia de nuestra *situación* explica en parte por qué no hemos podido tener una filosofía propia. (Zea 1952a: 33)

Not having wanted to become aware of our *situation* partly explains why we have not been able to have our own philosophy. (Emphasis in the original)

The first statement is inspired by Ortega y Gasset, the second by Jean-Paul Sartre, great philosophers whom Zea cultivated in his youth, together with José Gaos, starting from the end of the 1930s. His is thus a project inspired by thinkers within a tradition of "Continental" philosophy, as Anglo-Americans usually call it. Therefore, positivist historians as well as analytic philosophers (who are presently going through a crisis of foundation, as is illustrated by Richard Rorty's work, among that of many others) cannot help considering Zea's project as one of doubtful methodological consistency. Criticism is not infrequent, from the perspective of historical positivism, like that of Charles Hale or William Raat, or from that of the nascent analytical thought in Mexico.[1] Zea defends himself from such criticism by distinguishing between the "History of Ideas" in Latin America (which can, with absolutely no contradiction, be classified together with Hale's or Raat's position) and a Latin American "Philosophy of History" (see his treatment of the subject in 1974: 11), for whose construction he takes inspiration from authors such as Hegel (his disagreement with Hegel does not imply a difference in method, quite the contrary), Dilthey, Toynbee, Schweitzer, Sorokin, and many others. He returns to the subject several years later:

> La interpretación filosófico-histórica de la relación que, desde el punto de vista cultural, ha venido guardando América Latina con Europa y Occidente es lo que dará originalidad a la filosofía que parece ser la propia de esta nuestra América, al decir de Gaos. El punto de vista propio sobre la más propia realidad, incluyendo la conciencia de la relación de dependencia. (1978:27)
>
> The philosophico-historical interpretation of the relation that, from the cultural point of view, Latin America has maintained with Europe or the West is what will give originality to the philosophy that seems to be specific to this America of ours, according to Gaos. One's own point of view on one's own reality, including an awareness of the relation of dependency.

Zea had discovered this theme right from the beginning. That is why he defines himself as "historicist": "The scholars of philosophy in Mexico are situated in the group that is oriented toward the second current," the historicist one (1953a: 11). In his first texts, furthermore, we can observe a direction that he himself designated as that of the philosophers who embark upon "the path of universality" ("el camino de la universalidad";

1953a: 11). His article entitled "Superbus philosophus" is a good example, in which, taking inspiration from the *Imitatione Christi*, he dismisses the pride of the Greek philosopher, the escapism of the Christian, and the Jewish emphasis on the terrestrial, to affirm the position of Augustine ["The philosopher stops being the proud one who knows everything and becomes the modest interpreter of Divinity" ("El filósofo deja de ser el soberbio que todo sabe y se convierte en el humilde intérprete de la Divinidad"; 1942a: 30]. In other philosophical works, Zea explains this "path of universality" (for example, in *La conciencia del hombre en la filosofía. Introducción a la filosofía*, in which he gives us an overview of Western philosophy up to Pascal),[2] and shows us the theoretico-philosophical categorical horizon within which he situates himself methodologically. Zea does not classify these works of his when he speaks of his philosophical project:

> ¿En qué sentido tenían que ser continuados mis
> anteriores trabajos? Estos han marchado, relativamente y
> veremos por qué, en *dos direcciones*. Una, la empeñada
> en elaborar una *historia de las ideas de nuestra América* . . .
> Otra, buscando una *interpretación de esta historia*, su
> sentido como totalidad y como parte de la historia
> universal, la historia del Hombre. (1976a: 10)

> In which way did my earlier work have to be continued?
> It went relatively, and we will see why, in *two directions*.
> One that was concerned with elaborating a *history of ideas
> of our America* . . . And another that involved searching
> for an *interpretation of this history*, its meaning as totality
> and as part of universal history, the history of
> Humanity. (Emphasis in the original)

Three texts belong primarily to the history of ideas in a more positive sense (and these would be the most acceptable for Hale and Raat): *El positivismo en México, Dos etapas del pensamiento en Hispanoamérica. Del romanticismo al positivismo*, and *El pensamiento latinoamericano* (although 1953a, 1956, 1968, and some other texts also belong to this category). Those related to the Latin American philosophy of history are more numerous (1953a, 1953c, 1955b, 1957, 1960, 1971, 1976a, 1976b, 1978, 1981, and, to a certain extent, as prehistory, 1988). We can see that, biographically, this second direction will increasingly occupy Zea, more precisely from the end of the 1950s (his text of 1965 is an expansion of that of 1949, which is also the case with his book of 1975 with respect to his 1943-44 text).

I believe that, although it does not seem to acquire the same importance, there exists besides the third direction (the universalist) a fourth direction, which I would call the definition of a problematic horizon ("la definición de un horizonte problemático"). This subject is always present in all of Zea's texts, but becomes explicit in works such as his 1941 essay (published more than fifty years ago, which is why I indicated this date in the dedication of this short essay), expanded in 1942b and reedited in 1945, as well as in other works: 1952a, 1952b, 1969a, and 1974, among others. In the texts of this fourth direction (the "definition of a problematic horizon," which Zea himself calls "a form that combines both forms" previously mentioned; 1976a: 10), he posits the philosophical project that is developed within the second direction (the Latin American "philosophy of history"). I think that in this "problematic horizon" one can observe a certain change of perspective around 1973, a period when "dependency" (seen primarily in a cultural dimension; the subject was already present since 1949: 15) is now conceptualized from the perspective of its overcoming as "liberation" (see, for example, "La filosofía latinoamericana como filosofía de la liberación," 1974: 32-47). This is the result of a discussion begun in 1969, no longer with positivists or analytical philosophers, but with Latin American philosophers who were aware of elaborating, and claimed to elaborate, a Latin American philosophy, but who situated themselves differently with respect to historico-philosophical interpretation and philosophy itself (see the treatment of the subject in 1969a; in the conference quoted in 1974: 32-47; and in other texts written during these years).

I therefore believe that, in order to conduct a fruitful dialogue, everything should be centered around the project of a "Latin American philosophy of history," which is Zea's main contribution and has a definitive character (and which, it is not superfluous to say, consecrates Zea without any doubt as one of the great Latin American thinkers of the twentieth century). Our philosopher has continued this project with great firmness and constant fidelity for more than fifty years, and developed it in an

exemplary and inimitable fashion [in everything that characterizes it as positive and situational, that is to say, as elaborated by
a philosopher who is the product of his time, as they all are, and
who was primarily formed during the 1930s and 1940s, especially by his master José Gaos, who, in *Carta abierta*, considered
the youthful work of Zea as "a new Spanish American philosophy of history" ("una nueva filosofía de la historia Hispanoamericana")].

Furthermore, Gaos believed that this early philosophy elaborated by Zea (1949) "could be considered as particular to this
America" ("podría ser considerada como propia de esta América"; *Carta abierta*); that is,

> una filosofía de la historia que, por serlo de la realidad
> de esta América, se expresará en forma distinta de lo que
> ha sido la filosofía de la historia europea u occidental.
> (1978: 19)
> a philosophy of history that, because it is a philosophy
> of the reality of this America, will be expressed in a
> different form from the European or Western philosophy
> of history.

One must remember, however, that Gaos is referring to a work
belonging to the "history of ideas" (1949)—the first direction of
Zea's work—and not to what Zea considers as a Latin American
"philosophy of history," which is the second direction (the first
of these is only formally considered as such in 1953a, or even in
1952b).

Let us now ask ourselves: In what does this Latin American
philosophy of history consist? I think that it is a historical hermeneutics, interpretation as self-consciousness of one's own history. History is taken here in the sense of "happening" or
"event" (*acontecimiento*; *Geschichte* in Heidegger), or situated on
the level of the "world of everyday life" ("mundo de la vida
cotidiana"; Husserl's or Habermas's *Lebenswelt*); as well as in the
sense of history as the account of "historical science" (*Historie*);
and, in a third sense, as a history already thought by Latin
American thinkers (not necessarily philosophers in the strict
sense of the term), whom Zea studies in a positive manner as an
indefatigable reader, in order to write his works related to the

"history of ideas." One must keep in mind as theoretically central the concept of "consciousness" [*conciencia*; with a specific and increasingly Hegelian content: as historical "self-consciousness" (*auto-conciencia*)]. This is carried out in four concentric circles:

Nuestra historia como mexicanos, como latinoamericanos, como americanos y como hombres sin más.
Preocupación que se encuentra en la totalidad de mis
trabajos. (1976a: 10)
Our history as Mexicans, as Latin Americans, as Americans, and simply as humans. A preoccupation that is
found in most of my writings.

This enables Zea to affirm the concrete level (Mexican, Latin American, and American), but always tending toward the universal [the "simply" ("sin más"), which one finds so frequently in his work].[3] Here we would have to ask ourselves whether this universal dimension is concrete ["all humanity" ("toda la humanidad")] or abstract ["humanity as such" ("la humanidad en cuanto tal")].

Zea uses different materials for this historical hermeneutics, this interpretation of historical self-consciousness that he calls "Latin American philosophy of history": writings particularly by Latin Americans (or by people coming from elsewhere), historiographers, sociologists, specialists in literature, thinkers, philosophers, and so forth. His methodology depends on the philosophies of history elaborated by the thinkers he studied since his youth (from Ortega y Gasset or José Gaos to Hegel, Toynbee, and others). His short text entitled *El Occidente y la conciencia de México*, which is not unrelated to Octavio Paz's *El laberinto de la soledad* (originally published in 1950), is an excellent methodological example of Zea's work as he passed the threshold of forty years of age.

Maybe this methodological complexity frightened Luis Villoro, but it is to this that Zea's success as an interpreter of the culture of our continent can be attributed (he is universally recognized today in all centers dedicated to Latin American studies). It is obvious that for "analytic reason" ("razón analítica"; that of Mario Bunge, for example) even psychoanalysis could not have the status of a "science." It was thus a question of the definition of "science": for a purely instrumental and mathematical reason psychoanalysis cannot be a science (and neither can Marxism), whereas for a "more general" ("más amplia") definition of science (with a stricter sense of "rationality" as practical, hermeneutic, or pragmatic reason), psychoanalysis acquires the status of a "hermeneutic science" (that is Paul Ricoeur's position). Analytic philosophy itself, that of the linguistic turn, has now been integrated within a much richer and more profound practico-pragmatic philosophy (in the tradition of Austin and Searle, and radically transformed by Karl-Otto Apel and Jürgen Habermas). Zea would thus have the support of many good philosophers today, and even the "hegemonic Euro-North American philosophical community" ("comunidad filosófica hegemónica europeo-norteamericana") would be in his favor. Simply abandoning "Latin American thought" for a project of historical positivism or analytic philosophy finally ended up without the expected results. Zea continued in the direction he had started from.

The same could be said of the criticism that philosophico-economist Marxism (even that of Althusser) directed at Zea with respect to the methodology of the "history of ideas." I do not want to suggest that Zea had no limitations, but it has been demonstrated that one cannot study the history of ideas only as a reflection of the processes of the "infrastructure." It is also clear today that the criticism of economist Marxism, including the Latin American version, should be the task of the Latin American philosopher who claims that he is producing a Latin American philosophy, for there is the need for a "reconstruction" of Marxism itself that Zea did not include in his hermeneutic project (but which, once realized, helps to provide a better grounding for this project of a Latin American philosophy).[4]

In a third stage (after the criticism of positivism, analytic philosophy, and Marxism), a new debate arises, as I have already indicated, on which Zea, as a philosopher of Latin American history, takes position in *La filosofía latinoamericana como filosofía sin más*. The central argument, which had been evolving in Zea's thought since 1941, consists in affirming that the Latin American past cannot be negated (as Augusto Salazar Bondy apparently claimed in his short work entitled ¿*Existe filosofía en América Latina?*).[5] As Zea put it:

> Pasado propio y pasado impuesto y, por impuesto,
> también propio, han de formar el pasado que ha de ser
> dialécticamente asimilado por pueblos como los nuestros.
> De allí esa lucha con la filosofía y la cultura occidentales
> que parece propia del pensamiento latinoamericano.
> (1978: 32)
> One's own past and an imposed past, and as it is
> imposed, it is also one's own, must form the past that
> has to be dialectically assimilated by cultures such as
> ours. That explains the battle with Western philosophy
> and culture that seems peculiar to Latin American
> thought.

Yet it seems strange to criticize the negation of the past in historians who have repeatedly dealt with Latin America. Salazar Bondy (1965) has two admirable volumes on the history of Peruvian philosophy, on the level of the history of ideas.[6] In my own case,[7] I have more than a dozen works on Latin American history, in some aspects of the area of historical science;[8] several on the interpretation of Latin American history[9] starting from its protohistory;[10] and even some on the history of ideas (Dussel 1968, 1979, 1982).

I do not want to refute the history of a liberating Latin American thought. What I do refute, together with Salazar Bondy, is the existence of a Latin American critical philosophy that is in a "stage of philosophical normalcy" ("etapa de normalidad filosófica")[11] and has been able to affirm itself as Latin American philosophy, while being recognized as an expression of universal philosophy, one that is practiced in the main programs of philosophical studies and not in the specialized area of Latin American studies, or in a program related to a specific university chair; in other words, philosophy in a *restricted* sense (*restringido*), according to the definition of the "hegemonic Euro-North American philosophical community." This philosophy in the restricted sense must be distinguished from philosophy as "Latin American philosophy of history" ("filosofía de la historia latinoamericana") or as a historico-fundamental hermeneutics of the "world of everyday life" [Husserl's *Lebenswelt*, starting from

Die Krisis der europäischen Wissenschaften, certainly because of the impact Heidegger's *Sein und Zeit* (*Being and Time*) had on it]. Zea's "Latin American philosophy," according to my interpretation, is a hermeneutics that makes explicit a presupposed attitude in the "understanding" of the world (*Verstehen* in the Heideggerian sense) from which the work of philosophy itself "in a restricted sense" can start. (I am saying "restricted sense" in order not to judge whether it is philosophy "in the strict sense.") Zea's project is in a stage of "pre-comprehension," which is really fundamental in the historical and daily weltanschauung (in Dilthey's sense), and which is always present at the beginning of the act of philosophizing. The imitative and Eurocentric philosopher in Latin America (who is supposedly "universalist") is already outside Latin America when starting to philosophize. On this point, Salazar Bondy (and I myself) proposes the same thesis as Zea, when the latter writes:

> México, como el resto de los países de Iberoamérica, no ha dado aún origen a una filosofía a la que se pueda llamar propia. Más bien ha venido glosando las grandes corrientes del pensamiento europeo. (1955: 47)
>
> Mexico, like the other countries of Iberoamerica, has not yet produced a philosophy that it can call its own. Rather, it has glossed the great currents of European thought.[12]

Is this not exactly Salazar Bondy's position, and my own? On the one hand, we all think that it is necessary to be aware of reality or of the "world of everyday life" in Latin America (as its past), and in this sense there have been some authentic Latin American thinkers [not "normalized philosophers" ("filósofos normalizados")]. On the other hand, philosophy in the restricted sense (which affirms itself as universal and is recognized by the "hegemonic Euro-North American philosophical community") has not produced its "own" philosophy in Latin America. Is this a contradiction? I do not think so, because we are talking about two levels: on one we can situate the authors interpreted in Zea's "philosophy of history," and on the other, the philosophers of "normalized philosophy" to which I, together with Salazar Bondy, am referring.

Latin American philosophers must elaborate a hermeneutics that can discover[13] the *meaning* of their own history and own reality, an impressive task carried out by Zea, in the way that Aristotle emphasized that in the use of the most fundamental method of all, the dialectic method, neither science nor philosophy was useful, because it was necessary to reflect directly on *tà éndoxa* (the opinions of the "world of everyday life" from which the "principles" of science and even of philosophy in the strict or restricted sense can be thought) (*Topicon* I.1: 100 a 18-b: 23; I have discussed this in Dussel 1974: 17ff.), and only *paideia* was useful for that (a *paideia* that was like a fundamental "culture").[14] I think that Zea's "Latin American philosophy of history" is situated on this historico-fundamental level, as philosophers, who are aware of their self-consciousness, reflect on the "world of everyday life" (*Lebenswelt*), always already presupposed a priori beneath one's feet as a dependent and marginal world that is historically situated as Latin American. I think (against all those detractors who demand specific methods) that Zea is right in this. In this sense all the great Latin American thinkers (to name only a few: Bartolomé de Las Casas, Clavijero, Bolívar, Alberdi, and Martí) have thought on the basis of their own reality and with the purpose of affirming "Latin Americanness" (*lo latinoamericano*). It is not in this sense that Salazar Bondy and I have spoken of "imitative philosophy" (or as Zea writes, philosophy that "has glossed the great currents of European thought"). In what sense were they inauthentic "glossers" of "imitators"? Not finally in the sense of authors who enable one to elaborate a historical hermeneutics (in the manner of Zea's "Latin American philosophy of history"), but in something quite different that I would like to explain in some detail.

The "hegemonic Euro-North American philosophical community" (Popper, Austin, Ricoeur, Vattimo, Habermas, Charles Taylor, and Rorty, to name some philosophers from philosophically "hegemonic" countries) and even the hegemonic "philosophical community" in Latin America (in faculties, institutes, research councils, and so forth) *ignore* all peripheral philosophical thought (from Latin America, Africa, or Asia) and dismiss it as not relevant, pertinent, or central. The *"outside* of history" ("el *fuera* de la historia") that Zea discovers in the European "philosophies of history" (like that of Hegel) is now interpreted as an "outside," as an "exclusion," as an "exteriority" of the *"community* of philosophical *communication* itself" (*"comunidad de comunicación* filosófica"); that is to say, of the community that dominates philosophical discourse (and that is why we call it hegemonic) situated on the Europe-United States axis. It is a position of exclusion that is imitated by the colonial "universalist" philosophers. And it is with respect to this supposedly universal "philosophy" (to be precise: European and North American) that we are excluded.

The problem is threefold: (1) we have to think in a self-conscious manner "from Latin America" ("desde América Latina"), with an awareness of our place in world history; (2) we have to think philosophically "about our reality" (from our positivity, but also as dominated, impoverished, and so forth); and (3) we have to think in such a way that we can "enter" the discussion with this "hegemonic philosophical community." Because we are "excluded" from it, we must "interpellate" it so that our own philosophical discourse will be "recognized." The "recognition" of this hegemonic community is not the origin of our philosophizing (which starts from our negated reality, from ourselves), but given the colonial condition of our "normalized" philosophy (or academic: "philosophy as compromise . . . but not as some professors of philosophy understand it"; Zea 1952b: 11), it is necessary to proceed by self-affirmation and the recognition of this hegemonic community in order to establish among ourselves the conditions for a philosophical dialogue that is creative, respectful, and rigorous.

In this aspect, a "history of Latin American thought" (even in the form of a "Latin American philosophy of history") is not sufficient anymore. It is now necessary to resort to the whole range of discourse, the problematics, and the methods of this "hegemonic philosophical community," in order to elaborate our challenge on the basis of its own rules: as a distinct reality (marginal, dominated, and exploited) and as a philosophy in the strict sense that is still excluded. This need for an argumentation that makes use of the discourse of hegemonic philosophy from the position of *"a reality as an exteriority not thought by its thinkers"* (*"una realidad como exterioridad no pensada por ellos"*) forces us, at the same time, to construct and reconstruct new universal categories, and develop new methodological aspects (valid for Africa and Asia, but also for Europe and the United States). We have advanced considerably since Salazar Bondy's question was formulated in 1968. I think that, little by little, this challenge of a Latin American philosophy will be "received" by the "hegemonic philosophical community,"[15] and this will force it to "include" a problematic, a thematics, some categories, and so forth, that it had not thought before. Eurocentrism and the fallacy of development, so characteristic of contemporary Euro-North American philosophy, will thus be problematized from something like an *outside* of history (mentioned by Zea).

I think that both projects, that of a "Latin American philosophy of history" as a historical hermeneutics of the concrete presuppositions of the "world of everyday life" in Latin America (Zea's project), and the elaboration of a philosophy that, starting from this hermeneutics, proposes to construct a Latin American philosophy orchestrated with the language and the discursivity of the hegemonic philosophical community,[16] are complementary (and in no way mutually exclusive).[17]

These pages are, once again, dictated by a feeling of respect for the great master of Latin American thought, and by appreciation for my first reading of his works, when, in Paris at the beginning of the 1960s, I discovered myself as "outside of history," thanks to Leopoldo Zea. It is the affirmation of our Latin American exteriority, as the Other, as the poor one, that has urged me on in a philosophical project that I have been working on for the past thirty years, one that attempts to negate this negation and subsume it in a future universality (that is as much human in a general sense, as philosophical in the strict sense, and I believe this is the case with Zea's project as well).

Notes

1. See, for example, Luis Villoro's judgment when he writes, speaking of Mexican philosophy in the decade following his own: "They will be works with scarce *local color* and the Mexican philosophical production will be like that existing in any other part of the world" (1972: 3; emphasis in the original). It is difficult to formulate a philosophical project more opposed to Zea's [although Zea defends a certain universalism, in his expression "simply philosophy" ("filosofía sin más") directed against Salazar Bondy]. For Villoro, this decision

was clear, because he had produced in his youth excellent works in the line of Zea, such as *Los grandes momentos del indigenismo en México* (1950), and also studies, in the tradition of the history of ideas, on ideology in the process of national emancipation.

2. I would like to point out that Zea does not pose the question of Latin American philosophy here. It is obvious that this is an early work of his, but it should always be important to introduce the question of Latin American thought into "universalist" philosophical works, because introducing it is inevitable if we think from our reality.

3. "Latin American philosophy? No, simply philosophy, for its being Latin American is inevitable. It will be the reply of Latin American philosophy to the question concerning its own existence" (1971: 186). Universality is the pretension toward which we strive from a particularity that starts from a specifically Latin American reality.

4. This was my intention in the three books on Latin American philosophy entitled *La producción teórica de Marx* (1985), *Hacia un Marx desconocido* (1988), and *El último Marx* (1990), in which I ask questions that Zea does not include as the task of a Latin American philosophy.

5. Salazar Bondy wrote: "Our philosophy with its own peculiarities has not been a genuine and original thought, but one that was inauthentic and imitative in what was fundamental" (1968: 131). To which I added: "If that is so, is an authentic philosophy possible in our continent, which is underdeveloped, dependent (and underdeveloped because of its dependency), and oppressed, even culturally and philosophically?" (Dussel 1973: 154). See "The Destruction of European Philosophy" (Schelkshorn, chapter 2: 31ff.) and "About the Philosophico-historical and Historico-philosophical Conception of E. Dussel" (Schelkshorn, chapter 3: 57ff.).

6. In his conclusion, Salazar Bondy writes the following on Peruvian philosophy: "Meditation has essentially had an imitative character; its evolution can still be reduced to successive foreign influences . . . Because of this it has largely lost its sense of authentic reflection, only repeating and divulging ideas and doctrines" (1965, 2:456). Critical of his own national reality, he also writes: "The frustration of the historical subject in Peruvian life has been especially serious for philosophy up to the present time" (1965, 2:459). Here we already find all the theses of his later work with which Zea enters into a polemical discussion. When I met with Salazar Bondy in Buenos Aires in 1973 we had thought of starting to collaborate actively on a future philosophical construction. Augusto died "too early," at the height of his creative youth, in 1974.

7. Zea repeatedly criticizes my position, although I can only appreciate the tone with which he does so, for example when he writes: "Salazar Bondy, Dussel, Fanon, and those who like them fight or have fought for a philosophy of liberation" (1974: 42).

8. See, for example, the first of the nine volumes of Dussel 1969-71, the result of four years of research in the Archivo General de Indias in Seville (and presented as a thesis in *history* at the Sorbonne).

9. See, for example, Dussel 1965. I must point out that in these years Zea's book *América como conciencia* had such an influence on me that since that time until today my entire purpose has been precisely to make possible the "entry" of

Latin America into world history (with respect to the historical self-interpreta-tion of Humanity, and with respect to the "hegemonic philosophical commu-nity," to which I will return later). I must thank Zea, and that is why I express my appreciation in the dedication, for having taught me that Latin America was *outside* history. Years later he repeated: "Asia on account of its anachronism, and America and Africa on account of their being young or primitive, remain *outside*" (1978: 36; emphasis in the original). I return to this theme in my latest work, "1492. El encubrimiento del Otro. Hacia el origen del 'mito de la Modernidad.' "

10. Dussel 1969, 1974, and 1975, as well as the unpublished *Hipótesis* (1966). As one can observe, not only have I not negated our history, but I have dedi-cated, as few philosophers have done, many years and books to it, and have started, in order to situate Latin America in World History, from several millen-nia B.C., as I pointed out explicitly in the prologue to *El humanismo semita*, and as a presupposition for a Latin American philosophy.

11. This is Francisco Romero's expression; see "Sobre la filosofía en Iberoamérica," *La Nación* (Buenos Aires), 24 December 1940; quoted by Zea 1945: 20.

12. It is obvious that Zea uses "philosophy" in this quotation in a restricted sense, which does not include Bolívar, Alberdi, or Martí; otherwise the state-ment would be contradictory.

13. This discovery is like an inversion of the original discovery of America. Zea writes: "The discovery of America had really been a concealment [*encu-brimiento*]. A concealment of the reality of the people and cultures of this Amer-ica" (1981: 53).

14. "In every kind of speculation and method, from the most quotidian to the most elevated, there seem to be two types of attitude: the first could be called the science of the *ente*, and the other something like a culture (*paideia*). In fact, it is the cultivated man (*pepaideuménou*) who can carry out criticism (*krísis*). And it is precisely this attitude that I think belongs to the man who possesses universal culture and that is the result of culture" (Aristotle, *De Partibus Animalium* I.1: 639 a: 1-10).

15. Maybe Karl-Otto Apel's (1992) article is indicative of this advance; or that of Paul Ricoeur (1992).

16. One calls "philosophy of liberation" a philosophy that uses categories that can be universalized, from the situation of dependency, domination, and exploitation in Latin America, but also, at the same time, of any other position of oppression: of women, nonwhite races, youth, popular culture, workers ex-ploited by capitalism, continents excluded from the benefits of central capital-ism, and so forth. It is a metalanguage that can be universalized and that starts from Latin America.

17. There are still many other themes to discuss, such as the difference be-tween an "assumptive project" ("proyecto asuntivo"; Zea 1978: 269ff.) and a popular "project of liberation" (which is not the project of the Creoles, fighting for independence, or that of conservatives or liberals, but of the ethnic groups, exploited classes, marginal persons, and the "social block of the oppressed": the Latin American people); the problem of the mestizo and the necessary inclusion of Indians and blacks in a Latin American project; the articulation of cultural to-gether with economic dependency (which explains the continuing importance of

Marx today), and so forth. There is a dialogue to be created even on the level of a historical hermeneutics of the world of everyday life, or Zea's "Latin American philosophy of history."

Works Cited

Apel, Karl-Otto. "Die Diskursethik vor der Herausforderung der Philosophie der Befreiung." *Diskursethik oder Befreiungsethik?* Aachen: Augustinus, 1992. 16-54.

Aristotle. *De Partibus Animalium.* Vol. 1. Berlin: De Gruyter, 1960. 639-697.

_____. *Topicon.* Vol. 1. Berlin: De Gruyter, 1960. 100-164.

Dussel, Enrique. "Iberoamérica en la historia universal." *Revista de Occidente* 25 (1965): 85-95.

_____. *Hipótesis para el estudio de Latinoamérica en la Historia Universal.* Vol. 1. Resistencia (Argentina): Universidad del Nordeste, 1966. Unpublished.

_____. "Sentido de una historia de las ideas dentro de una teoría de la cultura." *Cuyo* (Mendoza, Argentina) 4 (1968): 117-119.

_____. *El humanismo semita.* Buenos Aires: Eudeba, 1969. Written in 1963.

_____. *El episcopado hispanoamericano, institución misionera en defensa del indio (1504-1620).* 9 vols. Cuernavaca: CIDOC, 1969-71.

_____. *Para una ética de la liberación latinoamericana.* Vol. 1. Buenos Aires: Siglo veintiuno, 1973.

_____. *El dualismo en la antropología de la Cristiandad. Desde los orígenes hasta antes de la conquista de América.* Buenos Aires: Guadalupe, 1974.

_____. *Método para una filosofía de la liberación.* Salamanca: Sígueme, 1974. Reedited by Universidad de Guadalajara (Mexico) in 1992.

_____. *El humanismo helénico.* Buenos Aires: Eudeba, 1975. Written in 1961.

_____. "Francisco Romero, un filósofo moderno en Argentina." *Cuyo* (Mendoza, Argentina) 4 (1979): 79-106.

_____. "Hipótesis para una historia de la filosofía en América Latina (1492-1982)." *Ponencias.* Bogotá: USTA, 1983. 405-436.

_____. *La producción teórica de Marx. Un comentario a los Grundrisse.* Mexico City: Siglo veintiuno, 1985.

_____. *Hacia un Marx desconocido. Un comentario de los manuscritos del 1961-63.* Mexico City: Siglo veintiuno, 1988.

_____. *El último Marx (1863-1882) y la liberación latinoamericana.* Mexico City: Siglo veintiuno, 1990.

_____. "1492. El encubrimiento del Otro. Hacia el origen del 'mito de la Modernidad.'" Paper read at Goethe Universität, Frankfurt, October 1992. Published in Madrid: Nueva Utopía, 1992.

Gaos, José. *Carta abierta.* Mexico City: n.p., 1978.

Hale, Charles. "Sustancia y método en el pensamiento de Leopoldo Zea." *Historia Mexicana* 20, 2 (1970).

Heidegger, Martin. *Sein und Zeit.* Tübingen: Niemeyer, 1963.

Husserl, Edmund. *Die Krisis der europäischen Wissenschaften.* Vol. 6. The Hague: Nijhoff, 1962.

Paz, Octavio. *El laberinto de la soledad.* Mexico City: Fondo de Cultura Económica, 1976. First published 1950.

Raat, William. "Ideas e Historia en México. Un ensayo sobre metodología." *Latinoamérica* (Mexico) 3 (1970).

Ricoeur, Paul. "Filosofia e Liberazione." *Filosofia e Liberazione. La sfida del pensiero del Terzo-Mondo*. Lecce: Capone, 1992. 108-115.

Salazar Bondy, Augusto. *Historia de las ideas en el Perú contemporáneo*. 2 vols. Lima: Francisco Moncloa, 1965.

_____. *¿Existe filosofía en América Latina?* Mexico City: Siglo veintiuno, 1968.

Schelkshorn, Hans. *Ethik der Befreiung. Einführung in die Philosophie Enrique Dussels*. Freiburg: Herder, 1992.

Villoro, Luis. *Los grandes momentos del indigenismo en México*. Mexico City: El Colegio de México, 1950.

_____. "Perspectiva de la filosofía en México para 1980." *El perfil de México en 1980*. Mexico City: Siglo veintiuno, 1972.

Zea, Leopoldo. "América y su posible filosofía." *Letras de México* 11 (1941). Expanded in 1942b.

_____. "Superbus philosophus." *Trabajos de historia filosófica, literaria y artística del cristianismo y la Edad Media*. Ed. José Gaos. Mexico City: El Colegio de México, 1943. First published 1942, and referred to as 1942a.

_____. "En torno a una filosofía americana." *Cuadernos Americanos* (May-June 1942b).

_____. *El positivismo en México*. Mexico City: Fondo de Cultura Económica, 1943-44.

_____. "En torno a una filosofía latinoamericana." *Jornada* 52 (1945). First published 1942.

_____. *Dos etapas del pensamiento en Hispanoamérica. Del romanticismo al positivismo*. Mexico City: El Colegio de México, 1949.

_____. *La filosofía como compromiso y otros ensayos*. Mexico City: Tezontle, 1952a.

_____. *Conciencia y posibilidad del mexicano*. Mexico City: Porrúa, 1952b.

_____. *América como conciencia*. Mexico City: Cuadernos Americanos, 1953a.

_____. *La conciencia del hombre en la filosofía. Introducción a la filosofía*. Mexico City: Imprenta Universitaria, 1953b.

_____. *El Occidente y la conciencia de México*. Mexico City: Porrúa, 1953c.

_____. *La filosofía en México*. Mexico City: Libro-Mex, 1955a.

_____. *América en la conciencia de Europa*. Mexico City: Los Presentes, 1955b.

_____. *Esquema para una historia de las Ideas en Iberoamérica*. Mexico City: UNAM, 1956.

_____. *América en la historia*. Mexico City: Fondo de Cultura Económica, 1957.

_____. *América Latina y el mundo*. Caracas: Universidad Central de Venezuela, 1960.

_____. *El pensamiento latinoamericano*. 2 vols. Mexico City: Editorial Pormaca, 1965.

_____. *Antología de la filosofía americana contemporánea*. Mexico City: Costa-Amic, 1968.

_____. *La filosofía latinoamericana como filosofía sin más*. Mexico City: Siglo veintiuno, 1969a.

_____. "Definición de la cultura popular." In Zea, *Características de la cultura nacional*. Mexico City: UNAM, 1969b.

_____. *La esencia de lo americano*. Mexico City: Pleamar, 1971.

_____. *Dependencia y liberación en la cultura latinoamericana.* Mexico City: Joaquín Mortiz, 1974.

_____. *El positivismo en México. Nacimiento, apogeo y decadencia.* Mexico City: Fondo de Cultura Económica, 1975.

_____. *Dialéctica de la conciencia americana.* Mexico City: Alianza, 1976a.

_____. *Filosofía latinoamericana.* Mexico City: ANUIES, 1976b.

_____. *Filosofía de la historia americana.* Mexico City: Fondo de Cultura Económica, 1978.

_____. *Negritud e indigenismo.* Mexico City: UNAM, 1979.

_____. *Latinoamérica en la encrucijada de la historia.* Mexico City: UNAM, 1981.

_____. *Discurso desde la marginación y la barbarie.* Barcelona: Anthropos, 1988.

_____. "12 de Octubre de 1492. ¿Descubrimiento o encubrimiento?" *El descubrimiento de América y su sentido actual.* Ed. Leopoldo Zea. Mexico City: Fondo de Cultura Económica, 1989. 193-204.

Chapter 3

Modernity, Postmodernity, and Novelistic Form in Latin America

Françoise Perus

(translated by Amaryll Chanady)

I would like to examine the relationship between modernity and postmodernity in a specific area of cultural production: that of literature, and narrative poetics in particular. The potential interest of an investigation of this kind can be explained by the fact that the particular mode of apprehension and formalization of our imaginary relations with the natural and social world as it is constituted by the novel is not really ideological (in the sense of a conceptual systematization), but figurative. The novel elaborates and reelaborates, on the verbal level, "images" of the different social subjects, including accents, tonalities, and voices that, on account of their heterogeneity and diversity of aspect, echo those of the verbal texture of society. But the novel also maintains, with respect to its own representations, a specific relationship that some call "irony" (Lukacs), others "autoreflexivity" (Bakhtin), or *action en retour* of the subject of novelistic enunciation with respect to its object (Meschonnic). The novel can therefore become a historical and cultural document of great importance, because it is particularly sensitive to aspects of social life that other sources or forms of discourse (ones that are more conjunctural, as in the case of political discourse, or more

43

conceptual and abstract, as theoretical or philosophical discourse) cannot register.

These aspects of novelistic discourse obviously do not concern the information (in a narrow sense) that a fictional text can contain in its implicit or explicit references to a particular historical event, happening, or process. The referential mechanisms that solicit the virtual reader's empirical experience or historical culture have as their main function the production of a "truth effect" destined to reinforce the mechanisms of identification and recognition, and merely serve to situate the novel's referent in its concrete spatiotemporal dimension.

The documentary value of narrative fiction is situated on other levels: in the first place, on that of the configuration of *signs*, which is especially indicative of the historical and cultural forms of constituting subjects in their relation with time and space, and in their relation with that of "others"; and in the second, on the level of the combined artistic modalization of signs and properties of the referent on the compositional and stylistic planes. This modalization not only registers, in its particular sphere and according to its specific modalities, the concrete forms of social dialogism (or its absence), but also involves the crucial problem of historical and cultural forms of relationship with language itself.

Because we are talking about signs, the presence and recurrence of mythical figures, archetypes, "social types," "problematic individuals" in the process of formation, or simple "voices" lacking a practical dimension and associated with the conceptualizations of time and space involved by these different forms of subjective individuality, are not strictly "literary" problems in the technical sense of the word. They are rather artistic formalizations of specific and differentiated modes of being, existing and acting (or not acting) in the world, that the novel takes up, formalizes, and socializes anew. One can say the same thing about genres and subgenres that inform, confer ethical value on, and ensure the sociohistorical viability of such signs. The possibility or impossibility of an epic, as well as its drifts toward tragedy, lyrical poetry, the grotesque, parody, or the carnivalesque, do not reveal only one point of view, but also deeply entrenched tendencies of sociocultural processes and structures that go beyond the value systems of authors who narrate imaginary relations with the world, together with, and from the perspective of, their own fictional "children."

The joint artistic modalization of signs and referents on the compositional and stylistic levels maintains a close relation with the essentially "modern" character of the novel genre. Although the genre is not strictly speaking peculiar to "modernity"—characterized by the dissolution of forms of communal and relatively autarkic social organization, and by the expansion and generalization of relations of exchange—nevertheless modernity enabled it to become a predominant genre in Europe during the nineteenth century, and in Latin America in the twentieth. Modernity made possible not only the concretization of the virtualities of those "vulgar" and dialogical forms of classical antiquity and the Middle Ages in which the genre has its principal antecedents, but also the redefinition of the mode of existence of the great traditional genres (mainly the epic and tragedy). The novel genre is, according to Bakhtin, the only one capable of appropriating all genres, past and present, literary and nonliterary, and reelaborating them around what he calls "a zone of maximum contact with the present of culture in the becoming" (1978: 151). "Plurilinguism" and discursive heterogeneity, dialogism, and the structuring of literary representations around the present of culture in its becoming, thus constitute the distinctive traits of this genre whose zenith coincides with the ascent of modernity.

The correlation between these three fundamental aspects of the genre determines, theoretically at least, the relation that the novel establishes with language. In fact, these correlations imply a triple orientation of novelistic enunciation: toward its own object, toward the object of enunciation or discourse of the "Other," and toward itself. This in turn leads to other inferences with respect to (1) the possibility of a dissociation between language and its object, and thus the liberation of the object from the mythical power of language; (2) the recognition, tacit if not explicit, of the relativity of all language—thus, the recognition and the valorization of the object can only result from the dialogical confrontation within which it is situated; and (3) the possibility of escaping from the opaque and closed prison-house of language, or of discourse, that led Roland Barthes to claim, in his acceptance speech on entering the Collège de France, that "all language is totalitarian."

Unless we continue maintaining a linear and progressive conception of history, postmodernity cannot be understood as a new epoch that comes to replace modernity in the same way that the latter had replaced traditional societies. The relationship between modernity and postmodernity consists rather in a crisis of our episteme (in the sense that Foucault gave the term) primarily concerning notions of historical and progressive time, the individual or collective subject related to the previous notion, and finally knowledge, based on the separation between subject and object. In their mutual relations, all these concepts structure the horizon of "Western rationality," originating in the Enlightenment and now apparently in its last throes. More than the arrival of a new era, postmodernity thus consists of modernity's turning upon itself, once the instruments that fashioned it and legitimated it have been discarded. This explains its multiple paradoxes: the dissolution of the coordinates of time and space, the decentering or disintegration of the subject, the dissemination of meaning, and the rejection of all foundations of knowledge. The predomination of the "aesthetic" and even the "aestheticization" of politics in postmodern discourse are not gratuitous: they translate in their fashion the overlapping between spheres of human activity, and the modalities of formalizing our relations with the world that modernity had insisted on maintaining separate, based on an opposition between what is "rational" and what is not. We still have to determine, however, whether postmodernity does not run the risk of relegating political discourse, and politics itself, to pure fiction (in the traditional sense of the term), thus returning to a magical-mythical conception of language.

In fact, the particular slant acquired by impugning the episteme of modern rationality in the configurations of a discourse of "postmodernity" in search of itself simultaneously *within* and *against* what it feels in advance to be monolithical and already known (and what thus has no reason to be reconstituted in its heterogeneity and diversity of perspectives), complicates the delimitation of the contributions of postmodern thinkers to the crisis of civilization to which they allude, and to which they try hard to contribute. First, this is because of the impossibility of defining a precise object of knowledge that goes beyond the mere substantivization of an adjective: "modernity" is what is "modern." As such, this notion only "designates" what the subjectless discourse of postmodernity (another substantivized adjective) identifies and valorizes as "modern" on the margins of any precise temporal and discursive frame. But the procedure is not so new: it reminds us of the old problematic of the Zeitgeist of German philosophy. Second, the delimitation of the contributions of postmodern thinkers is difficult because of the refusal of these thinkers to consider themselves as part of a debate concerning a form of civilization no doubt in crisis, and to reestablish the links between *thinking* and *doing* in that form of civilization. Because it admits to neither exteriority nor contradiction, the discourse of postmodernity tends to become a monologic discourse that acquires, in spite of itself, the inverted form of substantialism and fundamentalism that it intends to attack.

The elucidation of the crisis that modern Western civilization is experiencing, and the search for viable alternatives to this crisis (if it really is a question of that), cannot do without a careful reconstitution of the debates and issues of this form of civilization in the double sphere of thinking and doing. There is not the least doubt that this revision implies special attention to the diversity and lack of linearity of its periods, to the resulting complexity and instability of the forms acquired by diverse agents and subjects, and to the relations between language (languages) and its "objects." If we do not want to return to the metaphysics that postmodern discourse claims to refute, we must start by refusing to convert modernity into a metaphysical entity.

Like the discourse that impugns it today, modern Western civilization—which initiated its expansion five hundred years ago with the great discoveries and was consolidated with the second industrial revolution—constructed an image of itself that affirmed its destiny to become universalized as civilization by antonomasia, exclusion, or abasement of what remained outside its orbit, or resisted absorption. On the one hand there was the East, around which all the attributes of "barbarism" (which the West claimed and still claims to have left behind) were crystallized and continue being crystallized; on the other there were the "backward peripheries," a mixture of the "promised land" (North America for a certain period of time) and irreducible "barbarism" (Latin America and then Africa). In particular contexts, all these images became the object of various acts of resemantization that served the internal questioning of an aspect of one's own civilization (Montesquieu's Uzbeks or Rica, Rousseau's "noble savage," or Chateaubriand's Chactas, not to mention the various ways of exalting exoticism in nineteenth-century European literature and culture), without involving a substantial modification of the structure of the semantic field thus constituted.

This construction of joint images of the "I" and the "Other" implied in the nineteenth century an ordering of the geographical and cultural space in function of a differential temporality according to what one judged to be their greater or lesser distance with respect to Civilization. In this aspect, the "I" was the measure of all things, and only conceded to the Other a formal existence, or an accidental character, destined to reaffirm its own preeminence and right to subordinate the Other.

Quite different, however, was the perception of the spatio-temporal relations in the periphery that had acquired formal independence and that, like it or not, was also part of "Western civilization." In the first place, the "modernizing" sectors' internalization of the superiority of the Atlantic and civilized West implied for them the representation of "universality" as something that should no doubt be attained, but that was for the moment situated outside its own geographical and cultural space. Second, given the highly uneven degree of international exchange within the different geographical and cultural areas of a nation within the periphery, a spatial representation of the various historical periods arose.

If we examine in this context Domingo Faustino Sarmiento's foundational text *Facundo* (1845) — which, in spite of not being a novel, is characterized by a high degree of formal and discursive heterogeneity that situates it close to narrative fiction — we can identify the following traits. First, "civilization" is read above all through its absence in the Argentine countryside: a lack of dams and navigation on the rivers, a lack of means of transportation, a

lack of villages and cities, a lack of industry, and so on. Everything is primarily a comparison with an *ailleurs* (an "elsewhere")
situated in Europe or the United States. When "civilization" becomes concretized in a positive manner on the level of images
and not merely on that of notions or valorizations, it cannot go
beyond the sphere of representation: it only manifests itself in
theaters, operas, and in the wearing of a dress coat or fashions
that conform to models brought from abroad.

The evocation of "barbarism," however, takes the form of a
spatial displacement in the pampa and an inventory of places
and social types described according to other images originating
in an encyclopedic knowledge (in the literal sense of the word,
that is to say, taken from encyclopedias): the entire accumulation of "known" representations of primitivism appears in
Sarmiento's discourse, with a predilection for Asia Minor. Apart
from some passing allusions to China, the Roman township, or
the European feudal system, Asia Minor provides the most varied and constant system of comparisons for the evocation of nomadic life and the desert: Persia, Mesopotamia, the Tigris, the
Euphrates, and Baghdad. Yet in spite of this intense mobiliza-
tion of elements of knowledge, images, and myths coming from
the most diverse horizons and without any other temporal connection besides that of designating the remote origin that "civilization" left behind, Sarmiento concludes that the Argentine
Republic in the middle of the nineteenth century, this "Thebes
of the River Plate," has a new and original ("inédito") character.
Revealed to European, and especially French, eyes, which are so
eager for new styles, it leaves them "astounded" (*Facundo*). In
other words, there is no "universal" language capable of describing this new reality.

Sarmiento admits that he proceeds like a chronicler, translating the "unknown" into the terms of the "known." The same
happens to him as had to the chroniclers of the Indies: when he
wants to describe the absence of civilization and culture of a geographic and human space that he considers "unpublished," but
of which he has practical experience, he ends up revealing the
existence of a different culture, and one certainly far less "foreign" than the bookish references that he uses in a barbarous
manner ("a lo bárbaro"), that is, without being able to establish

concrete historico-temporal connections between the different images of an identical "substance" existing in different areas. In fact, what his analyses of the gauchos' ways of life in the pampa demonstrate, beyond the apparent cultural "vacuum," are forms of knowledge, systems of values, aesthetic conceptions, and forms of social organization in accordance with specific and geographically determined conditions of life. (Here too Sarmiento leaves aside historical factors; or, when he does consider them, it is only as "idiosyncrasies" of the Spaniards and of the natives, the latter of whom lack, according to him, any desire for progress.) As a result, in this conjunction of "civilization *and* barbarism" (the emphasis is mine), which characterizes, according to Sarmiento, the supposedly "one and indivisible" Argentine Republic, the *cultural* image of "barbarism" is much more concrete, richer, and more valuable than that of its "civilized" counterpart, to the point that it "literarily" permeates the conceptual and rhetorical demonstration of the text with its lyrical accents, "oral" narrations, and even "fireside tales."

These ambiguities and paradoxes of the system of representation on the level of the enunciated reappear in the internal configuration of the writing subject. On one occasion, Sarmiento bases the conception of his relationship to the object of his writing (Argentine reality, considered mainly as a spatial and temporal disjunction between civilization and barbarism) on the model of the chroniclers of the Indies, but this is not the only representation he gives of this relationship. Besides the chronicler, we also find the opposing figures of the author of *La democracia en América* and the gaucho singer:

> A la América del Sur y a la República Argentina sobre todo, le ha hecho falta un Tocqueville, que presumido del conocimiento de las teorías sociales, como viajero científico de barómetros, octantes y brújulas, viniera a penetrar en el interior de nuestra vida política; como en un campo vastísimo y aun no explorado ni descrito por la ciencia. (Prologue to *Facundo*; Sarmiento 2)
>
> South America, and the Argentine Republic in particular, lacked a Tocqueville, who, presumptuous in his knowledge of social theories, would come as a scientific traveler with barometers, octants, and compasses, to

penetrate the interior of our political life, as if it were a
vast field, still unexplored and undescribed by science.

Meanwhile, in the absence of a Tocqueville,

> El cantor está haciendo candorosamente el mismo trabajo
> de crónica, costumbres, historias, biografía, que el bardo
> de la Edad Media, y sus versos serían recogidos más
> tarde como los documentos y datos en que habría de
> apoyarse el historiador futuro, si a su lado no estuviese
> otra sociedad culta con superior inteligencia de los
> acontecimientos, que la que el infeliz despliega en sus
> rapsodias ingenuas. (Part 1, chapter 2 of *Facundo*;
> Sarmiento 28)

> The singer is candidly accomplishing the same work on
> chronicles, customs, stories, and biography, as the bard
> of the Middle Ages, and his verses will be collected later
> as the documents and data that the future historian will
> have to use as a base, unless surrounded by another
> cultured society with a knowledge of events that is
> superior to that which the unfortunate man
> demonstrates in his ingenuous rhapsodies.

Obviously these two tutelary figures of the writing subject do
not have the same status in the text if gaucho life occupies the
place of interpreted culture and Tocqueville represents the perspective of the interpreting culture. Both, however, perceived as
simultaneously close and distant, illuminate the two separate
faces of that "historian" of the present that Sarmiento would
like to be: one who observes from the outside, applying notions
and value judgments coming from a "universal" and cultured
tradition that has still not arrived in Argentina, and one who
narrates and re-creates from a fundamentally oral tradition,
starting from his own experience and his own passions. Without
the instability of the subject of enunciation and its displacement
from one sphere to the next and from one perspective to another, one could explain neither the linguistic, discursive, and
formal heterogeneity of the text, nor the fact that the observed
culture can end up acquiring, at least sometimes, the character
of a "voice" capable of converting the interpreting culture into
the interpreted one (for example, Napoleon or Robespierre seen
as "bad gauchos").

These particular characteristics of enunciation and the wavering subject that it constitutes lead me to another figuration of the subject in the text: that of the author of *The Last of the Mohicans*, with whom Sarmiento partially identifies, not only because of the similitude between the Argentinean and North American referents, but also and above all because of the point of view that informs Cooper's fiction and the constitution of his characters. According to Sarmiento:

> El único romancista norteamericano que haya logrado hacerse un nombre europeo, es Fenimore Cooper, y eso porque transportó la escena de sus descripciones fuera del círculo ocupado por los plantores *al límite entre la vida bárbara y la civilizada*, al teatro de la guerra en que las *razas* indígenas y la *raza* sajona están combatiendo por la posesión del terreno. . . .
>
> Hay que notar de paso un hecho que es muy explicativo de los fenómenos sociales de los pueblos. Los accidentes de la naturaleza producen costumbres y usos peculiares a estos accidentes, haciendo que donde estos accidentes se repiten vuelvan a encontrarse los mismos medios de parar a ellos, inventados por *pueblos* distintos. . . . En fin, mil otros *accidentes* que omito, prueban la verdad de que modificaciones análogas del *suelo* traen análogas costumbres, recursos y expedientes. No es otra la razón de hallar en Fenimore Cooper descripciones de usos y costumbres que parecen plagiadas de la pampa; así hallamos en los hábitos pastoriles de la América, reproducidos hasta los trajes, el semblante grave y hospitalidad árabes. (Part 1, chapter 2 of *Facundo*; Sarmiento 21; emphasis added)
>
> The only North American novelist to have acquired European recognition is James Fenimore Cooper, and that is because he transposed the scene of his description outside the perimeter occupied by the planters, to the *border between barbarian and civilized life*, and to the scene of the war in which the indigenous *races* and the Saxon *race* are fighting for possession of the land. . . .
>
> One must mention in passing a fact that satisfactorily explains the social phenomena of societies. Accidents of nature produce customs and usages that are peculiar to these accidents, with the result that where these accidents are repeated, the same means of dealing with

them are to be found, although they are invented by
different *cultures*. . . . In short, a thousand other
contingencies that I will omit prove the truth that
analogous modifications of the *land* bring about
analogous customs, means, and measures. There is no
other reason why we find in Cooper descriptions of
usages and customs that seem copied from the pampa;
and that is why we find in the pastoral habits of
America, which are reproduced even in the costumes
themselves, the grave countenance and hospitality
proper to the Arabs.

Cooper's perspective, which leads one to consider the object
of fictional representation as a frontier between two cultures and
two worlds that are separated and in conflict, is, without doubt,
the same as Sarmiento's. But it could also be that of Bakhtin,
when he situates the structuring of literary representation
within a "zone of maximum contact with a present in its becoming" (1978: 150), and demonstrates how this form of structuring
entails not only "plurilinguism" or linguistic and discursive heterogeneity in any novelistic text, but also the configuration of an
essentially "dialogical" textual space. As we will recall, it is in
relation with the dialogical nature of this textual space that the
Soviet critic and theoretician posits the problematization of the
relationship between language and object, the relativization of
all language, and the self-reflexivity of the subject of enunciation. All these are aspects that Sarmiento does not explain with
respect to Cooper's novel, but that he puts into practice in his
writing of *Facundo*, even though he had not intended to write a
novel. It thus remains to determine whether, in situations of peripheral transition, the characteristics of the genre established
by Bakhtin do not also apply to other types of discourse. By "peripheral transition" I mean the constitution or reconstitution of
national culture and literature around a double dialogue, tense
and conflicting, and between spheres of culture: "universal"
culture on the one hand (or, that of the various metropolises,
past and present, that can in no way be considered homogeneous), and "autochthonous" culture, mainly oral and popular,
although not homogeneous either, on the other.

The "dialogism" in question is always determined in a specific manner, and occurs under concrete conditions. Although it subordinates vernacular culture and problematizes the two "languages" and perspectives between which it moves, Sarmiento's dialogism cannot escape these elements. Up to now, I have tried to show how disjunction, which is also discontinuity between two social and cultural forms in conflict, leads to a spatialization of temporal representation, or, in other words, to the neutralization of the historico-temporal coordinates through the distribution of these forms within differentiated and unconnected spaces. Therefore, although the historical and progressive time of the "center" constitutes without any doubt the *implicit* ideological horizon that structures the text, the latter's concretization on the American continent becomes the representation of what is actually unrepresentable.

This explains why the confrontation between present-day reality in Argentina and the "languages" that can depict it does not appear as a debate of ideas as much as a collation of images and myths, around which gravitate numerous notions and value judgments deriving from a Tocqueville-inspired positivism that is practically not subject to debate. The traces of enlightened thought in Sarmiento are therefore to be found in his accumulation of myths, rather than in his philosophical and political conceptions, and are thus far removed from Auguste Comte's form of positivism adopted in the middle of the nineteenth century. This is why the myths informing open-ended and progressive history in Latin America after Sarmiento do not all originate in the pre-Hispanic or vernacular tradition.

The same impossibility of representing historical and progressive time in a concrete manner also applies to the forms of representing biographical time. Between social and political events that are again primarily defined by the place of their occurrence and characterized by the blind forces that set them in motion, sweep them along, and confront them, Juan Facundo Quiroga's life appears as the reiteration of a single gesture that fixes him in the stereotyped image of a cruel and barbarous *caudillo*, that is, as a prototype in which races, natural surroundings, and circumstances are crystallized. The significant moments of his life are juxtaposed or ordered in a contiguous manner according to places and a purely external and chronological time, and only reiterate the same image of a "barbarous" essence that defines him as well as the background from which he comes. This is why he cannot evolve or change; with his excesses and accumulation of crimes, he seems to emerge from a Byzantine novel rather than from a history whose reconstitution and peaceful understanding are rendered impossible by those barbarous times, according to Sarmiento himself.

We thus find two different types of "subject" in Sarmiento's text: one is stable, represented, and fixed in its "essence" according to a basically positivistic conception, and the other is unstable, constituting itself in the process of writing and situated halfway between two sociocultural worlds that, in spite of their differences, alternately and jointly occupy the place of the "I" and the "Other." Both worlds thus create around the subject of writing a tense and conflicting dialogical space that not only relativizes both voices, but also contributes to the problematization of the desire to imprison the object of representation (the first "subject" in this case) in a static and positivistic manner.

Given the characteristics and the limitations of this incipient dialogism, however, it has no possibility of being developed at that time, because it lacks the interiorization of process that modernity associates with historical and biographical time. In Sarmiento, the justly detected structural heterogeneity remains a spatial juxtaposition and disjunction, which cannot be resolved except through the substitution of "civilization" for "barbarism." This explains the belief in the necessity of "importing" European immigrants and other signs of modernity.

In much of later Spanish American literature, this notion of process, which did not go beyond the form of a desired horizon that the substitution of "civilization" in *Facundo* was supposed to bring closer, becomes concretized precisely at the time when Sarmiento posits the disjunction between "civilization" and "barbarism." But this is done in a paradoxical fashion; the disjunction is reformulated in terms of "the barbarism of civilization," and runs through all social narrative of the first half of the twentieth century, although in fact the reformulation can already be found in José Hernández's *Martín Fierro* (1872). Instead of acquiring an open and progressive character, historical time thus takes on the form of a return to one's origins.

In the first part of *Martín Fierro*, a kind of "novelized" epic whose narrative structure constitutes an implicit dialogue ("external," in Bakhtin's terms) with Sarmiento's *Facundo*, Fierro, dispossessed and persecuted, takes refuge in the Indian camps that the law of the "civilizers" obliges him to exterminate. Thus, instead of leading to an appropriation of historical time, the narrated process ends up being its negation. Once again, the notion of open-ended historical becoming only informs the text from the outside, entailing the annulment of the gaucho's former free reign over the pampa. In the same way, Arturo Cova and his men, in Eustacio Rivera's *La vorágine* (1924), surrounded by the "vortex" represented by the penetration of commercial and financial capital that destroys the semifeudal structure of the Colombian flatlands from the borders of the nation, are "swallowed by the jungle," that is to say, by "nature" spoliated and violated by "civilization." The same happens to the protagonist of *Canaima*, by Rómulo Gallegos (1935), who ends up stranded in the Upper Orinoco in an indigenous community that gives him shelter.

There are many examples of this thematization of the return to one's origins under the impact of the arrival of "modernity." This return entails the cancellation or reversal of historical time as well as the loss of space (territory) in several senses of the word. The culminating point is Alejo Carpentier's *Los pasos perdidos* (1953) and the poetics of "marvelous American reality" (*lo real maravilloso americano*), illustrated to a certain degree by this and other novels by the Cuban author.

Obviously this thematization does not always lead to the same configurations of meaning: "civilization" can even win over "barbarism" again, sending it back to its origins in the jungle, as in Gallegos's *Doña Bárbara* (1929), without entailing a substantial alteration of the kind of chronotype I am trying to define.

The discovery of the types of juxtaposition or superposition of different historical periods within the same national territory in *Los pasos perdidos* takes the form of a spatial displacement in search of lost musical instruments and voices, starting in New

York City and ending with the encounter with the original tribe on the edge of the Venezuelan jungle. The journey tends to make different areas and epochs coincide as they are connected by the sole presence of the traveler, who confronts both enlightened rationalism and its surrealistic counterpart with experiences that end up transforming the intellectual and anthropological voyage into a mythical one. Traveling backward in time and coming face to face with myth (or myths) once again places historical and progressive time outside the time and space of the novel.

The treatment of this theme is even more interesting and complex in Rómulo Gallegos's novel *Canaima*, which is a direct antecedent of Carpentier's text. In *Canaima*, the disjunctions between nature and culture (an ideological space that is complementary to the opposition between "civilization" and "barbarism") and between historical and mythical time are first solved (in the double sense of resolving and dissolving) through a particular configuration of time in the landscape. The different time periods and "ages" of humanity, as well as the various myths associated with them, are not juxtaposed or superposed, but blended in the intermingling and reflecting waters of the Orinoco delta, whose sandbar impedes free passage toward the open sea (or open-ended historical becoming). Likewise, the form of narration mirrors the diegesis (which is structured around a double movement of ascending and descending the current of the Orinoco and its tributaries between rapids and stagnant water) by alternating between acceleration, stagnation, and regress in historical and biographical time. The narrative proposes two opposing and mutually contradictory denouements: one that puts an end, with the sigh of the Guyanese from the deserted villages and the return of myth, to the desolation of a new cycle of international relations, and another that describes the ship's escape from the sandbar of the Orinoco and its passage to the open sea, to which it conveys the mestizo son of the protagonist who remained stranded with the indigenous tribe in the Upper Orinoco. Although the surroundings and the narrative content are different from those of *Cien años de soledad* (first published 1967), where the extinction of the Buendía family and the stagnation of Macondo contrast with the problematic decipherment (of the past or of the present?) of Melquíades's manuscripts, the structure of the chronotope and its double resolution seem rather similar to those of García Márquez's novel.

These reformulations of Sarmiento's thesis of "civilization and/or barbarism" in the different forms of the Spanish American narrative chronotope since the end of the nineteenth century and in the novel of the first part of the twentieth, situate the problem of interpreting Latin American "modernity" with respect to a repeated desire to liberate open-ended and progressive history (always on the point of occurring) from the accumulation of myths that place obstacles in its course or impede its emergence. One should point out that in this desire, the function of the progressive perspective of the Enlightenment only consists in the subordination of the complex and greatly varied accumulation of mythical representations that the protagonists bring into contact with a present whose becoming and openness toward the future always remain uncertain. Therefore, this perspective does not entail an extensive debate of ideas with the Enlightenment on the philosophical, ideological, and political level, as was the case in Russia at the end of the nineteenth century with Dostoyevski's polyphonic novel and poetics, analyzed by Bakhtin. In fact, such a *debate* of ideas and "consciences" does not appear in the Spanish American novel, and then, with *Yo el Supremo* by Augusto Roa Bastos, only in a carnivalized form rather than a polyphonic one in the strict sense. Maybe this was not gratuitous: the Jesuit missions were the main source of enlightened thought. In this aspect at least, Roa Bastos's novel surpasses Carpentier's *El reino de este mundo, El siglo de las luces*, and *El recurso del método*, which tried to illustrate the avatars of rationalism in contact with "marvelous American reality" or, inversely, question the supposed linearity of European time.

Apart from these examples that come from highly intellectual and transcultural writers, Latin American fiction tends above all to reactivate, apply to its own context, and confront with its own traditions, the mythological beliefs and practices that enlightened rationalism claims to have left behind, and the myths that this same rationalism created in order to distinguish itself from its origins or to represent its own periphery. This particular dialogic and doubly peripheral confrontation with the culture of the Enlightenment entails a series of peculiar characteristics in the configuration of the fictional character-signs. Formed by the confluence of a historical perspective that is simultaneously open and truncated, and various mythological traditions ("universal" and vernacular), these characters generally and jointly participate in the archetype and the "social type" (pertaining to a region, ethnic-cultural type, or class). In their frequently erratic trajectory, two antithetical narrative forms often converge: the initiatory quest and the bildungsroman. In this convergence, the epic and tragic character of the mythical archetype (which involves neither the appropriation of a heterogeneous space nor the internalization of historical and biographical time, but the reiteration of an abstract destiny) stands in contradiction to the notion of concrete and open-ended process inherent in the bildungsroman. For that reason, the internal transformation of the protagonist can only acquire the form of a violent and tumultuous catharsis, in which the mythical takes the place of a kind of collective unconscious.

On account of the multiple mythological elements and historical epochs thematized in *Canaima*, the problematic acquires its clearest formulation throughout the greater part of this novel, especially when directly related to autocratic political leadership (*caciquismo*), the absence of stable political and juridical institutions, the precariousness of the very concept of justice, and the predomination of essentially oral and pragmatic cultural forms (see Perus, "Universalidad del regionalismo"). In the European bildungsroman, the figure of the subject and the different value systems suppose not only the internalization of a juridical norm that makes possible the articulation of the notion of the individual subject with that of a universal and abstract human essence, but also that of relatively stable institutional frameworks within which tradition and memory are articulated and conflicts between value systems are resolved. In other words, the bildungsroman and the autoreflexivity inherent in it are inseparable from the constitution and appropriation of a written tradition and, at the same time, from the elaboration of a universalist conception of the human being in philosophy. The passage from orality to writing, and from the spatial and regional to the "universal" (articulated around political, juridical, and cultural institutions proper to the nation-state), thus brings with it the first deterritorialization of the identity of the subject and its rearticulation around temporal, historical, and/or biographical axes.

Agustín Yáñez treats the problematic in *Al filo del agua* (1947) in the context of the modernization and institutionalization of the Mexican Revolution (see Perus, "La poética narrativa"). In this novel, the narrator from Jalisco contrasts the rituals of an ecclesiastical culture of colonial origin and based on transcendental faith, which has established itself in a small village with an essentially oral tradition, with the penetration of the multiple forms of a modern and written culture (newspapers, novels, and so on). The transformation of the forms of subjective individuality, formerly ruled by "fears and desires," are situated on two levels: first, as a collective catharsis effected by the encounter of sacred music with profane music (the sphere of orality), and second, as a movement of secularization of faith, morals, and art that is related to the penetration of written cultural forms, and that makes possible new forms of individuality related to uprootedness and the subjective appropriation of historical and biographical time. There is a fundamental difference, however, between the ways in which Yáñez and Gallegos treat the subject. Gallegos bases the catharsis on the intermingling with natural forces and the association with an animistic conception of the world originating in indigenous tradition, and rejects, at least partially, the deterritorialization of subjective identity and the forms of individualism proper to modern Western civilization. Yáñez has recourse to the cultural context of the disjunction between the sacred and the profane, thus allowing for forms of individualism questioned by Gallegos. Similar scenarios are also found in *Los ríos profundos* by José María Arguedas, and especially in his *El zorro de arriba y el zorro de abajo*, where the deterritorialization of individual and collective identity related to the migration of the indigenous population to the coast takes the form of a reaffirmation and redefinition of indigenous cultural identity in new places and territories.

These particular forms of figuring the relationship between space, time, and character-signs in Spanish American narrative corresponding to the phase of the instauration of "modernity," also involve specific relationships between the narrator and the "languages" that contribute to the artistic modalization of a dialogism that is to a large extent problematic. The absence of the constitution of a fully national culture until very late in the twentieth century in most of the Latin American countries implies the coexistence, in the same national geographic space, of cultural elements that not only belong to (theoretically) different historical periods, but are also unequally distributed among the different regions and social and ethnic strata that participate (or do not participate) in national culture in the process of formation. For that reason, each one of these elements (formally distinct and implying worldviews at different stages of elaboration) necessarily carries the marks of its historical and cultural origins and its sedimentation in a certain social or ethnic stratum. In other words, such elements do not have the universally abstract character that they acquire in European culture. To the problem of "plurilinguism" postulated by Bakhtin in terms of internal differentiation in the concrete usages of a national language, related to the different spheres of social and human activity and the resulting social disparities, one must add the problem of cultural heterogeneity and its deep internal disjunctions (which can even reach linguistic difference in the literal sense).

In this context, and owing to their juxtaposition or confrontation with other "languages" of vernacular provenance, even the "universal" or universalized languages (including canonized literary genres) tend to lose their "universality." All languages appear as relativized here, although not fully dialogized, as is proven by the difficulty that many Spanish American authors have in sustaining a uniform point of view and style with respect to the object of representation. Obviously, this uniformity does exist, but it is either circumscribed to lyrical subjectivism and the stylization of past genres from a nostalgic or tragic perspective, in which plurilinguism and dialogism are absent (Jorge Isaacs's *María* or Ricardo Güiraldes's *Don Segundo Sombra*), or projected from the outside onto the object of representation (structures, processes, and social agents) in the form of a monologic and positivistic conception, resulting in a naturalistic and purely formal differentiation between the "written" style of the narrator and the "oral" and regional style of the characters (Esteban Echeverría's *El matadero*, Gallegos's *Doña Bárbara*, or Jorge

Icaza's *Huasipungo*). But as soon as the object of representation is constituted by the artistic formulation of the relationships between cultural spaces that are heterogeneous (and perceived as such), and the subjective aspects of these relationships, another type of narrator appears, whom we could call ubiquitous. This narrator alternates between positions of exteriority with respect to the characters and the narrated world, and positions of complete identification with them. The former positions correspond to the open-ended historical vision foreign to the represented world, and the latter force the narrator not only to step back in order to let the characters speak, but also to blend his or her own discourse with theirs. In this way, the "written" language of the narrator (who, as such, tends toward monolinguism and monologism) is contaminated, at least stylistically speaking, by the multiple registers of orality of the fictional characters who are frequently popular, or at least immersed in the life of the street, the public square, or the different spheres of practical life.

This type of narrator, found in many Spanish American novels, does not correspond to other types of narrators found in the European tradition, such as the "omniscient" narrator, who reproduces the dialogues of the characters among themselves and reconstitutes his or her own psychological processes by analyzing the characters, or the subjective narrator of the so-called stream-of-consciousness technique, which transforms the characters and subject of enunciation into a purely "internal voice." The kind of narrator we find in Gallegos's *Canaima*, Asturias's *El Señor Presidente*, Yáñez's *Al filo del agua*, or Juan José Arreola's *La feria*, to give only a few examples, is quite different, because the conceptions both of the character-signs and of narrative time are different. As I have already mentioned, the characters, which are generally numerous, episodic, and not situated hierarchically, are constituted neither as individual psychological entities subject to development nor as "consciences" or "ideologues" (in the Dostoyevskian or Bakhtinian sense of the term). Rather, they are archetypes, social types and supports for "languages" and worldviews in different stages of elaboration and originating in heterogeneous and largely unconnected spaces and temporalities. As such, these characters do not lead to the construction of a uniform, progressive, and open-ended narrative time, but to a conjunction of diverse historical and mythical temporalities, which the narrator structures around a zone of contact with a present whose becoming always remains uncertain. By alternating between external characterization and identification with the characters, the subject of enunciation thus depicts local and very diverse aspects of ubiquitous social and cultural conflicts.

On the strictly linguistic level, this leads to a noticeable plurality of language registers and an accentuated dialogism, which profoundly enrich and renew literary language, that is to say, writing. On the compositional level, however, the characters do not reach their full development as "voices" ("consciences" or "ideologues"), with the result that the dialogism tends to limit itself to the confrontation between the historical conscience of the narrator and the multiple forms of a kind of "collective unconscious" that the latter tries to investigate and express through the characters in an operation that is cathartic both for the narrator and for the reader. More than the characters as such, it is thus the "languages" that they represent and the difficulties of dialogical interrelation between them that constitute the primary object of these poetic narratives. Yet these narratives evince a sustained effort to liberate for the reader the different "objects" figured by the mythical power of language that imprisons them and makes social subjects reiterate "useless" or tragic gestures and actions, through the systematic confrontation of social discourses and multiple points of view that the social structures tend to maintain separate.

This strategy is usually symbolized in the text itself. But as soon as the artistic project goes beyond stylization (or parodic accentuation) of the different discourses involved in order to introduce a questioning of the discourse and practices of domination, whether religious or political, the symbolic figuration is generally situated in the context of the public square or the popular fair, with the resulting parody and carnivalization of all the crystallizations or solidifications of dominant discourse. That is the case with the novels I last mentioned, and probably *El Señor Presidente* (1946) displays the most characteristic formulation. In this novel by Miguel Ángel Asturias, the figure of the dictator has a contrasting double, the puppeteer, who makes his puppets move in the fair theater in the same way that the president makes his subjects move. The puppeteer, however, who wants to make children cry and only makes them laugh, and ends up insane because of a reality that exceeds his fiction, also represents the narrator. At the same time that the narrator stylizes, parodies, and carnivalizes all the forms of dominant culture, he constructs his characters like real puppets distributed in unconnected and timeless places, and situates literary representation within the confusion of the real and the unreal, laughter and absurdity. The parodic and carnivalesque theatricalization of discourses that are solidified and lack any correspondence with the practices that they legitimate and hide, and their contrast with the reality of dreams that transfigure repressed fears and desires, no doubt constitute the main antecedent not only of the dictator novels but also of the particular form that the historical novel takes in Latin America, where it is more present and in vogue than ever.

Literary discourse, and more specifically narrative fiction, is not conjunctural. Because of its artistic formalization of cultural and subjective realities, it is inscribed instead in the large domain of mentalities. In contrast to the various kinds of ideological and political discourse, Spanish American novelistic discourse emphasizes the precariousness of the notion of historical and progressive time (or, in other words, the difficulties of its concretization) in the subcontinent's culture. Although the educated elite is aware of a tacit horizon without which a properly novelistic perspective would not even be possible (that is to say, an openness toward the present in its becoming), such a notion tends to remain outside the narrated world, thus indicating the persistence of a profound cultural separation between the represented sectors, popular or not, and the "cultivated" elite. Whereas the latter frequently have an epic-tragic conception, associated with "barbarism," the conquest(s), or political change, in the former there tend to predominate mythical traditions of diverse origins and nature, vernacular (forms of animism, or cosmologies of pre-Hispanic origins) as well as "universal." What is repeatedly perceived as a historical blocking of an open and progressive perspective (and the concomitant questioning of the results and values on which such a perspective is based) tends to give rise to an equally repeated movement of return to one's origins that is simultaneously a descent to Hell and a voyage to the territorial borders, as well as a crossing of the frontiers of the zone of cultural influence of the Western world. The pre-Hispanic cultural heritage, associated or not with the premodern humanism of Dante, thus establishes the basis for a questioning of modern Western civilization. Therefore, by means of a dialogism that is more formal than real, the (re)encounter with the subverted course of history involves either a hypothetical indigenous uprising designed to substitute one culture for another, or an equally hypothetical process of maturation of a cultural miscegenation that is capable of assimilating both heritages in a critical manner.

The idea of the nation-state, which implies a separation between the subject (individual and collective) and his or her territorial foundations, as well as a rearticulation of individual and social identity in the more abstract and complex framework of national institutions, remains largely absent from the virtual subjects of the posited substitution. The process of "miscegenation" (*mestizaje*), which is generally linked to the loss of one's roots, gives rise to unstable forms of individuality, because an identification with separate and heterogeneous social and cultural contexts does not allow (or allows only with difficulty) processes that are centered and based on oneself, and that can lead to redefinitions of one's identity within the context of relatively stable frames of reference. The search for identity, which is usually erratic, violent, and related to various forms of the "unconscious" (simultaneously a remembering and a "forgetting") that are more cultural than individual, thus acquires the traumatic character of a catharsis or rupture, and lacks a clear perception of its possibilities of concretization and projection toward the future.

These manifestations of the precariousness of social dialogism (due to the persistence of profound internal sociocultural divisions) are accompanied by an acute consciousness of the relativity of the different social discourses, especially that of institutionalized ones. From various perspectives, their parodic, sarcastic, grotesque, or carnivalesque stylizations constitute the most frequent modalities of this relativization.

The limited assimilation of enlightened thought, and then only in a version that is more peripheral than central; the subverted perception of the notions of historical and biographical time; the repeated questioning of the bases of national history; and the precariousness of identity understood as an individual process related to a cultural tradition that is sedimented, systematized, and in a permanent process of reelaboration, an identity that serves as an alternative to forms of territorial, ethnic, mythical, or religious identification: all of these are factors that situate the Latin American "periphery" in a particularly complex situation with respect to the present changes in the world.

Works Cited

Asturias, Miguel Ángel. *El Señor Presidente*. Madrid: Alianza, 1982. First published 1946.

Bakhtin, Mikhail. *La poétique de Dostoievski*. Trans. Isabelle Kolitcheff. Ed. Julia Kristeva. Paris: Seuil, 1970.

_____. *Esthétique et théorie du roman*. Trans. Daria Olivier. Paris: Gallimard, 1978.

Carpentier, Alejo. *Los pasos perdidos*. Mexico City: EDIAPSA, 1953.

Gallegos, Rómulo. *Canaima*. Barcelona: Araluce, 1936. First published 1935.

_____. *Doña Bárbara*. Buenos Aires: Espasa Calpe, 1944. First published 1929.

García Márquez, Gabriel. *One Hundred Years of Solitude*. Trans. Gregory Rabassa. New York: Avon, 1971.

_____. *Cien años de soledad*. Barcelona: Argos Vergara, 1975. First published 1967.

Hernández, José. *Martín Fierro*. Madrid: Alianza, 1981. First published 1872.

Lukacs, George. *La théorie du roman*. Trans. Jean Clairevoye. Paris: Gonthier, 1979.

Meschonnic, Henri. *Pour la poétique*. Paris: Gallimard, 1970.

Perus, Françoise. "Universalidad del regionalismo: *Canaima* de Rómulo Gallegos." In *Canaima*, by Rómulo Gallegos. Archives. Paris and Caracas: UNESCO, 1991. 417-472.

_____. "La poética narrativa de Agustín Yáñez en *Al filo del agua*." In *Al filo del agua*, by Agustín Yáñez. Archives. Paris and Mexico City: UNESCO, forthcoming.

Rivera, Eustasio. *La vorágine*. Buenos Aires: Losada, 1953. First published 1924.

Sarmiento, Domingo Faustino. *Facundo (Civilización y barbarie. Vida de Juan Facundo Quiroga)*. Sepan Cuantos 49. Mexico City: Porrúa, 1966. First published 1845.

Yáñez, Agustín. *Al filo del agua*. Mexico City: Porrúa, 1969. First published 1947.

Chapter 4

Identity and Narrative Fiction in Argentina: The Novels of Abel Posse

Blanca de Arancibia

(translated by Amaryll Chanady)

> *If the past is only known to us today through its textualized traces (which, like all texts, are always open to interpretation), then the writing of both history and historiographic metafiction becomes a form of complex intertextual cross-referencing that operates within (and does not deny) its unavoidably discursive context.*
>
> —Linda Hutcheon, *A Poetics of Postmodernism* (81)

In the past few years, the problematic of identity in Argentinean literature has been the object of frequent debate in the academic media of Argentina. It has even approached the dangerous limit of more or less fugitive fashions that transform a subject of authentic interest into a rapid current that, after having reached a crest, disappears, only to be replaced by another intellectual trend. Although some have reviled it as irrelevant or even snobbish, others have defended its potential for explaining a perpetually conflictual present. In any case, the continuing interest that the subject suscitates justifies further attempts at elucidation. In fact, starting from the writing and reflections of Sarmiento, the Argentinean examination of our way of "being American" has found inexhaustible material in narrative fiction, as well as in essayistic and philosophical writing.

As part of the same endeavor of scrutinizing our origin and future, the *rewriting* of Latin American history has been no less popular. The texts and paratexts written by the continent's authors continue to question official history and their own resulting identity. Their objective is to "deflect" (or at least to decenter) historical, paternalistic, or totalitarian discourse, and the immediate result is the problematization of the legitimacy of this discourse and its ability to explain the present. We could mention in this respect the well-known Carlos Fuentes (with his *Terra Nostra*) and Gabriel García Márquez (*El general en su laberinto*), and also lesser-known authors such as Hector Tizón, Libertad Demitrópulos, Marta Mercader (who wrote a remarkable novel on Juana Manuela Gorriti), Ricardo Piglia, Rodolfo Rabanal, and Abel Posse. These authors belong to a large group of writers generally disappointed or dissatisfied with essayistic thought who are attempting to revise central or transversal master narratives of Argentine history.

Stimulated by a situation that compels it to rethink its mode of being, our literature expresses the conflictual nature of Latin American culture and reflects, usually in a critical manner, the ineluctable ethical component of an investigation of identity. In short, it obeys a necessity that can no longer be postponed: that of thinking itself in its social function as well as in its relationship to authority, paternity, and cultural filiations. It does this in the manner of a long adolescent crisis, characterized by manifestations that are uneven and multiform, sometimes brilliant and at other times ridden by doubt and striving for success.

Depending on the historical period, our literature has been alternately receptive to foreign influences (mainly European) and closed to anything but itself. Spanish American *postmodernismo* succeeded with relative ease in its proposal of a national model based on myths of the earth that would resolve nearly all conflicts concerning external influences by accentuating these myths (*Don Segundo Sombra*, by Richardo Güiraldes and published in 1926, is a good example), while differentiation with respect to the metropolis(es) was still possible. Today's problem is much more acute, however. On the one hand, myths alone no longer suffice for the location of meaning, or the justification of creating what is considered to be a "national style." On the other, contemporary civilization with its mass media makes total introversion impossible and enmeshes all writing in the web of other writing and other perceptions of the world. Nothing can henceforth escape the intercultural dynamic. This almost-tragic impossibility is the reason why Argentinean literature, in its desire to constitute itself as a specific and singular form of writing, no longer believes, and is no longer capable of believing, in the exclusiveness of an "original discourse" that it constantly demands of its thinkers. Although it shares with the rest of Latin America certain thematic obsessions and formal traits, and although Argentinean fiction has created a personal voice (thematically and formally) with respect to the rest of Spanish America, the impossibility of eluding the intercultural movements of the West creates a fault within the project itself and makes it extremely difficult to elucidate one's own identity and not just engage in a mere game of construction, or echo other Western voices. This is all the more inevitable when Latin American philosophy does not seem to have found the voice and roots of an authentic thought, in spite of the notable quests undertaken by intellectuals such as Rodó, Korn, Zea, or the philosophers of liberation, to name only some (in an unjust list) of those who, starting from the pioneering work of Juan B. Alberdi, have pursued the search for a discourse based on specifically Latin American axiologies.

When transculturation is considered as the "menace of deculturation" (Todorov 425), assuming one's identity becomes a manifestation of the will and an exercise in self-affirmation. A conspicuous example of this phenomenon is Quebecois literature. An analogous situation characterizes Argentine fiction, with its equally solipsistic emphasis, although the linguistic question central to Quebecois literature is irrelevant here. In the case of Argentina, self-affirmation and solipsism are also caused by the peculiar inefficiency of political and economic projects, the adoption of cultural models that are profoundly antithetical to national customs, and the exodus of people. These phenomena are perceived as a menace to the integrity of society. Narrative fiction reflects (sometimes with an exasperating narcissism) the lack of horizons, or rather of projects, which seems to characterize daily life and the cultural sphere. It seems as if the lack of a project makes the country appear eternally provisional. That is the interpretation of Osvaldo Soriano in *Una sombra ya pronto serás*, a gloomy title taken from a tango for a narrative about a group of emblematic characters, lost in a labyrinth of paths and always trying to escape. It is a tragic variation of the theme of the *ailleurs*, or elsewhere, which tends toward a deliberate self-absorption, and is found in other novels, such as *En otra parte* by Rodolfo Rabanal.

We must ask ourselves, however, how it is possible to investigate literature from the perspective of the problematic we propose, at a time when the affirmation of identity in contemporary texts can be considered as a belated "modernist nostalgia" or an "invitation to exclusion" and "closure." It would be legitimate to reflect on the relevance of these issues in a world that is becoming increasingly international, and in which pluralization sometimes makes ethnic groups invisible. Yet there are urgent needs that are unknown by theory, or known only in the "parlor of Sunday visits."

For the purposes of my investigation, I will consider paratextual and even extratextual material, and confront it with certain rhetorical and structural procedures activated in the novels to be examined, thus acting on Hayden White's incitement to identify codified elements that betray the appearance of ideologies. Searching for implicit, incorporated, subverted, or parodied narrative models would lend a greater degree of credibility to this investigation and simultaneously open up a dimension that is not only rich but also expressive and significant, but a detailed study of this kind would exceed the dimensions of this chapter. I will have recourse to all these aspects as much as possible, in an alternating and complementary fashion, using a theoretical model that somewhat eclectically combines contributions from different approaches, in order to examine from the angle of the identity problematic four texts of Abel Posse: *Daimón* (1978), *Los perros del paraíso* (1983), *Momento de morir* (1979), and *La reina del Plata* (1988). The four novels appear as thematic pairs; the first two narrate the discovery and colonization from the angle of the event (in the case of the second novel) and the "repeatable fact" (in the case of the first), and the last two explore more specifically the aporias of Argentine history. The lack of diffusion by international media of three of these novels will necessitate a more descriptive study than usual.

Interest in Posse's work in Argentine universities has so far been limited. *Los perros del paraíso* and *Daimón* have aroused the most attention in academic commentary. Together with the two novels on Buenos Aires that we will discuss, these works weave an inconsistent interpretation of the historical referent and are, to a more or less obvious degree, what we call "historiographic metafictions" (Hutcheon 105-23), which interrogate, problematize, subvert, and reelaborate official, supposed, and possible history. Behind each of these novels stands the shadow or memory of other texts. *Los perros del paraíso* is a complex rereading of historiography proper and of the chronicles, thus inevitably reminding us of Carpentier's *El arpa y la sombra*; *Daimón* creates an allegory of South American destiny based on the Spanish rebel Lope de Aguirre, whose demonism (an ambiguous characteristic evoked by the title) has fascinated the imagination in the way Sade and Gilles de Rais have done. *Momento de morir* evokes for the Argentine reader the narrative world of Bioy Casares, particularly that of two of his novels, *El sueño de los héroes* and *Diario de la guerra del cerdo*. Finally, *La reina del Plata*, unjustly neglected, is woven around a multiplicity of texts and discourses, historical and literary, that reread the past and present of the country.

The four texts propose an examination of identity based paradoxically on two formal-thematic traits that can presently be considered as universal: the rereading of history and the infinite library. In Posse's narrative, both practices are related through the author's belief in the social role of literature, which he has repeatedly expressed in interviews and essayistic texts.

Contemporary Spanish American narrative has inherited the preoccupation with history from a long tradition of interaction between the novel and historical reflection that Asturias already referred to [150ff.; see also Gómez-Moriana (63) on the subject of the selection of "facts" for the purpose of the argument] and of which *Facundo* is our prototype. Chronological experimentation, characteristic of Posse's work, indicates a very particular relationship with the past, seen from our present situation. This relationship, which is not just limited to humorous play (see *Papeles para el diálogo*), was already present in Leopoldo Marechal's *Adán Buenosayres*, another possible narrative intertext of *La reina del Plata*.

Los perros del paraíso, a kind of cosmogonic and carnivalesque myth, incorporates into the story instances of quoted discourse in the citations that introduce it and the "Chronology" that is presented in the form of annals summarizing the subsequent narrative. The quotations are ironically decontextualized, as is the selection and combination of reported events in the "Chronology" itself (cf. Gómez-Moriana 63). While the farcical component arises from narrativized history, the ironic distance is a result of the annal-like "Chronology."

The two long movements that completely divide the rhythm of *Los perros del paraíso*—the time before and that after the voyage of discovery—tense and relax the narrative voice. In the before, we have carnival, joyful abandon, and ludic irreverence; in the after, we have an atmosphere of lyricism and elegy. This distinctive tone is what transforms the text into a genuine piece of fiction, and even a work of art, in opposition to essayistic or historiographic texts. During the voyage of discovery, for example, time concentrates its infinite clusters in a kind of magical space, and this configuration perfectly expresses the moment of an authentic transition. The anachronisms and other chronological games carry the most obvious ideological weight. The novel is a message undermining itself, ambiguous and unstable, in which the narrator proclaims his presence (and thus denounces authorship as authority). His intrusions from an enunciative position in the present concur with other analogous techniques to destabilize the official historiographic account, as well as the fictional (and marginal) narrative itself. They cancel the narrative contract, impede abandonment to novelistic illusion, and relativize or defer all interpretations, at least on a first reading. One of the strategies, as I have mentioned, is the constant intrusion of the present: "Isabel partió a revienta caballos desde su campamento sito donde hoy es Venta del Prado (sobre la Nacional 630)" (92) ["Isabel rode off in a whirlwind from her campsite situated where there is a Prado sale today (on national highway 630)"] and

> Nota del autor: Se ha podido situar el lugar de la descrita escena. Queda a pocas millas de Alcalá (donde residía entonces Isabel), entre Leches, hoy Loëches, y Torrejón de Ardor, un poco al norte de Torrejón del Rey. En la colina funciona hoy un taller de gomería y vulcanizado. (88)
>
> Author's note: We have been able to situate the location of the described scene. It is a few miles away from

Alcalá (where Isabel was residing at that time), between Leches, today Loëches, and Torrejón de Ardor, a little to the north of Torrejón del Rey. On the hill a workshop of rubber and vulcanization is operating today.

This implies a resistance to sacralize a past that fascinates us nevertheless (we need only think of the lyrical power and the density of values synthesized by Isabel of Castille). This type of marginal text, the footnotes, is the "dialogic form" that, according to Hutcheon (105-23), permits the parodic inversion of sources and the ridiculing of erudition.

The collage of real and fictitious texts, the hidden or apocryphal quotations, and the use of capital letters to designate important abstractions turn out to be highly confusing. One of the basic problems faced by readers of these historiographic metafictions is the high degree of cultural competence and erudition that must be mobilized in order to disentangle the play of collage and the distortion of the authentic texts used. The two techniques of collage and distortion become aggressively active in the transgression of traditional historiography. They also become iconoclastic, because they affect the grounding of a large number of sacralized discourses and beliefs to such a degree that they undermine the "dignity" of written tradition. The novel is transformed by these two techniques in a highly desacralizing epistemological exercise that proposes the deauthorization and the rejection of canonized authority (commonly practiced historiography) as a criterion of truth and coherence, at the same time that it promotes disbelief as a theoretical activity and practice necessary for scrutinizing History.

Through the use of Marseilles tarot cards to provide chapter headings that comment on and annotate the story, *Daimón* refers to initiation and revelation. The specific semantic production is provided by the dexterous game of *brouillage* of textual sources, the deliriously and stereotypically baroque view of the American continent, and the transformation of Aguirre effected by America. Foundational violence, the tradition of anarchy, and the transgression of filiations are the main structures of signification in this novel, which has remained, like *Los perros del paraíso*, relatively unaffected by European transculturation in an all-absorbing continent. Although "official history," as well as the narrative transformations, has pointed to the "demonism" of Lope de Aguirre, the protagonist of Posse's novel acquires an almost positive character, based on the ambiguity of the title *Daimón* (demon or daemon), which de-emphasizes the evil nature of the figure and accentuates the foundational violence he perpetrates.

Both of these novels propose a mythical reading of America. This substitution of myth for History reveals the rejection of the West as a model and also reader of our reality. The mythical aspect is essential in both texts in order to understand their profound meaning, and it corresponds to the textual and extra-textual desire for regeneration. The dialogues of *La reina del Plata* expressly refer to this initiatory aspect: "The primordial child, you will say. But no. Rather the mandala . . . It's not a matter of wanting to return, no. Rather a union of essences, something else. The attraction of something that is contained in the magic circle of the mandala. The opposite of a black hole . . . " (214; see also 224). Alvin Kernan, in his study of myth in literature and the latter's social power, affirms that "only in the Third World, Latin America, Africa, and Asia, do the novel and poetry have something like the cultural power they exercised in the West as recently as two or three generations ago" (33).

The preponderance of parody is overwhelming. In fact, the two novels related to the Spanish conquest present themselves as epic parodies that illustrate the Bakhtinian notion of festival or carnival and the semantic value of the ludic dimension. Hilariously combining learned and popular texts (in the manner of Manuel Puig), the narrators of both stories not only contribute to the destruction of the book, understood as the official history of priests, military heroes, and battles, but also demonstrate the impossibility of the Book (as a legitimation of knowledge, according to Lyotard's interpretation of the word: the right to decide what is true). The entire text is thus transformed into a "border zone" that makes meaning vertiginously unstable. It de-doxifies, as Linda Hutcheon would say.

Humor and eroticism are basic in the novels' semantic organization. The first is fundamental for the destitution of the historical (essentially serious) account; the second, exacerbated and provocative, is an important interpretative key that joins the iso-topic network composed of hyperbole, exuberant language, and some thematic antinomies, in order to signify (through mimesis) the essentially excessive character of the American continent. The ample spaces of indeterminacy and play that appear in both texts support the ludic (and not factual) character that the nar-rative voices themselves attribute to American existence.

The protagonists of *Momento de morir* and *La reina del Plata* are typical inhabitants of the barrios and cafés of Buenos Aires: tav-ern "philosophers," members of the middle class, including nu-merous petty lawyers (a common immigrant's dream was seeing one's son become *un doctor*), bohemians, and pseudointellectu-als. The first novel, which is profoundly disconcerting, is the paradoxical account of a barrio lawyer who, involved in a story of revolutions, persecution, and death, is propelled by events he does not control to the ultimate position of leader of the country. In the second, the voice of an outsider (*externo*), that is to say someone expelled from the system, narrates what happened during a so-called postrevolution and the failed attempt of a new revolution. In the two narratives, the leitmotiv is a humor-ous game, a wink to the reader based on an entire national cul-ture very difficult to translate.

Everything in *Momento de morir* is predictable and trivial: the discourse of the narrator, the characters, their actions, and even the structure. The discomfort felt by the reader has an explana-tion, however. This novel is an exercise in style, entirely con-structed of linguistic clichés, Spanish American ways of think-ing, and typically Argentine literary and cultural stereotypes. The use of clichés produces a "reality effect" that leads one to assume that the author's intention was to reproduce the speech of a certain sector of the Argentine population, without any other goal than simple mimesis.

This strategy creates a certain kind of pastiche—and here we touch upon the second characteristic of Posse's project, namely, the infinite library. The singular form of pastiche found in the novel is a reference to Argentine literary tradition, as it evokes one of the greatest contemporary Argentineans, Adolfo Bioy Casares. The latter is alluded to by a particular atmosphere, cer-tain human types, specific places, frequently used clichés, Argentinean myths such as *el doctor* and the café, the language of the barrio in Buenos Aires, the passion for soccer, the role of the tango, the kitsch of the surroundings, national customs, and walking tours through a fantastic city. We are presented with a double pastiche, very close to facetiousness and caricature, when certain autochthonous ways of expressing oneself and thinking are caricatured through the work of Bioy, who had himself condensed a tradition of *sainetes* and tangos. It is a curious and interesting phenomenon of "transmigration" of traits to genres that are different from those in which they originated.

The differences on the technical level between Bioy and Posse betray the dissimilarity between their respective narrative projects. In Bioy, clichés function as quotations (Béhar 186), that is to say, as a distance established by the narrator between triviality and himself. Michael Riffaterre describes this practice as an "ill-intentioned strategy," because it focalizes the character "in the abdication of his personality" (176-81). In contrast, the narrator of Posse's novel appropriates linguistic clichés and mental stereotypes. He enunciates and thinks in that way himself, together with the other characters. This means that the reader does not judge the intellectual poverty on the basis of the text's construction, but on that of the writer. In the use of this strategy, which is even more "ill-intentioned" because it is the compositional principle of the novel, Posse is closer to Puig than to Bioy, on account of his use of a discourse that he claims to be a "facsimile of the model" (see Lusson), not to mention his stealing of characters from other literary works or deliberately erroneous allusions to the texts of other writers. The rewriting of the ancestors implies the transformation of a text A into a new text B: a "palimpsestic" phenomenon, as Genette would say. It is a phenomenon of filiation, of paternity, and of belonging.

One aspect that will probably become outmoded, and that risks going unnoticed in one or two generations owing to its excessive contextualization, is related to the references to more or less recent Argentine history. I am referring to dated expressions arising from military or even political discourse and taken up and repeated by the communication media, such as "national essence" ("ser nacional," 53), "the people's prison" ("la cárcel del pueblo," 75), "old conservative fox" ("viejo zorro conservador," 25) or "old radical fox" ("viejo zorro radical," 74), "moments of struggle lived by the country" ("momentos de lucha que vive el país," 47), or the phrase that is very familiar to Argentines of a certain generation: "May this blood that is spilled here unjustly serve to guarantee the justice and order of the institutions left to us by the architects of the Fatherland" ("Que esta sangre que se derrama aquí, injustamente, sirva para afianzar la justicia y el orden de las instituciones que nos legaron los constructores de la Patria," 63). These phrases are ridiculed and degraded in the novel. Densely contextualized political discourse is also used in other works written by Posse.

The narrator of *Momento de morir* finds it impossible to perceive reality, which is filtered, transformed, and made unrecognizable by the public media. News on the radio and images repeated on television disseminate violence, while the incessant information duplicates reality, converting it into its opposite, a reflection. Soon this duplication eliminates reality itself, as is depicted in the following sharp reading of political activism: "I pointed out to Natalio that the racket of the loudspeakers, the clamor of the megaphones, and the confusion of the public media were much greater than the noise of reality (I clearly remembered the large Peronist crowds)" (106).

Far from belonging to the tranquilizing domain of the historical novel with its canonical use of facts, the relationship between Posse's narratives and historical themes demonstrates that History in our countries is not only the fruit of chance, but also a kind of entelechy in which human beings do not intervene—on the contrary, things happen to them, such as time or death. This conception is dependent on that developed in texts such as *Daimón*, where Latin America continues to expel active people, especially those who *make* history.

La reina del Plata is a complicated novel because of the interweaving of different discourses, the complex structure, and the two narrative threads (the first concerning the protagonist's amorous relationship and the dealings of the couple with government deputies, and the second revolving around Café Sudamérica, with its patently emblematic name and its crowd of stereotyped customers). Numerous discontinuities in the temporal succession make it difficult to re-create the chronology of the story, and suggest a theme similar to that transmitted by the structure of *Daimón*: the infinite spiral that repeats history and its evils with only minimal variation. The impression that time does not progress is accentuated by the circular political evolution of the female protagonist. Motifs that recur in Posse's other narratives linked to the identity project (inaction, the desire to be reborn as a kind of inescapable destiny imposed from the outside) reappear in this novel, thus creating a labyrinthine intertextual interplay. There is an undeniable rewriting of certain discourses of modernity and their political projects, through the inclusion of historically impossible or deformed texts that are parodied by becoming the object of pastiche; an example is the exchange of correspondence between Rosa Luxemburg and the Argentine ex-president Hipólito Yrigoyen.

The excess of its intertextual practice and the multiple forms that it assumes in Posse's fiction draw all discourse, all possible narrative—and History—into an abyss. Parody, pastiche, apocryphal references, and the interplay of modification and falsification to which Borges had accustomed us, characterize a form of writing that is as evasive as its own discursive limits. The title of *La reina del Plata* alludes to the semantic field of the tango and to a national myth (Carlos Gardel, the best-known singer of tangos). At the same time, it announces a place (Buenos Aires) and an almost hybrid type of discourse situated between multiple configurations.

In the two novels by Posse that we are examining whose action is situated in the Argentine capital, and in which the quest (as investigation or inquiry) is essential, the paradise indefatigably pursued by the protagonists in their peregrinations through Buenos Aires is found in the neighborhoods where the childhood years of each character were spent. This transformation of the paradisiacal space—the city, and not the pampa, as it was for the generation of *Raucho* and *Don Segundo Sombra*—is important and characterizes the affirmation of urban narrative as well as the definite acceptance of the metropolis for the production of meaning. The didactic element has disappeared.

In Posse's narratives, childhood is the key to identity, if that is possible. In childhood, Posse also perceives "the dimension of the Fiesta," the "appropriation of the Kingdom," and (echoing

Heidegger) "What is Open" ("Lo Abierto"): a paradisiacal nostalgia that, transferred to the cultural sphere, is the desire for a specific origin and is thus intertwined with the interest in History. Because it is linked in these novels to the presence of the father, childhood implies the certainty of origins. The inability to recuperate these origins implies harboring doubts about the identity of one's father. The entire problematic of *Los perros del paraíso* is based on the questioning of paternity; *Daimón* recounts the rebellion against it; and *La reina del Plata* depicts the nostalgia of certainty concerning one's paternal filiations. This is clearly visible in some of Posse's other narratives, especially *Los demonios ocultos*.

An almost impossible endeavor, the construction of identity is problematized in its temporality: in these narratives, History *writes itself*, and the inconstancy of the aleatory dimension marks its writing. The narrator organizes the account of the events (always a posteriori), and entertains the illusion of playing the role of protagonist, from which his real function of mere narrator disqualifies him: "I, Doctor Medardo Rabagliatti, was the witness of events and horrors . . . It is normal that I should narrate them" (*Momento de morir* 15). Because they maintain the hope of discovering the logic of what happened, and thus of their own function, the narrators fill gaps and weave explanations in an interpretation of the reality they live in, a reality that is constantly destroyed or made uncertain by subsequent events and discourses.

Therefore, if the scrutiny of historical extravagance and the quest for identity go together, the conclusion suggested by a reading of Posse's texts is aporistic: if History is not made by the people of America, if it has the magical power of a living force, there is no other way of discovering identity than through the moment of initiatory access, the sphere of sudden, imperious, and inevitable revelation.

"Expressing the identity of an individual or community," according to Ricoeur in the context of his discussion of Hannah Arendt's *Human Condition*, "means answering the question: Who perpetrated a particular action? Who is its agent or author?" (3:355). But if we believe the reading of History effected by Posse's protagonists, identity becomes disturbingly problematic. For Rabagliatti in *Momento de morir*, and for Aguirre in *Dai-món*, human beings are not the agents of History. The identity question is thus deferred, in all senses of the term.

I am left, however, with the voluntarist affirmation with which I began and which applies to a specific conception of the social function of literature. In Posse's fiction, cultural identity takes the form of an adherence to particular models, the adoption of a stereotyped Latin American and Argentinean voice, and the creation or reinforcement of a "space" or sum of spaces and voices that concede a specific domain to our literature in the Western concert. For such a project (proclaimed by Posse in numerous paratexts) to be effective, the narrative voice must be easily recognizable in all forms through a limited number of necessarily exaggerated traits. The project specifically requires a literary family, a genealogy assumed in Argentina by Arlt, Bioy Casares, Manuel Puig, and a popular culture represented by the tango, the bolero, and mass media.

Posse's objective, expressed in his theoretical as well as fictional writings, is the institutionalization and universal recognition of this "verbal continent" (Lusson), this "Latin American voice" that Cortázar had already recognized in 1949, when he stated: *"We are creating a language*, as much as it may displease the necrophages and ordinary professors of literature . . . It is a turbid, hot, clumsy, and subtle language, but one that is increasingly adequate to our literary expression" (27; emphasis in the original). Asturias expressed an analogous view when he claimed: "we have created a language" (148, 149).

In order to strengthen this objective and with the stated conviction that all shared language "transmits a form of being" (cf. Lusson), Posse adopts a kind of "formulaic" style that has recourse to the reutilization of expressive and conceptual patterns selected from a common tradition ("un pozo común"), namely, *Spanish American literature* in the broad sense. Posse insists on some writers he considers most representative; in interviews and reports, he mentions Carpentier, Rulfo, Arguedas, Sarduy, and Guimarães Rosa, and the Argentineans already mentioned, among others. Revendicating what he calls "creative delirium," he characterizes this common tradition as "a system of poetical figures that form a network, connected to the submerged imaginary of the reader," and that facilitates "the creation of a space through narrative language" (*Papeles para el diálogo* 30-37). The "stereotype" I am referring to alludes to a literary activity anchored in this particular imaginary and that indicates a metonymic relationship between literature and identity. In this space, identity arises as a consequence of reading and recognizing oneself and one's specificity. It is significant that meaning is appropriated. What is important here is not *what is said*, because the *manner of saying* it constitutes the most relevant level of expression. "Stereotype" is as much a mental image (of reality, the Other, oneself) as a literary manner, and this mental image is sufficiently empty that one can flesh it out with different traits, while still being able to recognize it.

The use of literary stereotypes, which Marchese and Forradellas compare to the practice of pastiche on account of the mimetic component, has the advantage of effectiveness. This seems to have been well understood by some writers, such as Isabel Allende (*La casa de los espíritus*) and María Granata (*El jubiloso exterminio*), who successfully adapt the atmosphere and language of García Márquez, which leads to profitable sales and positive critical acclaim. In Latin American literature there seems to be a tendency to repeat certain types of formulas that, like the "literature of exile" at its time, and today the stereotype of Argentine failure, assure a good academic reception, better sales, and translations in the countries of the Northern Hemisphere. This practice, based on imagology, ensures recognition on account of the previous diffusion of a model of unequivocal identity. We can recognize the "novel of exile" because its examples have multiplied, thus producing a general category. The same occurred with indigenist fiction and with the novel of the *caudillo* or tyrant. The stereotype is impossible as long as the class does not exist, that is, the general category of which we recognize a new element.

By having recourse to similitude, an analogical system operating within tradition, through a practice in which stereotype and pastiche are mixed, Abel Posse situates himself within a Latin American baroque characterized by a strong stamp of identity and almost always related to extratextual teleologies, as we can see even in a writer like Carpentier. The "Latin American baroque," a kind of linguistic revelry, functions as an excess of energy and "represents" or "reproduces," on the level of the signifier, a particular referent, something external to the text: the world to which it corresponds. It is not, however, an image of America, but a phenomenon structured *like America* ("a imagen de América"). Together with surrealism, the baroque is, according to Posse, a "door of access" to American reality (cf. Mundó).

This baroque is characterized by proliferation, collage, ludic condensation, and dialogism; sometimes by parody; and always by ex-centricity, pomp, and excess that oppose it to *homo faber* (cf. Lusson). In it we find myth, humor, wild fantasy, and rootedness in history. It contributes toward the creation of the clichés suggested by "Spanish America" and "Spanish American literature," and thus gives rise to a particular kind of mimesis. The "excessive language" does not reproduce "the real," but a stereotyped idea of America as the "continent of excess," or Polyphemus's provision bag. In this way the desired referent is directly indicated, even if it becomes more unreal and *imaginary* than ever.

Now that the debt of continental identity has been paid, what remains of national identity? The two novels set in Buenos Aires cannot avoid considering it. Posse's treatment of the subject here does not only entail the blurred reading of history, but also a double articulation concerning myth. The first movement of articulation consists in a devalorization of myths that inform certain moments of Argentine history and ones that are perpetuated in the country's popular culture. Some examples are the bad men ("los malevos") and the barrio (which was so dominant in Borges's writing), the gaucho, the Argentinean in Paris, the *bandoneón* of Aníbal Troilo (a popular myth in Buenos Aires), the gurus of national culture, "patriotic kitsch," as Abraham Moles (22) calls the sentimental attachment for the native country, utopias, important causes, and reforms. Relativizing and degrading the emotional value of the myths and causes considered important by tradition, Posse proposes, in the second moment of articulation, their use as "topics": "material" matter, or threads of fictional web that form the story, acting as structural and semantic elements. As in the case of *Daimón*, where the figure of the eternal rebel is contextualized within Spanish American history in general (part of our identity is related to the repetition of phenomena that have given us form in the manner of "laws"), the figure of the "bad man" ("malevo") emblematically concentrates the aporias of our situation. Metaphors of absurd or useless causes are transformed into humorous myths invented by Posse, and this procedure lends force to the operative and formal capacity, while it contributes through variation to the reinforcement of the "Latin American" or "Argentinean voice." It is an interweaving of historical (because symbolical) and ahistorical systems that would attract the attention of Vattimo (see 40). Through these strategies, identity becomes cultural memory, rather than the ritualized memory of cults.

Yet the undeniable technical modernity of Posse situates his fiction within a writing community that does not recognize borders. His is a "modern" project served by "postmodern" writing that, reflecting on difference, emphasizes the problem of alterity, and where imagology and forms serve a sociopolitical purpose that is not a proposal of a way of thinking or behaving, but that of a simple consciousness-raising. This singular aporia explains not only Posse's entire fictional work, but also the difficulties that arise when one speaks of "narrative identity." Furthermore, in their relationship to history, his novels are intended not so much to rewrite it or to recognize an Otherness (that of historiography as another discourse or another form of knowledge different from the world of fiction) than to become substitutes for historical discourse itself. This is because their resistance is more radical: it is a rebellion against History. The "Fiesta," a central concept in Posse's work, implies the suspension of time and simultaneously the impossibility of History, a negation of projection as well as memory. History, for the protagonists of these novels, is suffered (*La reina del Plata* 105). It is not even possible to narrate it, in a definitive liquidation of the myth of transparency to which Vattimo alludes.

We must situate Abel Posse's narrative project and his conception of the function of literature within this complex problematic. Does literature have a usefulness? Ricoeur and Angenot have approached this from different angles. Angenot states: "It is only in this case, when we entertain this kind of hypothesis, that we have the right to claim that literature is in fact useful for something. It says, it often ends up saying: that does not make sense, that is not all you could say about it, there are other things besides this, 'There are more things on Heaven and Earth . . . ,' we can see things differently, 'It ain't necessarily so' . . . " (16).

Works Cited

Angenot, Marc. *Que peut la littérature? Sociocritique littéraire et critique du discours social.* Working papers 5. Montreal: CIADEST (McGill), 1991.

Asturias, Miguel Ángel. *América, fábula de fábulas.* Caracas: Monte Avila, 1972.

Béhar, Henri. *Littéruptures.* Paris: L'âge d'homme, 1988.

Cortázar, Julio. "Leopoldo Marechal: *Adán Buenosayres.*" In *Las claves de Adán Buenosayres,* by Leopoldo Marechal. Mendoza: Azor, 1949. 23-30.

Genette, Gérard. *Palimpsestes.* Paris: Seuil, 1982.

Gómez-Moriana, Antonio. "Narration et argumentation dans les Chroniques des Indes. Le Journal de Colomb 12 octobre 1492." *Parole exclusive, parole exclue, parole transgressive. Marginalisation et marginalité dans les pratiques discursives.* Ed. Antonio Gómez-Moriana and Catherine Poupeney-Hart. Montreal: Le Préambule, 1990. 53-86.

Hutcheon, Linda. *A Poetics of Postmodernism: History, Theory, Fiction.* New York and London: Routledge, 1988.

Kernan, Alvin. *The Death of Literature.* New Haven and London: Yale Univ. Press, 1990.

Lusson, Fernando. "Abel Posse: 'La literatura de América Latina está atravesando su siglo de oro.' " *Lanza* (Ciudad Real), section "El tema del día" (27 July 1988): 3.

Lyotard, Jean-François. *La condition postmoderne. Rapport sur le savoir.* Paris: Minuit, 1979.

Marchese, Angelo, and Joaquín Forradellas. *Diccionario de retórica, crítica y terminología literaria.* Barcelona: Ariel, 1986.

Moles, Abraham. *El kitsch. El arte de la felicidad.* Trans. Josefina Ludmer. Buenos Aires: Paidós, 1973.

Mundó, Josep. "Entrevista con Abel Posse: de Latinoamérica con voz distinta. Los caminos del lenguaje." *Llibreria* 123 (November 1988): 6-10.

Posse, Abel. *Momento de morir.* Buenos Aires: Emecé, 1979.

―――. *Daimón.* Barcelona: Argos, 1981. First published 1978.

―――. *Los demonios ocultos.* Buenos Aires: Emecé, 1987.

―――. "Discurso de recepción del premio Rómulo Gallegos." *Revista Argentina* (Caracas) (2 August 1987): 28-31.

―――. *Los perros del paraíso.* Buenos Aires: Emecé, 1987. First published 1983.

―――. "La libertad no es sólo un delirio literario." Nota de fondo. *Papeles para el diálogo* 1 (Caracas) (1988): 30-37.

―――. *La reina del Plata.* Buenos Aires: Emecé, 1988.

Ricoeur, Paul. *Temps et Récit.* 3 vols. Paris: Seuil, 1983-85.

Riffaterre, Michael. "Fonction du cliché dans la prose littéraire." In Riffaterre, *Essais de stylistique structurale*. Paris: Flammarion, 1971. 161-181.

Todorov, Tzvetan. *Nous et les autres. La réflexion française sur la diversité humaine*. Paris: Seuil, 1989.

Vattimo, Giorgio. *La société transparente*. Paris: Desclée de Brouwer, 1990.

White, Hayden. *Tropics of Discourse*. Baltimore and London: The Johns Hopkins Univ. Press, 1978.

———. *The Content of the Form: Narrative Discourse and Historical Representation*. Baltimore and London: The Johns Hopkins Univ. Press, 1978.

◆ Chapter 5

The Construction and Deconstruction of Identity in Brazilian Literature

Zilá Bernd

(translated by Amaryll Chanady)

> *Identity cannot have a different form from that of narrative,*
> *because to define oneself is, in the last analysis, to narrate.*
> —Paul Ricoeur, *Temps et récit* (317)

Although the question of identity is always intimately associated with the act of narrating, as Ricoeur claims, it becomes central to emergent and peripheral literatures (as in the Americas), whose main preoccupation frequently is to provide an explicit or implicit definition of its communities in its narrative. As Edouard Glissant pointed out in his study of the formation of national literatures, literature has two main functions:

> It has a desacralizing function, one of heresy and
> intellectual analysis, which deconstructs the organization
> of a particular system, exposes its hidden mechanisms,
> and demystifies it. It also has a sacralizing function,
> which reassembles the community around its myths, its
> beliefs, its imaginary, and its ideology. (192)

A literature that attributes to itself the mission of articulating a national project, and recuperating the foundational myths of a community as well as other aspects of its collective memory, only has a sacralizing and unifying function that tends to perpetuate sameness, monologism, or the construction of an ethnocentric identity, and thus circumscribes reality to a single frame of reference.

In Brazil, the foundational epics of the colonial period (eighteenth century) and romanticism (nineteenth century) acted as sacralizing forces indicating a "naive conscience" (Glissant 192), because they only recuperated and solidified the country's myths. On this level, literature incorporates an invented image of the Indian that excludes his or her voice, and that is most consistent with the construction of the national project. The Brazilian *modernismo* of the 1920s, however, conceived of national identity as a desacralization, which corresponds, according to Glissant, to a politicized perspective that is continuously open to difference, and that enables a culture to establish relations with others.

In particular historical periods, literature tends to unify the community around its foundational myths, its imaginary, or its ideology, and this leads to discursive homogenization, or the creation of an "exclusive voice" that practices a systematic concealment or misrepresentation of the Other (see Gómez-Moriana and Hart, especially 53-176). In the case of Brazilian literature, these Others are the Afro-Brazilian and the Indian, who are often represented in a marginalized space and from a deforming perspective, if they are represented at all.

This sacralizing or "celebrative" function "recalls the sacred origins of all poetry and seems to consolidate the ideological basis of literary practice" (Dubois 74). Within this sacralizing function (either epic or tragic), however, literature "must signify . . . the relationship of a culture with another in difference" (Glissant 193), unless it wants to remain folkloric or backward.

Certain authors who invest their writing with a mythology of origins and closeness to one's roots initiate the construction of the idea of the nation, for it is true that "literature makes the country and the country makes the literature," to quote Gilles Marcotte (82). In this essay I will discuss some of these texts that are characterized by a primarily sacralizing function.

Figurations of American Space and the Invention of the Indian in the Epic

Retracing the history of Brazilian literature involves the identification of successive stages that go from the recognition of the earliest writing as literary manifestations and the subsequent process of institutionalizing these as national literature, to their transformation into an object of study and knowledge. It is in the eighteenth century that the "literary manifestations acquire the organic characteristics of a system" (Cândido 1964: 45).

I am interested in delineating the paradigms through which each period articulates its project of constructing a national literature, and will develop the hypothesis that, from the eighteenth to the twentieth century, a strong principle of cohesion oriented this process, transforming literature into a hegemonic discourse in which ruptures and dissidences were brought about with great difficulty.

The epic poem is the appropriate genre for the description of foundational historic events that it associates with mythical elements and the feats of heroes or "beings of superior physical and psychological strength." This genre had a celebrational function that was essential for the creation of a minimum focus of cohesion capable of unifying the members of a community in the early stages of the process of identity formation.

Two epic poems in particular, O Uraguai (1769), by José Basílio da Gama, and Caramuru (1781), by Santa Rita Durão, besides celebrating the feats of the conquistadors, fulfill the function of creating common cultural roots and symbolizing national identity. These poems extol American geography and choose nature as their protagonist. The main project, namely, the celebration of the epic feats of the European invader, is sabotaged by the power of the marvelous character of the American continent. The poet inscribes nature as the founding element of his discourse, instead of introducing it as a simple scenic background, as he would have done if he had adhered to the canons of the traditional epic genre.

This is especially evident in O Uraguai, in which we can discern a progressive development of national consciousness: the mythical dimension of the epic material

> apelando para o maravilhoso nativo integra na
> perspectiva indígena a brasilidade e põe em cena o
> colonizado como herói. (Silva 31)

requires the native dimension of the marvelous to incorporate the Brazilian national character [*a brasilidade*] within an indigenous perspective and represent the colonized as a hero.

Although the epic narrates the feats of the conquistador Gomes Freire de Andrade and his expeditions to the Jesuit mission in order to subdue the last resisting Indians and enforce the Treaty of Madrid, the cultural perspective of the colonized is contrasted with that of the colonizer. This makes possible the emergence of a Brazilian national consciousness in narrative, as Anazildo Silva demonstrates in *A formação épica da literatura brasileira*. As an analysis of Brazilian literature will confirm, the American mythical referent informs the epic project of eighteenth-century writers, who are seduced by the idea of a novel and surprising New World. This emphasis on the wonderful nature of the continent finally displaces the initial project, which consisted in consecrating the Portuguese colonial enterprise. A good example is the following poem, in which the introduction of the magical world of the seer Tanajura clashes with the European rationality of the protagonist, Gomes Freire de Andrade, and with that of the poet himself, who is influenced by the European Enlightenment:

> Mas a enrugada Tanajura, que era
> Prudente e experimentada (e que a seus peitos
> Tinha criado em mais ditosa idade
> A mãe da mãe da mísera Lindóia)
> E lia pera história o futuro,
> Visionária, supersticiosa
> Que de abertos sepulcros recolhia
> Nuas caveiras e esburgados ossos
> A uma medonha gruta, onde ardem sempre
> Verdes candeias, conduziu chorando
> Lindóia, a quem amava como filha;
> E em ferrugento vaso licor puro
> De viva fonte recolheu. (*O Uraguai* 3:65-66)

But the wrinkled Tanajura, who was
Prudent and experienced (and who at her breast
Had suckled in a happier age
The mother of the mother of the wretched Lindóia)
And read the future through history,
Visionary, superstitious
Who gathered from open sepulchers
Bald skulls and picked bones,
To a dreadful cave, where always burn
Green candles, she led the crying
Lindóia, whom she loved as a daughter;
And in a rusty cup collected
Pure liquor from a running spring.

The Indian in *O Uraguai* is valorized according to the axiological paradigms of the Westernized white population, and this entails the systematic negation of indigenous culture, as is indicated by such expressions as "uncultivated America" ("inculta América"), "crude masses" ("povo rude"), "seven villages inhabited by the barbarians" ("sete povos, que os bárbaros habitam"), "coarse Indians, without discipline, without value, without weapons" ("índios rudes, sem desciplina, sem valor, sem armas"), and "uncultivated and simple people" ("a inculta gente simple"). The national consciousness that is developed during the eighteenth century is thus ambiguous: the colonizers' values are praised at the same time that the American continent is glorified by authors who "take an aesthetic and human interest in the natives" ("interessando-se estetica e humanamente pelos nativos"), as António Cândido pointed out in his article "Literatura e consciência nacional" (9; see also Cândido 1987).

This ambiguity is obvious in the lines of *Caramuru*, which, in spite of their construction of indigenous images based on a phobic perspective ("barbarous people," "cruel people," "coarse and brutish people," "cruel savage," and so on), provide an exhaustive catalog of American geography, fauna, and flora, thus revealing the poet's strong attitude of wonderment with respect to the country's natural attributes. The use of language is also characterized by a certain ambivalence. Although Santa Rita Durão affirms that the language of the Indians is "obscure," the large number of indigenous terms incorporated in the text indicates a gradual process of hybridization, rendered necessary by the limitations of the Portuguese language, which did not have adequate terms to designate the numerous indigenous referents of the New World. By naming America with words and expressions taken from autochthonous languages, the poet is conceding a certain validity to the indigenous symbolization of the continent.

In general, however, American culture is focalized from an ethnocentric perspective, according to which what is different can only be inferior to one's own culture. The poet is thus incapable of considering anthropophagy as a ritual (as the *modernistas* of the 1920s were to do), but describes it as an "abominable" practice:

Companheiras de oficio tão nefando
Seguem de um cabo a turba e de outro cabo
Seis torpíssimas velhas aparando
O sangue sem um leve menoscabo.
Tão feias são que a face esta pintando
A imagem propríssima do diabo. (*Caramuru* 1: LXXX)

The assistants to this so abominable task
Follow on the one side the crowd and on the other
Six very filthy old women who remove
The blood without the least disgust.
They are so ugly that their faces imitate
The very image of the Devil.

As in *O Uraguai*, the Indian is given certain heroic dimensions in *Caramuru*. Besides describing the courage of the Portuguese protagonist, Diogo Alvares Correia, the poet describes that of his wife, Paraguaçu. Her beauty, however, is hardly acknowledged, and then only when it corresponds to Western standards:

Paraguaçu gentil (tal nome teve)
Bem diversa de gente tão nojosa,
De cor tão alva como a branca neve
E donde não é neve, era de rosa. (*Caramuru* 2: LXXVIII)

Polite Paraguaçu (that is her name)
Very different from those who are so disagreeable
Her heart is as pure as the white snow
And where it is not snow, it is like a rose.

Paraguaçu accompanies her husband to Europe and is given the name Catarina. The loss of her name corresponds to the loss of her identity and symbolizes the alienation of the indigenous inhabitants, who had to divest themselves of their identity in order to be accepted by the colonizers in what was frequently a unidirectional process of transculturation.

To summarize, literature in the colonial period is characterized by the following traits:

1. The appropriation of American space as a marvelous-mythical reality.
2. A conceptualization of time based on the nostalgic return to the past, which corresponds to a desire to recuperate an original unity and the beginnings of history.
3. The construction of a monolithic and marginalizing discourse, which misrepresents the native inhabitants of the continent and judges them from an external perspective based on European axiological paradigms.
4. The emblematic hero continues to be Portuguese.
5. A contemptuous attitude toward the indigenous Other, whose culture is considered inferior to that of the white colonizer.

The Figuration of Origins: The Invention of the Indian and the Concealment of the Afro-Brazilian: José de Alencar (1829-1877)

As I have already mentioned, phenomena of hybridization characterized Brazilian literature since the earliest moments of its formation, and maintained a significant presence throughout the romantic period, in which authors openly expressed their intention to contribute toward "the slow gestation of the Brazilian people" ("a gestação lenta do povo brasileiro"), to quote José de Alencar.

An initial stage, corresponding to a certain extent to a cartographic necessity (see Sussekind 35) that led writers to symbolize the national space in a euphoric representation of Brazil, was followed by a foundational stage (of which Alencar's work is representative) characterized by an exhaustive textualization of origins, roots, foundational myths, and genealogies. The novelistic production of Alencar bears testimony to the simultaneous movements of deculturation and acculturation of two of the founding ethnic groups in Brazil: the Whites and the Indians.

In an ambitious literary project, Alencar attempted to reconstitute the process of nation building in Brazil. This project, characterized by the romantic sensibility of the majority of writers at that time, was based on the idealization of the founding figures of the Brazilian "nation," who were considered as heroes in the classical sense of the term, that is, people who possessed qualities that were superior to those of common mortals. Imbued with the desire to produce what Alfredo Bosi calls a novelistic summary ("suma romanesca") of Brazil (151), Alencar, like his eighteenth-century predecessors, did not situate the Afro-Brazilian on the same level as the inhabitant of the *sertão* (hinterland), the gaucho, the Indian, the *bandeirante* (member of an armed band), not to mention the European colonizer, all of whom were portrayed more or less in detail in the literature of the period.

Alencar's work demonstrates the difficulty of significantly transforming a dominant paradigm and articulating a dissident perspective in the field of ideas, as well as the longevity of hegemonic discourse that imposes and legitimizes certain ideas that are repeated by succeeding generations. The discursive dominant based on the conception of the Indian as a symbol of nationness (which dates from the eighteenth century) is reinforced in Alencar's work, which eulogizes the autochthonous inhabitant of the nation as the mythical ancestor and hero who has the extraordinary advantage of being "free of any stain," to use

António Cândido's expression, since the enslavement of Indians was abolished in the seventeenth century.

With Alencar and Gonçalves Dias, *national literature* is finally born (Cândido 1969), thus making possible the expression of the "Brazilian spirit" ("gênio brasileiro"; for a study on "national character," see Moreira Leite). Alencar himself, in his preface to the novel *Sonhos d'ouro* (1872), uses the expression "national literature":

> A literatura nacional, que outra coisa não é senão a alma da pátria, que transmigrou para este solo virgem com una raça ilustre, aqui impregnou-se da seiva americana desta terra que lhe serviu de regaço, e cada dia se enriquece ao contato de outros povos e ao influxo da civilização. (34)
>
> National literature, which is nothing but the soul of the nation that migrated to this virgin land with an illustrious race, was impregnated with the American sap of this soil that welcomed it, and every day it is enriched by contact with other cultures and the influx of civilization.

Alencar identifies three phases in Brazilian national literature, which he illustrates in his novelistic production: (1) a primitive or aboriginal phase, characterized by legends and myths of a savage land (*Iracema*); (2) a historical phase, in which the invading conquerors appropriate the land and make possible the "slow gestation of the American people" (*O Guarani* and *Minas de Prata*); and (3) the infancy of our literature (*Tronco de Ipê, Til,* and *O Gaúcho*).

Alencar initiates his project of symbolizing national identity through his Indianist writings, represented by *Iracema* (1857) and *O Guarani* (1865). He situates his characters in a distant past that coincides with the beginnings of colonization, and depicts the first violent clashes between the invading and the conquered peoples. The harmonious and even Edenic vision of life before the conquest, the positive representation of the indigenous population, and the national pride of the author (who constantly extols nature and the noble savage) are interwoven in this narrative characterized by a euphoric conscience in which the valorization of the regional and natural aspects of the Brazilian nation compensate for its backwardness.

Parodying Hegel, Edouard Glissant affirms that the sacralizing function of literature is representative of a "collective consciousness that is still naive" (192). In spite of the terminological variations (Cândido's euphoric consciousness, Glissant's and Darcy Ribeiro's naive consciousness), the observations made by these authors point to the same phenomenon: a new nation's urgency to name itself before the rest of the world and to be seen and heard as a specific collectivity frequently gave rise to a literature characterized by a form of exoticism that differs very little from that of colonial literature.

Alencar's work, in fact, remains faithful to the discursive hegemony established by travel literature written by European discoverers since the sixteenth century. The main emphasis of his narratives is on the description of the exotic aspects of the inhabitants of the New World. Rather than describe the ways of life and difficult conditions of the indigenous inhabitants, who were very much marginalized in the nineteenth century, Alencar paints an idealized portrait of the "savages," to use a term that was common in all travel narratives between the sixteenth and eighteenth centuries as well as in Alencar's texts. Exoticism, in which the author concentrates on local color and on what is unexpected and surprising, generally involves the valorization of the exterior aspects of a country or culture as it is defined (exclusively) by an external observer (see Todorov 1989 for a lengthy analysis of the West's relationship to its Other).

According to Todorov, the principle that rules exoticism is paradoxical: if it is impossible to praise the Other without knowing it, detailed knowledge is incompatible with exoticism. The exotic vision consists of a eulogy based on incorrect or insufficient knowledge of what the Other presents as immediately and obviously different. In the case of the Indians, the differences that fascinate the European are usually related to their supposed closeness to nature. The myth of the noble savage arises as an indirect criticism of one's own society: because the latter is considered corrupt (by thinkers such as Rousseau, for example), one nostalgically imagines a society characterized by plenitude and harmony. Alencar describes the Tabajara people as living in a paradisiacal society, in which men are "generous," virgins have "honeyed lips," warriors are courageous, the sand on the beaches is soft, and the rivers supply an abundance of fish.

The valorization of a mythical past provided Alencar with an indispensable basis for anchoring the construction of national identity. The son of pain, Moacyr (born of the love between the "beautiful" Indian woman Iracema and the "noble Portuguese warrior" Martim), is represented as the founding father of the Brazilian race, and becomes a source of pride, especially to the dominant sectors who are in the process of constructing the young nation. What an analysis of Alencar's work demonstrates is that it adheres very closely to the dominant conventions of not only Brazilian but also European literature, some of whose common topoi (the noble savage, the idealization of the "state of nature," the nostalgic view of the past) are incorporated in the narratives of the Brazilian author.

If we return to the colonial paradigm, we realize that it remained practically unaltered, in accordance with Angenot's hypothesis (1989; see also Angenot 1988 for a more general discussion of "social discourse") that the "new," not-yet-expressed, or destabilizing structures have great difficulty in penetrating the ensemble of discourses circulating in a given society. Contrary to the widespread belief that romanticism brought about a literary revolution in Brazil, I would claim that this literary movement did not transgress the principle of discursive acceptability and that, in spite of the variation of several motifs, it is possible to detect the perpetuation of the doxa, or "eternal return" of certain paradigms. The following aspects of eighteenth-century narrative did not change in Alencar's period: the textualization of American space as mythical and marvelous; the conception of time based on a nostalgic attitude toward the past; and the construction of an exclusive discourse, based on a misrepresentation of the Indian.

As Flora Sussekind observed (190), the figuration of the narrative voice in Alencar is characterized by the choice of a historico-genetic perspective that is blinded by a nostalgic search for origins, inaugural frames of reference, sources, roots, and primordial time. The Greek etymology of nostalgia (*nostos*, return) refers to the melancholy produced in exile by homesickness for the native land. Alencar's ingenuous attitude does not allow him to realize (as the *modernistas*, with their greater critical consciousness, were able to do in the 1930s) that "neither time, neither history, neither individual nor collective identity, can return to its origins, and that on the contrary, the *one* incessantly produces the *multiple*" (Cambron 180; emphasis added). The Indian is elevated together with the Portuguese forefathers to the position of an emblematic hero who becomes a symbol of the origin of the Brazilian people.

The devalorization of the indigenous inhabitants in the initial stages of identity construction is replaced by an obsessive hypervalorization of the culture of the Other. Nevertheless, the cultural elements valorized in Alencar's Indianist narrative are ones that no longer existed three and a half centuries after the arrival of the European conquerors, and thus merely provide illustrious mythical origins for our ancestors.

In conclusion, the cultural dialogue established between the colonized (Iracema, Poti, Araquém) and the colonizer (Martim) gives rise to a double process of deculturation (the loss of one's original culture) and acculturation (the adaptation to a different culture). The process is obviously unequal; while Martim adheres to some local customs, his values—the values of the hegemonic culture—end up being imposed as the dominant values of the Brazilian nation, as we can see in the conclusion of *Iracema*:

> A mairi que Martim erguera à margem do rio, nas praias do Ceará, medrou. Germinou a palavra do Deus verdadeiro na terra selvagem e o bronze sagrado ressoou nos vales onde rugia o maracá. (57)
>
> The *mairi* that Martin had planted at the edge of the river, on the banks of the Ceará, grew. The word of the true God was propagated in the savage land and the sacred bronze reverberated in the valleys where the maraca was rattling.

The death of Iracema (an anagram of America) is symbolic of the death of the mythical America that succumbed in the confrontation between "civilization" and "barbarism," in which civilization was supposedly represented by European culture and barbarism by the indigenous culture.

As I have tried to show, until the beginning of the twentieth century, Brazilian literature adhered fairly closely to the hegemonic national project oriented toward the formation of a mestizo nation, but one that adopted predominantly European values. It fulfilled a sacralizing function, because it contributed toward the solidification of this project. The Afro-Brazilian was "absent from history," as was the Indian; the latter only served the function of justifying an original ancestry, which was rapidly neutralized by the supposed ethnic and cultural supremacy of the colonizer.

The authors of previous centuries were interested in symbolizing collective memory, and aimed at a mythical totalization of the present, the past, and the future, given that continuity and a certain amount of repetition are essential to the national conception of time. Starting with *modernismo* in 1922, Brazilian literature had a preponderantly desacralizing function; it claimed to reject the excessive crystallization of discourses that were dominating the artistic scene, and the institutionalization of works that supposedly reflected "the national character" or the "collective spirit." Through their integration into narrative of heterogeneous discourses, and through their ironic and parodic strategies, the Anthropophagy Movement and Pau-Brazil poetry—in short, the work of Mário and Oswald de Andrade—initiated the process of destabilizing a homogenizing perspective that had become consolidated.

Between the forms of construction (the sacralizing function), which tend toward homogenization and even the radical negation of Otherness, and the forms of deconstruction (the desacralizing function), which introduce heterogeneity and were considered by Régine Robin as an essential condition of literary production (171), in this in-between space, a synthesis of the two poles begins to take shape. In works written after 1980 and thus after the beginning of the process of democratization, contemporary Brazilian literature sees the emergence of texts that associate the recuperation of myths with their constant demythologization, and the rediscovery of collective memory with its continuous rewriting, implying an incessant questioning of oneself.

Following in Mário de Andrade's footsteps in *Macunaíma*, João Ubaldo Ribeiro is able to relive, in the 1980s, the revolutionary *modernista* experience of bringing about a revision of Brazilian historical and cultural formation, and problematizing the traditional figure of the hero. *Viva o povo brasileiro* thus returns to the decisive moments in Brazilian history, dislodging hegemonic knowledge from its position of unquestioned truth and bringing to the forefront obscure characters from the popular sectors of society whom it depicts in their search for self-affirmation. The result is a vast multifaceted panorama in which the hegemony of the educated part of the population is relativized and in which the role of the Afro-Brazilian in the construction of national identity is revalorized.

The dominant discourse of the aristocracy is sabotaged by the author's corrosive treatment of it, while popular speech is recuperated and integrated within the textual weave in a conscious project on the part of the author to recuperate the "native originality" of which Oswald de Andrade wrote, and through which the critical consciousness of the oppressed sectors of society is constructed. Like the Caribbean authors who emphasized the marvelous dimension of orally transmitted popular tales and myths in their search for a version of Caribbean history that differed from that of written texts privileging the hegemonic perspective, João Ubaldo Ribeiro turns his attention to Bahia, a veritable crucible of popular cultural manifestations.

Letting himself be "contaminated" by the language and worldview of characters from the most humble strata of society, the author identifies with their interpretation of Brazil and adopts the marvelous, which enables him to rediscover and revalorize Brazilian culture. *Candomblé* and other rituals practiced by the descendants of slaves are thus not described as barbarous, or even presented as exotic in an effort to provide local color; on the contrary, they are fully integrated within the narrative structure and constitute alternative forms of narrating a different Brazil.

According to Hubert Fichte (17), rituals are forms of organizing the relations between human beings and the world. Fichte, who studied the poetic anthropology of Afro-American religions, considers ritual as a space where the time of individual life is connected to collective universal time, and as a structure of support with a function analogous to that of psychiatry or mental hygiene. In *Viva o povo brasileiro*, João Ubaldo Ribeiro depicts numerous initiation rites, describing them in a manner consonant with Fichte's point of view. In the case of the people who practice popular religions, the experience of salvation occurs by means of a trance or rather through the transformation of the believer, contrary to Christianity, which considers redemption as coming from above. In Afro-American religions, the trance transforms the believer into a god capable of vanquishing death, misery, and other ills.

Eusébio Macário, the only character of *Viva o povo brasileiro* belonging to the elite who is interested in popular knowledge and who decides to undertake an epic voyage of return to his origins, going back to his "native land" (the island of Itaparica) in order to understand his past, is totally transformed during an initiation rite. He learns that

> a magia não é feita de fora, mas de dentro. Por isto é
> que se fala tanto da necessidade de ter fé para que as
> coisas aconteçam, pois a fé, afinal, não passa de uma
> maneira de ver o mundo que torna possíveis aquelas
> coisas que se deseja que aconteçam. A fé, portanto, é um
> conhecimento, conhecimento que ele não tinha e que
> ninguém poderia lhe dar, só ele mesmo, embora pudesse
> ser ajudado. (595)
> magic is not created from the outside, but from the
> inside. That is why we speak so much about having faith
> so that things will happen, for faith, in the final analysis,
> is nothing more than a manner of seeing the world that
> makes possible those things that we want to happen.
> Faith is thus a knowledge, a knowledge that he
> [Macário] did not have and that nobody can give him,
> only he himself, even though he could be helped.

This passage and others in which the narrator describes the metamorphoses occurring during the Afro-Brazilian rituals situate the author within the Latin American current of marvelous realism, whose objective is, as Irlemar Chiampi explains, to

problematizar os códigos sócio-cognitivos do leitor, sem
instalar o paradoxo, manifesta-se nas referências
freqüentes à religiosidade, enquanto modalidade cultural
capaz de responder à sua aspiração de verdade supra-
racional. Em *El reino de este mundo*, de Alejo Carpentier, a
série de acontecimientos legendários que antecederam a
independência do Haiti é sistematicamente vinculada ao
pensamento mítico dos negros, para evitar o efeito de
fantasticidade que converteria a própria História num
impossível referencial. (63)

problematize the sociocognitive codes of the reader
without creating a paradox. It [marvelous realism]
appears in the references to religious faith, because it is a
cultural modality capable of corresponding to a society's
aspiration to suprarational truth. In *El reino de este mundo*
by Alejo Carpentier, the series of legendary events that
precede Haitian independence is systematically
connected to the mythical thought of the Blacks, in order
to avoid the effect of the fantastic, which would
transform history itself into an impossible referent.

The recurring descriptions of apparitions, metamorphoses,
deep trances, and other supernatural effects in the Latin American novel, including *Viva o povo brasileiro*, are not inserted for
their local color or exoticism, but in order to problematize the
rationality of the European tradition, and especially to name
everything that defines the American continent as completely as
possible through "the voices whose discourse was not troubled
by the temptation to dominate the world," as Wolfgang Bader
writes in his preface to Hubert Fichte's book.

João Ubaldo Ribeiro's work attempts a recuperation of religious beliefs and popular myths and traditions with the intention of restoring the people's capacity for recovering what is lost,
and bringing back the "collective consciousness" that was repressed by rationality. The project is completed by the integration of the reader as a "collective being, a member of a (desirable) community without monolithic and hierarchical values"
(Chiampi 69). According to Irlemar Chiampi, marvelous realism, which characterizes the literary production of the best Caribbean authors (writing in Spanish or in French), such as Alejo
Carpentier and Jacques Stephen Alexis, has an

> efeito de encantamento [que] restitui a função
> comunitária da leitura, ampliando a esfera de contato
> social e os horizontes culturais do leitor. (69)
> effect of enchantment that restores the communal
> function of reading, enlarging the sphere of social
> contact and the cultural horizons of the reader.

The formation of Brazilian literature is thus characterized by a kind of errancy, constituted by the alternating movement between the predominance of sacralizing forces and that of desacralizing forces that favor interrelation, or, in other words, the construction of a form of collective identity that does not exclude the Other.

Works Cited

Alencar, José de. Preface. *Sonhos d'ouro*. Rio de Janeiro: Garnier, 1872.

_____. *Iracema*. Ed. Silviano Santiago. Rio de Janeiro: Francisco Alves, 1975.

Angenot, Marc. "Pour une théorie du discours social." *Littérature* 70 (1988): 82-98.

_____. "Hégémonie, dissidence et contre-discours." *Etudes littéraries* 22, 2 (1989): 11-24.

Bosi, Alfredo. *Historia concisa da literatura brasileira*. São Paulo: Cultrix, 1976.

Cambron, Micheline. *Une société, un récit*. Montreal: Hexagone, 1989.

Cândido, António. *Formação da literatura brasileira*. Vol. 1. São Paulo: Martins, 1964.

_____. "Literatura e consciência nacional." *Suplemento literário de Minas Gerais* 156 (6 September 1969): 8-11.

_____. "Literatura e subdesenvolvimento." In Cândido, *A educação pela noite e outros ensaios*. São Paulo: Atica, 1987. 140-162.

Chiampi, Irlemar. *O real maravilhoso*. São Paulo: Perspectiva, 1980.

Dubois, Jacques. *L'institution de la littérature*. Brussels: Nathan, 1978.

Durão, Santa Rita. *Caramuru*. Rio de Janeiro: Agir, 1957.

Fichte, Hubert. *Etnopoesia*. Preface by Wolfgang Bader. São Paulo: Brasiliense, 1987.

Gama, José Basílio da. *O Uraguai*. Rio de Janeiro: Agir, 1964.

Glissant, Edouard. *Le discours antillais*. Paris: Seuil, 1981.

Gómez-Moriana, Antonio, and Catherine Poupeney Hart. *Parole exclusive, parole exclue, parole transgressive. Marginalisation et marginalité dans la production discursive*. Longueuil: Le Préambule, 1990.

Marcotte, Gilles. "Les problèmes du capitaine." *Liberté* 111 (1977): 78-86.

Moreira Leite, Dante. *O caráter nacional brasileiro*. 4th ed. São Paulo: Pioneira, 1983.

Ribeiro, Darcy. *Las Américas y la civilización*. Vol. 1: *La civilización occidental y nosotros. Los pueblos testimonio*. Buenos Aires: Centro Editor de América Latina, 1969.

Ribeiro, João Ubaldo. *Viva o povo brasileiro*. Rio de Janeiro: Nova Fronteira, 1984.

Ricoeur, Paul. *Temps et récit*. Paris: Seuil, 1983-85.

Robin, Régine. *Le roman mémoriel*. Longueuil: Le Préambule, 1989.

Silva, Anazildo V. da. *A formação épica da literatura brasileira*. Rio de Janeiro: Elo, 1987.

Sussekind, Flora. *O Brasil não é longe daqui*. São Paulo: Cia. das Letras, 1990.

Todorov, Tzvetan. *La conquête de l'Amérique. La question de l'autre*. Paris: Seuil, 1982.

―――. *Nous et les autres*. Paris: Seuil, 1989.

◆ **Chapter 6**

A Nahuatl Interpretation of the Conquest: From the "Parousia" of the Gods to the "Invasion"

Enrique Dussel

(translated by Amaryll Chanady)

> *In teteu inan in tetu ita, in Huehuetéutl*
> *[Mother of the gods, Father of the gods, the Old God],*
> *lying on the navel of the Earth,*
> *enclosed in a refuge of turquoises.*
> *He who lives in the waters the color of a blue*
> *bird, he who is surrounded by clouds,*
> *the Old God, he who lives in the shadows*
> *of the realm of the dead,*
> *the lord of fire and time.*
> —Song to Ometeótl, the originary being
> of the Aztec *Tlamatinime*[1]

I would like to examine the "meaning of 1492," which is nothing else but "the first experience of modern Europeans," from the perspective of the "world" of the Aztecs, as the conquest in the literal sense of the term started in Mexico. In some cases I will refer to other cultures in order to suggest additional interpretations, although I am aware that these are only a few of the many possible examples, and that they are a mere "indication" of the problematic. Also, in the desire to continue an intercultural dialogue initiated in Freiburg with Karl-Otto Apel in 1989, I will refer primarily to the existence of reflexive abstract thought on our continent.[2]

The *tlamatini*

In nomadic societies (of the first level) or societies of rural planters (like the Guaranis), social differentiation was not developed sufficiently to identify a function akin to that of the "philosopher," although in urban society this social figure acquires a distinct profile.[3] As we can read in Garcilaso de la Vega's *Comentarios reales de los Incas*:

Demás de adorar al Sol por dios visible, a quien
ofrecieron sacrificios e hicieron grandes fiestas, . . . los
Reyes Incas y *sus amautas, que eran como filósofos*,
rastrearon con lumbre natural al verdadero sumo Dios y
Señor Nuestro, que crió el cielo y la tierra . . . al cual
llamaron Pachacámac: es nombre compuesto de *Pacha*,
que es mundo universo, y de *Cámac*, participio presente
del verbo *cama*, que es animar, el cual verbo se deduce
del nombre *cama*, que es alma. Pachacámac quiere decir
el que da ánima al mundo universo, y en toda su propia
y entera significación quiere decir el que hace con el
universo lo que el ánima con el cuerpo . . . Tuvieron al
Pachacámac en mayor veneración interior que al Sol,
que, como he dicho, no osaban tomar su nombre en la
boca . . . y por esto no le hacían templos ni le ofrecían
sacrificios, mas que lo adoraban en su corazón (esto es,
mentalmente) y le tenían por Dios no conocido. (Book 2,
chap. 2: 74; emphasis added)

Besides worshiping the sun as a visible god, to whom
they offered sacrifices and in whose honor they
organized great festivities, . . . the Inca Kings and their
amautas, who were like philosophers, traced with natural
lucidity the true supreme God and Our Lord, who
created heaven and earth . . . and whom they called
Pachacámac. It is a name composed of *Pacha*, which is
the universe, and *Cámac*, present participle of the verb
cama, which means to animate; that verb comes from the
noun *cama*, which means soul. Pachacámac means he
who gives a soul to the universe, and in its proper and
complete signification, it means he who does to the
universe what the soul does to the body . . . They held
Pachacámac in greater internal veneration than the Sun;
they did not dare pronounce his name . . . and thus
built no temples and offered no sacrifices, but they
worshiped him in their hearts (that is, mentally) and
considered him as an unknown God. (Emphasis added)[4]

The *amautas* had specific functions in the empire and proposed
Pachacámac (from coastal Peru), the *Illa-Ticsi Huiracocha Pachay-
achic* (Originary Splendor, Lord, Master of the Universe), as the
first principle of the universe. From the Aztecs we have more
testimony: the *tlamatini* has a much clearer social definition.[5] In
his *Historia general de las cosas de Nueva España*, Bernardino de

Sahagún refers to the *tlamatini* when he speaks of the various occupations, after his descriptions of the carpenter, the stonecutter, the mason, the painter, and the singer (Book 10; chap. 7: 555).[6] Thus, there were perfectly defined classes, functions, and occupations—the governors, judges, warriors, priests, and, specifically identified as such, the "wise men" ("sabios"; Sahagún writes "philosophers" in the margin), of whom Fernando de Alva Ixtlilxochitl tells us:

> Los filósofos o sabios que tenían entre ellos [los aztecas] a su cargo pintar todas las ciencias que sabían y alcanzaban a enseñar de memoria todos los cantos que conservaban sus ciencias e historias. (2: 18)

> The philosophers or wise men who among them [the Aztecs] had the duty of painting all the knowledge that they knew and managed to teach from memory all the songs that preserved their knowledge and stories.

We have a splendid definition of the *tlamatinime*, who were educated in the *Calmécac* (a scrupulously regulated school of wise men, and as such a strong argument for the demonstration of the existence of Aztec philosophy):

> El *tlamatini*, una luz, una tea, una gruesa tea que no ahuma. Espejo horadado, un espejo agugereado de ambos lados. Suya es la tinta negra y roja . . . El mismo es escritura y sabiduría. Es camino y guía veraz para otros . . . El sabio verdadero es cuidadoso y guarda la tradición. Suya es la sabiduría trasmitida, él es quien la enseña, sigue la verdad. Maestro de la verdad, no deja de amonestar. Hace sabios los rostros de los otros, hace a los otros tomar un rostro, los hace desarrollarlo . . . Pone un espejo delante de los otros . . . Hace que aparezca su propio rostro . . . Aplica su luz sobre el mundo . . . Gracias a él la gente humaniza su querer y recibe una disciplinada enseñanza. (León Portilla 1979: 65-74)

> The *tlamatini*, a light, a torch, a big torch that does not smoke. A pierced mirror, a mirror perforated on both sides. His is the black and red ink . . . He himself is writing and wisdom. He is a path and a true guide for others . . . The genuine wise man is careful and preserves tradition. His is transmitted wisdom, he is the

one who teaches it, he follows truth. A master of truth,
he does not cease admonishing. He makes the
countenances of the others wise, he makes others
assume a countenance, he makes them develop it . . .
He places a mirror in front of the others . . . He makes
his own face appear in it . . . He applies his light to the
world . . . Thanks to him the people humanize their love
and receive a disciplined education.[7]

Just as important as the positive description of the wise man is
the negative description of the "false wise man" ("falso sabio"),[8]
which confirms my opinion that a form of thought existed that
was not only mythical, but strictly "conceptual," although
based on metaphors (conceptual, and not merely mythical, metaphors).[9]

One element that must also be taken into consideration is the
existence of a particular social institution: the *Calmécac*, a school
of *momachtique* (students). There the young boys, who left their
families between the ages of seven and nine to be integrated into
a "community" (*Icniuhyotl*), had an absolutely regimented life,[10]
whose center consisted of "dialogues" or "conversations"
among the wise men (*Huehuetlatolli*).[11] The purpose of schooling
was to learn "knowledge that was already known" ("la sabi-
duría ya sabida"; *momachtique*), in order to be able to produce
"adequate speech" ("palabra adecuada"; *in qualli tlatolli*) with
rhetorical discipline (as in the Academy or the *Liceo*). This
knowledge was articulated in the major work of the *Calmécac*,
the "flor y canto" (*in xóchitl in cuícatl*). Expressed aloud or written in the codices (*amates*), the "flor y canto" was recited or sung
with or without music, rhythmically punctuated, and even accompanied by dance; it was the place par excellence of communication between "the terrestrial" (*tlaltícpac*) and the divine, for
which the interpretation of dreams was also used.[12]

I believe that among the Aztecs in the fifteenth century a
great tension existed between what we could call the "sacrificial
myth" of Tlacaélel, a myth of domination and militarism (which
was replaced by the "myth of Modernity"), and the "protophi-
losophy" of the *tlamatinime* (which was ignored by the emancipation movement of the Enlightenment in Europe and Latin
America).[13] This explains the vacillation of Moctezuma—who

was more a *tlamatini* than a soldier. The admiration accompanying the "discovery" by the European navigators and cartographers can be correlated with the interpretive confusion of the *tlamatinime*, who initially interpreted the "discovery" as a "parousia" of the gods. The sacrificial violence of the "conquest" can be correlated with the inevitable acceptation by the vanquished of the brutal experience of "invasion"; "colonization" can be correlated with the "sixth sun" or the period of servitude; the "spiritual conquest" with the "death of the gods"; and so forth.

The "Parousia" of the Gods

Many of the beliefs of the *tlamatinime* coincided with popular ones and those of the dominant political, warrior, and commercial classes (as is the case, for example, with the belief in the existence of the "five suns").[14] Other beliefs, however, were the product of the highly conceptualized and abstract rationalization that was developed by the *tlamatinime* in the *Calmécac*, and I will briefly summarize this rationalization in order to understand "how" the *tlamatinime* interpreted the arrival of the travelers from the East, where the Sun rises every morning (*Huitzilopochtli*).

Beyond any myth, Aztec rationality affirmed, as the absolute and eternal origin of everything, not the "One," but the "Two" (*Ome*).[15] At the beginning, there was the "place of duality" (*Omeyocan*) in the thirteenth sky, where the "Divine-Duality" (*Ometeótl*), or simply the "Duality" (*Oméyotl*), resided.[16] It was not as it was for Hegel: first Being and Nothingness, and then becoming or movement in second place, Being-there or *Ente* (*Dasein*). For the *tlamatinime* the origin is already codetermined (*i-námic* means "shares"),[17] in the metaphorical[18] sense of "woman-man,"[19] but it received other meanings of a high degree of conceptual abstraction: "And they also called it (1) *Moyucayatzin*; (2) *ayac oquiyocux*; and (3) *ayac oquipic*, which means that nobody created or formed it" (Mendieta 95). Mendieta could not imagine the level of ontological abstraction of these terms (because mythical reason had clearly been exceeded, it must therefore be called strict philosophical reason). The first term means "the

Lord who invents himself" ("Señor que se inventa a sí mismo");[20] the second indicates that "nobody made him" ("nadie lo hizo a él"); and the third means "nobody gave him form" ("nadie le dió su forma"). Only the "flor y canto" of the *tlamatini* can provide an expression for *Ometeótl* that is more or less comprehensible: "night-wind" (*Yohualli-Ehecátl*);[21] "he who is close and surrounds us" (*in Tloque in Nahuaque*);[22] "he who gives us life" (*Ipalnemohuani*). It is now possible to read the text quoted as the epigraph of this essay, although it is necessary to continue the explanation in order to understand the passage.

How did the *tlamatinime* explain the relation between the "Divine Duality" (an absolute ontological principle) and "phenomenal," "temporal," and "terrestrial" reality (*tlaltícpac*), in which we live "as if in a dream" ("como en sueños")? The autopoetic Divine Duality then unfolds itself, operating a *Diremption*[23] or *Explicatio* (like the pseudo-Dionysius the Areopagite or John Scotus Erigena): "This god-goddess engendered four sons . . . " ("Este dios-diosa engendraron cuatro hijos . . . ") (García Icazbalceta 228ff.), each of whom was called Tezcatlipoca.[24] They are the originary concrete principles of the universe, and are situated at the "four cardinal points" (as in Chinese ontology, Polynesian traditions, and American cultures, from the Eskimos to the Incas and Araucanos): that of the East, which is red; that of the North, which is black, the realm of the dead; that of the West, white Quetzalcóatl, fertility and life; that of the South, blue Huitzilopochtli of the Aztecs. As with the pre-Socratics, there are four ruling principles: earth, air, water, and fire. Each one also dominated an "epoch" of the world. Five epochs had already passed, "five Suns." The present age was that of the "Sun in movement," the age of Huitzilopochtli, the warrior god of the Aztecs:

> Este Sol, su nombre 4 *movimiento*, este es nuestro Sol, en el que *vivimos* ahora . . . El quinto Sol . . . se llama Sol de *movimiento* porque se mueve, sigue su camino. (León Portilla 1979: 103, 333)

> This Sun, whose name is 4 *movement*, this is our Sun, in which we now *live* . . . The fifth Sun . . . is called the Sun of *movement* because it moves, it follows its path. (Emphasis in the original)

"Movement" (*Y-olli*) is related to "heart" (*Y-ollo-ti*) and to "life" (*Yoliliztli*).[25] It is for Ometeótl that "all live" (*Ipalnemohuani*), but they worship him through the Sun (one of the faces of Tezcatlipoca). Furthermore, these four "principles" are in continual "conflict." Humans, the *macehuales*,[26] enter this battle to preserve whatever they can from the existence of the "fifth Sun" in which they live; they lend their support and become accomplices of the reigning Sun. Human existence is always regulated, *necessarily* ruled by the rhythm of time or "of the years." The Aztecs had a "tragic" vision of existence, as there was no room for any freedom in human events and everything was predetermined in advance, according to the "old rule of life" ("vieja regla de vida"; *Huehuetlamanitiliztli*).

On the earth (*tlaltícpac*), everything is regulated according to Ometeótl's wishes:

> Nuestro Señor, el Señor que está cerca y nos rodea (*in Tloque in Nahuaque*), determina lo que quiere, lo planifica, se divierte. Como él quiere, así querrá. En el centro de la palma de su mano nos tiene colocados, nos está moviendo a su antojo. (*Códice Florentino*, book 6, folio 43: v; León Portilla 1979: 199-200, 349)

> Our Lord, the Lord who is close and surrounds us (*in Tloque in Nahuaque*), determines what he wants, plans it, amuses himself. As he wants it, he will want it. He has us placed in the center of the palm of his hand, he is moving us according to his whim.[27]

In the heavens above the stars continue their necessary "path" (*camino*), as do human beings.[28] That explains the obsession with finding the "ground" (*fundamento*) of things,[29] which constituted truth: "Are men perhaps *real*? Therefore our song is no longer *true*? What is left *standing*, by chance?" ("¿Acaso son *verdad* los hombres? ¿Por tanto ya no es *verdad* nuestro canto? ¿Qué está de pie por ventura?") (Ms. *Cantares Mexicanos*, folio 10: v; León Portilla 1979: 61).[30] For the *tlamatini*, the "flor y canto" (communicating with the divinity in the community of wise men) is finally "lo único *verdadero en la tierra*" ("the only *true* thing on earth") (*nelli in tlaltícpac*) (Ms. *Cantares Mexicanos*, folio 9v: 142). But if the wise man can live the mystical-philosophical experience of grounding himself in the divinity, or the "world of life" (*Lebenswelt*), there were other ways of attaining the desired grounding, such as through the structuring of the divisions of time according to the divine calendar. That is why the Aztecs had an exact knowledge of the measurement of sacred time: the time of day, the days, the weeks (thirteen days each), and the years (the lunar year, the solar year, the year of Venus).[31] Each day had a tutelary divinity, as did each week, month, type of year, and their extremely complex combinations. An entire "procession," a hierarchical multitude of divinities "moved" along the "path" of the sky every day, from dawn to nightfall, and even during the night. It was necessary to worship these divinities (with songs, rituals, sacrifices, and so forth), in order to appease them and ward off their possible evil actions. That explains the festivals and celebrations[32] and the entirely "regulated" life. Furthermore, and this is fundamental, the "eternal return of the Same" was completed by "astrology,"[33] and by the "interpretation" (in fact, a hermeneutics) of "signs" that gave meaning to the events that were "apparently" not "grounded" in "truth."[34] Astrology was an a priori "divine" rule that was applied to every event in time (*in tlaltícpac*); the hermeneutics of "omens" was an a posteriori explanation of a concrete, empirical, and "apparently" new sign, in order to apply to it (the sign) an a priori rule and thus discover a "contingent" meaning. The "omens" predicted future (and past) events, but ones that were always "necessary" ("that cannot be otherwise," as Aristotle would say). In this way, the tragic Aztec conscience, from the oppressed masses to the ruling or warrior classes and even the *tlamatinime*, had the "grounding" of their existence "secured" in the "truth" of Ometeótl.

We can now attempt a certain understanding of what must have happened to Moctezuma when he heard the "news" of the appearance of the recent arrivals on the coast of *Cemanáhuac* ("the entire earth") from the infinite *Teoatl* (Atlantic):

> Y cuando fueron vistos los que vinieron por el mar (*teoatl*), en barcas van viniendo . . . Y cuando estuvieron cerca de los hombres de Castilla, al momento frente a ellos hicieron ceremonia de tocar la tierra y los labios . . .
> Tuvieron la opinión de que era Nuestro Señor Quetzalcóatl que había venido. (León Portilla 1978: 32-33)

And when those who came from the sea (*teoatl*) were
seen, they were arriving in ships . . . And when they
[the Aztecs] were close to the men from Castille, they
immediately conducted a ceremony in front of them of
touching the earth and their lips . . . They believed it
was Our Lord Quetzalcóatl who had arrived.[35]

Even when he receives Cortés in the City of Mexico, Moctezuma
believes (because of a conclusion he arrived at for strategic reasons, as we will see) that he is Quetzalcóatl. The attitude of the
emperor has been considered vacillating, contradictory, and
scarcely comprehensible (the reasons given by Todorov, Wachtel, León Portilla, Octavio Paz, J. Lafaye, and others do not explain the "rationality" of Moctezuma's behavior).[36] He received
Cortés with these words:

Señor nuestro: te has fatigado, te has dado cansancio: ya
a esta tierra tú has llegado. Has arribado a *tu ciudad*:
México. Aquí has venido a sentarte en *tu solio*, en *tu
trono*. Oh, por tiempo breve te lo reservaron, te lo
conservaron, los que ya se fueron, *tus sustitutos*. Los
señores reyes, Itzcaotzin, Motecuhzomatzin el viejo,
Axayácac, Tízoc, Ahuítzotl. Oh, qué breve tiempo tan
sólo guardaron *para tí*, dominaron la ciudad de México.
. . . No, no es que yo sueño, no me levanto del sueño
adormilado: no lo veo en sueños, no estoy soñando. Es
que ya te he visto, ¡es que ya te he puesto mis ojos *en tu
rostro*! Ha cinco, ha diez días yo estaba angustiado: tenía
fija la mirada en la Región de los Muertos (*topan mictlan*).
Y tú has venido entre nubes, entre nieblas. Como que
esto era lo que nos habían dejado dicho los reyes, los
que rigieron, los que gobernaron *tu ciudad*: que habrías
de instalarte en *tu asiento*, en *tu sitial* . . . Ven y
descansa; toma posesión de *tus casas reales*; da refrigerio a
tu cuerpo. (León Portilla 1978: 38; emphasis added)

Our Lord: you have tired yourself, you have given
yourself trouble: now you have already arrived in this
land. You have arrived in *your city*: Mexico. Here you
have come to sit on *your royal seat*, on *your throne*. Oh,
for a short period they who have already left, *your
substitutes*, reserved it, conserved it for you. The kings
and masters, Itzcaotzin, Motecuhzomatzin the elder,
Axayácac, Tízoc, Ahuítzotl. Oh, for what a short time

did they keep it *for you*, and ruled the city of Mexico.
. . . No, it is not that I am dreaming, I am not arising
still half asleep: I am not seeing this in dreams, I am not
dreaming. I have already seen you, I have already set
my eyes *on your face*! Five, ten days ago, I was worried: I
had my gaze fixed on the Realm of the Dead (*topan
mictlan*). And you arrived among clouds, among fog. Just
as the kings, those who governed, those who ruled *your
city*, told us: that you were to settle into *your seat*, into
your chair of honor . . . Come and rest; take possession of
your royal houses; give your body sustenance. (Emphasis
added)

Moctezuma offers the recent arrival nothing less than the
throne, the government, and dominion over the Aztecs! Was
this not exactly what Cortés wanted? On the contrary: Cortés
does not understand this offer and furthermore has no intention
of occupying the throne. This produces a new confusion in
Moctezuma—but it is neither the first nor the last, and that is
why he will continue to react to each "novelty" in a way that
disconcerted successive interpreters. Is Moctezuma's behavior
rational? I answer clearly and unambiguously: Yes! It was entirely rational and the most convenient, *if we take into consideration Moctezuma's "world" and do not project a Eurocentric perspective onto him* (as even the above-mentioned authors have done,
in spite of being the most critical ones we could encounter).[37]

Let us carefully analyze the various "possibilities" (in the
Heideggerian sense of *Möglichkeit*; see Dussel 1973: 65ff., "Las
posibilidades ónticas," and Luhmann); that is, what was possible for Moctezuma from the perspective of his "world" (correctly situated), the world of an Aztec emperor, who was a good
warrior but an even better *tlamatini* of austere moral education in
the best tradition of the Toltec wise men. Moctezuma, that "cultivated" and refined emperor, who was not in the least cow-
ardly (contrary to the inadequate interpretation of him that was
incorporated into history), was faced with the following "possibilities," after having informed himself with all the means provided him by his civilization:[38]

1. The recent arrivals were a group of human beings, which
   was the least probable "possibility"[39]—from the nahuatl

hermeneutic perspective—and would have to be confirmed by other events that had not yet occurred, and were thus "reasonably" to be discarded, at that time. It would turn out to be the beginning of an "invasion," but only on the basis of new data that Moctezuma necessarily did not have available at that time.[40]

2. Only one rational possibility remained: they were gods. If that was so, which ones? Everything indicated (according to the counsel of the astrologers as much as to that of the *tlamatinime*) that it had to be Quetzalcóatl. One possibility considered by the *tlamatinime* was Quetzalcóatl's return, after having been expelled from Tula by the Toltecs or other ethnic groups.[41]

3. The third "possibility," in the form of another alternative to the second, was that although Quetzalcóatl was returning, the prince was now fused with the divine principle, as one of the faces of Ometeótl. This was really disastrous, as it would be the "end of the Fifth Sun."[42]

Confronting these "possibilities," Moctezuma doubted, but he continued to make "rational" decisions. In the first place, it would be good to pay homage to the recent arrivals with gifts and propose to them that they return to their place of origin (whatever that may be). Moctezuma did not want to meet them "face to face," because that would be his end. This is what has not been interpreted correctly:

> Ahora bien, Moctezuma cavilaba en aquellas cosas, estaba preocupado; lleno de terror, de miedo: cavilaba qué iba a acontecer con la ciudad. (*Informantes de Sahagún*; León Portilla 1979: 35)
>
> Now, Moctezuma reflected deeply on these matters, he was preoccupied, filled with terror, with fear: he was wondering what was going to happen to the city.

And he had good reason for doing so. For the enemies of the empire, the oppressed (such as the people of Zempoala or Tlaxcala—and the same would happen to Atahualpa with the Incas), Cortés was an ally (whether he was a man or a god) who could emancipate them from Aztec domination.[43] The warriors faithful to Huitzilopochtli would "fight" as collaborators of their god, but they would have to act alone if Cortés's men were really human beings (the first possibility), or if Quetzalcóatl tried to put an end to the "Fifth Sun" (third possibility). The people of Mexico-Tenochtitlan did not stand to lose anything if Quetzal-cóatl resumed rule in "his" empire (second possibility). Everyone thus judged the possibilities in different ways, but only Moctezuma had to face an extreme decision.[44] He had very little room for maneuver: if Quetzalcóatl wanted to resume the rule of the empire, he would have to abdicate (second possibility); in all other cases Moctezuma could take his chance with his warriors (but only after making sure that the second possibility did not correspond to reality). That is why Moctezuma, the great *tlama-tini*, "rationally" and with clearly strategic reason, makes the decision of giving up the empire and leaving in his place Quetzalcóatl-Cortés: "Take possession of your royal houses!"[45]

Naturally the recent arrivals confuse him again. When the Aztecs offer them food with blood, these strange gods scorn it. They appeared even stranger when they became ecstatic at the sight of gold; they irrationally transformed precious jewels into ingots, thus destroying the immense work of refined goldsmiths (artistry that later would be admired by Dürer in Holland). Also, they absurdly killed enemies in battle instead of taking them prisoner and sacrificing them to the gods. Once again, Cortés does not assume power in Mexico! But at least Moctezuma comes to a first conclusion: Cortés is not prince Quetzalcóatl who wants to resume temporal power (*in tlaltícpac*). The other possibilities still remain, but the situation must be analyzed carefully, for Cortés could act in the name of the god and bring about the end of the Fifth Sun. This was the supreme danger, and that is why Moctezuma bore humiliation knowing that, if Cortés and his men were human, in the worst case his life was in danger, but it would only be his end as monarch, and the city of Mexico would not suffer.

The "Invasion" of the Empire

A new event, which could not be considered by Moctezuma previously because it had not yet occurred (and therefore could not be a historical or real "possibility" at that earlier time),[46] started to create a situation that would permit the posterior development of the "first possibility" (although the "third possibility" still continued to be a supreme danger):

> No fue bien llegado con el armada, cuando Motecuhzuma fue dello avisado a tiempo. [Y el emperador llamando a Cortés le dijo]: "Señor capitán, sabed que son venidos navíos de vuestra tierra, en que podréis [part]ir, por tanto aderezaos con brevedad que así conviene." (Torquemada, chap. 59: 184)
>
> He had hardly arrived with the armada [that of Pánfilo Narváez, who was sent from Cuba against Cortés], when Motecuhzuma was apprised of it on time. [And the emperor called Cortés, saying to him]: "Captain, Sir, you know that ships have come from your land, in which you can leave, so prepare them quickly, for that is the way it should be."

Now Moctezuma, knowing that the Spaniards are human beings,[47] is aware for the first time that there are others like Cortés, with numerous new soldiers accompanying them. If they return to where they came from, everything will turn out well (and the empire, traditions, gods, the Fifth Sun, and Moctezuma himself will be out of danger). But two new events (soon to be three) make him aware of an unexpected development of the "first possibility" (and really it is a new "fourth possibility" he never considered before): first, that Cortés did not only not return to his place of origin, but that, defeating Narváez, he reinforced his army (with which he returned triumphantly to Mexico); and second, and no less important, the massacre that Pedro de Alvarado perpetrated against the Aztec elite. These two facts "proved" that Moctezuma had been in error,[48] and inclined the balance in favor of the warriors inspired by the sacrificial myth of Tlacaélel, who, considering the Spaniards merely as human beings, had thought from the very beginning that it was necessary to fight against them. Moctezuma was finished. Cortés, who had understood nothing of the "argumentative world" of the Other,[49] of the highly developed world of Moctezuma, tries to use him as he did before, and thus loses precious time for his own cause.[50] It is now late; all the Aztecs have discovered, clearly and *for the first time*, that Cortés and his men are only a group of human warriors, and that they are the vanguard of an "invasion": the "invasion of *Cemanáhuac*," of the entire world "known" to the Aztecs.

The wisdom of the *tlamatinime* had been negated, destroyed; their entire "worldview" (weltanschauung) was now proved inadequate and incapable of accounting for reality. Moctezuma, in his function as *tlamatini*, had died. His physical death was a matter of hours. Thus ended the "Parousia of the gods." Pánfilo Narváez, and not Cortés (just as Amerigo Vespucci and not Columbus had discovered America), proved that the events were part of an invasion, and this was not known before that point.

Tlacaélel, the Romulus and Remus of the Aztecs,[51] had been born in the year 10-Rabbit (*10-Conejo*) (1398), defeated the Tepanecas of Azcapotzalco, the Albalonga of Mexico-Tenochtitlan, in the year 1-Flint (*1-Pedernal*) (1428), and was called the "Conqueror of the World" (*in cemanáhuac Tepehuan*) (Alvarado Tezozómac 121; on Tlacaélel see León Portilla 1979: 247ff.; and León Portilla 1990: 46ff., 92ff.). To him the Aztecs owed the "reforms" that gave the empire its great cosmopolitan vision, and its interpretation from the sacrificial paradigm of the dominating power in Mexico:

> Este es el oficio de Huitzilopochtli, nuestro dios, a esto fue venido a reunir y trae así a su servicio a todas las naciones, con la fortaleza de su pecho y de su cabeza. (Durán 95)
>
> This is the function of Huitzilopochtli, our god, for this he had come to unite and thus he brings all nations to his service, with the strength of his breast and head.

Ometeótl reveals himself for the Tezcatlipocas; the god of the "Fifth Sun," Quetzalcóatl, was reinterpreted by the Aztecs in a sacrificial paradigm: "And here is his sign, how the Sun fell into the fire, into the divine blaze, there in Teotihuacán" ("Y aquí está su señal, cómo cayó en el fuego el Sol, en el fogón divino, allá en Teotihuacán") (*Documento de 1558*; León Portilla 1979: 103-9). The small hummingbird god (*dios colibrí*), Nanahuatzin, offered his life in sacrifice, immolated himself for the salvation of all; then burnt in the divine fire, he appeared, after a long night,

as the rising Sun, which the Aztecs considered as their tribal
god: Huitzilopochtli. This secondary warrior god would become, because of the "Reform of Tlacaélel," the main god of all
Anáhuac. Tlacaélel would end up burning all the sacred codices
of the dominated people, and write them anew. It was a veritable domination of theogonies. The empire was now "grounded"
as the servant of the existence and life of the Sun. That is why
"movement" (of the Sun and all reality), "life," and the "heart"
are related to "blood" (*chalchihuitl*): the life of the Sun-Huitzilo-
pochtli depends on human sacrifice. The victims are obtained in
the "flowery wars" (*guerras floridas*), justifying the existence of
the empire:

> Allí donde se tiñen los dardos, donde se tiñen los
> escudos, están las blancas flores perfumadas, las flores
> del corazón: abren sus corolas las flores del que da la
> vida, cuyo perfume aspiran en el mundo los príncipes:
> es Tenochtitlan. (Ms. *Cantares Mexicanos*, folio 20v; León
> Portilla 1979: 257)
> There where the spears are dyed, where the shields are
> dyed, are the white perfumed flowers, the flowers of the
> heart: the flowers of the one who gives life open their
> corollas, whose perfume is inhaled by princes on earth:
> it is Tenochtitlan.[52]

Through the myth of the necessity of human sacrifice, proclaimed from the main temple of Huitzilopochtli, Tlacaélel thus
manages to transform the empire into a collaborator for the continuing existence of the universe and the prolongation of the life
of the "Fifth Sun." The discovery that Cortés was not Quetzalcóatl was the moment when the warriors tried to prolong the
"Fifth Sun" by defeating the intruders:

> En consecuencia luego salieron de noche. En la fiesta de
> Techílhuitl salieron; fue cuando murieron en el Canal de
> los Toltecas. Allí furiosamente los atacamos. [*Anonymous
> Ms. from Tlatelolco* (1528); León Portilla 1978: 43]
> Consequently they then went out at night. They went
> out during the festival of Techílhuitl; that was when they
> died in the Canal of the Toltecs. There we attacked them
> furiously.

It was of little avail to them to drive Cortés out of the city during the "Noche Triste" ("Sad Night" — sad for the Spaniards, of course).[53] The worse for Mexico, the plague breaks out, and this is interpreted as a bad omen for the empire. From Tlaxcala the invaders reorganized their forces, and Cortés started to "weaken" Mexico, as the Catholic Monarchs had done with Granada. The siege of Tenochtitlan lasts for months. Finally the Spaniards drive the Aztecs out of the city and surround them in Tlatelolco. They are defeated.

> En los caminos yacen dardos rotos; los caballos están esparcidos. Destechadas están las casas, enrojecidos tienen sus muros. Gusanos pululan por calles y plazas y están las paredes manchadas de sesos. Rojas están las aguas, cual si las hubieran teñido, y si las bebíamos, eran agua de salitre. (*Anonymous Ms. from Tlatelolco*; León Portilla 1978: 53)

> On the roads lie broken spears; the horses are scattered. The houses are without roofs, their walls are red. Worms teem in the streets and squares, and the walls are splashed with brains. Red are the waters, as if they had been dyed, and if we drank them they were saltpeter.

> El llanto se extiende, las lágrimas gotean allí en Tlatelolco. Por agua se fueron ya los mexicanos; semejan mujeres; la huida es general. ¿Adónde vamos? ¡Oh amigos! Luego ¿fue *verdad*? Ya abandonan la ciudad de México: el humo se está levando, la niebla se está extendiendo . . . Esto es lo que ha hecho el Dador-de-la-Vida en Tlatelolco. (*Cantares Mexicanos*; León Portilla 1979: 62)

> The wailing spreads, the tears are falling there in Tlatelolco. The Mexicans already left by water; they are like women; the flight is general. Where are we going? Oh friends! Then was it *true*? They are already abandoning the city of Mexico: the smoke is lifting, the fog is spreading . . . This is what the Giver-of-Life in Tlatelolco has done.[54]

The "invasion" has ended. The warriors have been routed. The same was to happen to the Mayas, to the Incas of Atahualpa . . . right to the confines of Patagonia in the South, or Alaska in the North, during the following years.[55] Modernity has been installed . . . it has emancipated the people oppressed by the Aztecs and victims of their bloodthirsty gods . . . and like a "Sixth Sun" that rises on the horizon of Humanity, a new god (capital) is inaugurating a new "sacrificial myth": the "myth" of Tlacaélel is replaced by the no less sacrificial "myth" of the provident "hand of God" that regulates Adam Smith's harmony of market forces.

Notes

1. In teteu inan in tetu ita, in Huehuetéutl
   [Madre de los dioses, Padre de los dioses, el Dios viejo],
   yaciendo en el ombligo de la Tierra,
   metido en un encierro de turquesas.
   El que está en las aguas color de pájaro
   azul, el que está encerrado en nubes,
   el Dios viejo, el que habita en las sombras
   de la región de los muertos,
   el señor del fuego y del año. (León Portilla 1979: 93)
   In the second line, the "Old God" is Ometeótl, a dual originary principle: Mother-Father, like the "Alom-Qaholam" (originary Mother-Father) of the Mayas (see *Popol Vuh* 23 and 164). It is the originary "divine duality" (reminding us of the "twins" of all other American cultures, from the North American prairies to the Caribbean, the Amazon, and even Patagonia). Heraclitus's dual principle refers to the same thing.
   In the third line, "lying": this "being stretched out," "resting," or "lying down" gives the idea of being below, of grounding, or being the ultimate reference in the sense of the Absolute as foundation (*als Grund*, in Hegel's major and minor treatise on Logic). "To be lying (down or below)" (*ónoc*) as the foundation of the universe means to provide it with its "truth."
   In the fourth line, "enclosed in a refuge" could be the concept of the "in itself" (*in sich*).
   In the fifth line, the "waters" are the ocean, or the North and South Seas of the Aztec empire.
   At the end of the sixth line, "clouds" refers to the sky "above," as the same waters "below," the oceans, continue in the sky as the waters above.
   The eighth line refers to the "nether world," the realm that completes the trilogy: Sky-Earth-Hades, as in the Mesopotamian cults. This nether world (*topan mictlan*) was the "realm of the dead," which must be distinguished from Tllocan or the paradise of the just.
2. In Mexico in 1991, I discussed with Karl-Otto Apel the existence or inexistence of philosophy in American protohistory before the arrival of the Europeans, and the possibility or impossibility of an "Enlightenment" (*Aufklärung*), at least in Jaspers's sense of an "axis time" (*edad eje, Achsenzeit*).
3. I am using the term "philosopher" in the original Greek sense of "one who loves knowledge," and thus in the present sense of the philosopher-theologian, before the secularization (a product of Christianity) that since the third

century A.D. transformed the philosopher into someone who was not a Christian theologian.

4. Garcilaso, the Inca, adds shortly thereafter: "which means that the God of the Christians and Pachacámac are one and the same" (75). He criticizes the interpretation given by Pedro de Cieza, who, "because he was Spanish, did not know the language as well as I do, I who am an Inca Indian" (74).

5. The word comes from *mati*, he knows; *tla*, a thing or something; and *ni*, which substantivizes *he who* knows. Thus *tlamatini* means "he who knows something."

6. It is important to point out that the occupation of painter was essential, because it meant painting the sacred codices. Also crucial was the singer, who had to intonate the "song," as with the Guaranis, but ritualized with a splendor that cannot be compared to the songs of the simple and poor villages of the tropical rain forests.

7. León Portilla (1979) indicates the extensive meaning of each word in nahuatl; I will provide commentary on only selected words and phrases.

"a big torch that does not smoke": because it does not smoke, it is clear, transparent, and lucid.

"a mirror perforated on both sides": the gods looked through a hole to see the earth, but the astronomers also observed the skies through a perforated object. "Perforated on both sides" signifies discovering the meaning of what is human from the perspective of the gods, and the meaning of the gods from a human point of view.

"he follows truth": truth is *Neltiliztli*, from the root *nelhuáyotl*, meaning cement or foundation (as in the Guarani "foundation of the word"), and also from *tla-nél-huatl*, meaning root. León Portilla writes: "We can conclude that the nahuatl preoccupation when inquiring whether something *was true* or *standing* (as in the case of the Guaranis) was directed toward wanting to know whether there was something fixed, well cemented, that escaped the *only a little here* [*sólo un poco aquí*], the vanity of things that are on earth (*tlaltícpac*), which appear as a dream" (1979: 61; emphasis in the original). That is the entire question of "grounding": "Are men perhaps real? Therefore our song is no longer true? What is left standing by chance?" (Ms. *Cantares Mexicanos*, folio 10: v; León Portilla 1979: 61).

"He makes the countenances of the others wise": *Teixtlamachtiani*, the person who makes rich or communicates something to somebody. *Ix* (from *ixtli*), meaning face, countenance; *te*, meaning the other. The expression *teixicuitiani* is still stronger, meaning: to make others acquire their own "face" or "countenance" (he or she personalizes or individualizes them). Finally, *teixtomani*, meaning developing the face of the other. A person "without face" is ignorant, drifting, does not find meaning in anything, not even in the self. The educated person "has a face," and can discover a critical sense that transcends mere *tlaltícpac* ("on the earth," the ephemeral, the "phenomenal," the Platonic "doxa"): "as in dreams." All wisdom consists of going beyond *tlaltícpac* (the terrestrial) in order to attain "what surpasses us" (*topan mictlan*), the transcendental. There is an explicit "Enlightenment" (*Aufklärung*) here. We are at least on the level of Parmenides's poems and Heraclitus's oracles (or in Jaspers's *Achsenzeit*), as with the pre-Socratics. León Portilla proves this abundantly and extensively; because of the limited space of this essay I cannot develop his arguments in greater depth here.

"He places a mirror in front of the others": *Tetezcaviani*, from *tezcatl* and *tezcavia*, meaning to place a mirror in front of others. The "mirror" is evidently critical reflection, the "speculative," the ability to look at oneself, the overcoming of meaninglessness. The *tlamatini* thus places a mirror before the face of the other in order to discover oneself, to reconstruct the face and develop it.

"He applies his light to the world": The world is a fundamental concept. *Cemanáhuac*, meaning the complete circuit of water, comes from *cem*, meaning entirely, completely; *a(tl)*, meaning water; and *náhuac*, meaning circuit. It is the whole "world," Mexico, from the North Sea (the Caribbean, the Atlantic) to the South Sea (the Pacific). The Ocean (*teócatl*) is divine water, which meets the sky (*ilhuicaatl*), which is also divine water, because both are identical (see Seler 3). To apply one's light to the world thus means to observe and discover with one's light, or one's intelligence, the mystery or the appearance of the world. *Tla-ix-imantini* means: he who with his face-appearance knows things.

"Thanks to him the people humanize their love": *Itech netlacaneco*. From *netlaca-neco: -neco* (he is beloved), *tlácatl* (human being), *ne-* (impersonal prefix), meaning: "the people are loved humanely" thanks to him (*itech*). In other words, he humanizes, makes civilized, educates, makes loving or love morally defensible.

8. Besides other meanings, this term referred to "the sorcerer who made the other's face turn around" (*teixcuepani*), that is to say, instead of showing the other his face so that he can fulfill it, he shows him the nape of the neck, so that he cannot see his face. We could say that the Europeans in their "discovery" of America only saw "a face turned backward" (concealed), or that they "made others lose their face" (*teixpoloa*) (León Portilla 1979: 73).

9. "All the songs of these people were composed of such obscure *metaphors* that there is hardly anyone who understands them without studying them and discussing them with the specific purpose of understanding their meaning. I started listening on purpose and with great attention to what they sing, including the words and terms of *metaphor*, and it seemed nonsense to me, and then, discussing and conferring with the people, I perceived their songs as *admirable maxims*, as much in the divine works they now compose, as in their popular songs" (Durán 21; emphasis in the original).

10. "They all cleaned the houses at four in the morning . . . The food that they prepared was cooked in the building of the *Calmécac* . . . Every night at midnight they got up to pray, and he who did not wake up and get up was punished by pricking the ears, the chest, the thighs, and the legs" (Sahagún 327).

11. In nahuatl a "philosophical treatise" should be translated by "dialogue" or "conversation" (like the Platonic Dialogues). These were essentially *Teutlatolli*, or "discourses on the divine," and had their discursive rules, their method of argumentation, and their required forms of articulation.

12. This was much more than a work of poetry: it was an expression of wisdom, a work in which the human communicated with the divine and vice versa, in short, the culmination of the entire nahuatl culture. It resembled the sacred "word" of the Guaranis, but was much more elaborate.

Regarding "the interpretation of dreams": "They were taught the *tonalphua-lli*, the book of dreams (*temicámatl*) and the book of years (*xiuhámatl*)" (*Códice Florentino*, book 3: 65; quoted by León Portilla 1979: 228).

13. In eighteenth-century Mexico, Clavijero recuperated these traditions and explicitly considered them as "philosophy."

14. As can be seen in the *Popol Vuh* and in the existence of four types of humanity preceding the Mayas, who constitute the fifth, the Mayas, as well as the Toltecs (who were to the Aztecs as the Greeks were to the Romans), had the same sacrificial vision of Tlacaélel. They believed that they were living in a "fifth age," and that "four ages" had already passed, each of which had a different "Sun."

15. The "One" was affirmed by Plato in *Parmenides*, Plotinus in the *Eneid*, Hindu thought, and Chinese Taoism. In all of these systems the problem was how to determine the "One" in order to attain "plurality," that is, the question of "matter."

16. According to the Aztecs, there were thirteen skies (remember that for Aristotle there were up to sixty skies or spheres). The first was that of the moon, the second of the stars (for the Greeks, this was the last sphere, that of "fixed" things), the third of the Sun, and so on. Ometeótl lived in the last sky, the thirteenth.

17. "There lives the founded [*fundado*] god and his co-principle" (León Portilla 1979: 151). The "Old God" always has his own co-principle.

18. The "metaphor" is no longer simply mythical, but "conceptually" metaphoric.

19. There were different ways of saying this term: *Omecíhuatl* (Dual Lady); *Ometecuhtli* (Dual Lord); *Tonacacíhuatl* (Lady of Our Flesh); *In Teteu Inan* (Mother of the Gods); *In Teteu Ita* (Father of the Gods).

20. This would be a case of absolute autopoiesis. What is most relevant is that the "self-production" occurs through thought (*yucoya* means to produce through thought).

21. In the originary "night" everything is invisible and mysterious; in the originary "wind" everything is impalpable, imperceptible, not present to the senses. It is a case of absolute transcendance.

22. This may be the most extraordinary attribute of Ometeótl. *Tloc*, near; *náhuac*, surrounds, like a ring; the ending *-e* indicates abstraction (similar to *-dad* in Spanish or *-heit* in German): "closeness-surrounding." The originary "divine duality," Ometeótl, is the absolute in which we live. It is near, it surrounds us, and the *tlamatini*, who is close to it, has the mystical-ontological experience of the great thinkers of the great civilizations in their "axis time" (*Achsenzeit*). It is similar to Augustine's expression: "In him we live and exist."

23. We could not apply Hegel's concept *Entzweiung* (becoming two) to this process, because they are already "two" at the beginning. *Entvierung* (becoming four) would be more correct. According to Hegel: "The absolute is the night and the light preceding it, the difference between both" (1962: 65). See Dussel 1974: 89ff. It is interesting that the metaphors are identical ("night," "light"). I hope to analyze all these elements of the ontological reflection of the nahuatl culture in more detail in the future, in order to demonstrate more convincingly before

skeptics the existence of an explicit formal beginning of philosophy in Latin American protohistory before 1492.

24. "Smoked mirror," one that does not reflect, or that does not allow one to see because it is dark. The opposite is *Tezcatlanextia*, "a mirror that makes things appear" (a quality of Ometeótl, who produces things as their reflection). The "mirror" fulfills the function of "reflection," of "divinity's turning upon itself," or of the philosophical subjectivity of the *tlamatini*: "he who is conversing with his own heart" (*Mayolnonotzani*).

25. "Life," in fact, means "mobility" (*Bewegenheit*)—as Marcuse demonstrated in his thesis on the meaning of Being for Hegel. Life, for the Aztecs, was "mobility"; the heart was the organ that "moved." The Sun moved in the sky as it followed its "path" (*Iohtlatoquiliz*), "moving" or giving life to all living beings (those that move on their own). The latter had to offer their lives in sacrifice so that the Sun could live. It was a "vital-sacrificial" circle (as in the metaphors concerning capital in Marx's interpretation).

26. "Those that were worthy," because Quetzalcóatl resuscitated them when he "bled his member" (*Manuscrito de 1558*; León Portilla 1979: 184). *Mazehualtin* thus means "those whom the god merited through his bloody self-sacrifice." All humanity is thus born with a blood debt to Quetzalcóatl (who is like a Prometheus, but divine and not in chains, or like a Christ covered in blood).

27. "Our Lord . . . determines what he wants": *Moyocoia* indicates that the "plans" of the divinity produce what it wants. This is very similar to the concept of "providence."

28. *Iohtlatoquiliz* means "movement along the path of the sky." The "path" (*ohtli*) is necessary, and in a certain way each person also follows his or her "path" from the day of birth; each person's "name" was astrologically chosen according to the "signs" of the day, and the person's entire life was already "marked" in advance.

29. *Anáhuac* (the earth surrounded by the Ocean: *Teoatl*), like the known world (*Cemanáhuac*), was "grounded," placed on the "navel of the earth" (*Tlalxicco*), which rested on Ometeótl, who "was lying" (*ónoc*) below.

30. *Nelli* (truth) has a particular meaning in Nahuatl: it is what is "grounded," what has permanence, what exists forever. The first question has the following meaning: Do humans have something stable in their being, something well rooted? For Hegel, this would be a question about the "essence" (ground, foundation) in its dialectic-ontological sense (and not in its traditional ontic or metaphysical one).

Regarding the third question, for the Guaranis, "standing" means being "grounded" in Ometeótl, or the Absolute.

31. The solar year corresponded to a cycle of 4 times 13, or 52, years, which the Aztecs considered a century, or a time period after which a new story was added to all the existing temples, with the lighting of the "new fire."

Every 104th solar year coincided with a Venus year, and this was called "an old age" ("una vejez"; *huehueliztli*).

32. Bernardino de Sahagún dedicates his entire book 2 to this subject: "Which deals with the calendar, festivals and ceremonies, sacrifices and solemnities" (73ff.).

33. See "About judicial astrology and the art of divination" (Sahagún, book 4: 221ff.). "Astrology" determined the content of each day of the year, and of the time of year, for the purpose of births or consultation concerning events situated in time, and therefore valid forever.

34. "Which deals with omens and predictions, which these natives took from some birds, animals, and insects, in order to predict future things" (Sahagún, book 5: 267ff.). In a way Sahagún is incorrect, because these omens and predictions were used to discover present events "as past events," not as "future things." In the cycle of the eternal return of the Same, every "future" event was for the Aztecs a "past" event (in the circle the future point is simultaneously a past event of a future present, but a future present that will be identical to the present present and all the present pasts). There is no historical sense of events, and this is the difference between the tragic (Promethean) conscience of Moctezuma, and the dramatic conscience (Christian and modern; see Paul Ricoeur's *La symbolique du mal*, or my *El humanismo semita*) of Hernán Cortés.

35. The *Códice Florentino*, book 6, chapter 2 (León Portilla 1979), gives the names of the Aztecs who climbed onto the ships: Píntol huasteco, Yoatzin de Nuctlancuahtla, the man from Teuciniyocan, and Cuitlapíltoc and Téntitl, who were guides. This is a story seen "from the other side": with names and "real" people.

36. Todorov's *La conquête de l'Amérique*, especially the chapter entitled "Moctezuma et les signes," is close to my interpretation, but Todorov attributes Moctezuma's vacillation to the fact that the Aztecs had a different type of "communication." He does not draw adequate conclusions from his hypothesis that everything had always already been determined. Tzvetan Todorov and Georges Baudot (1983) have published a collection of Aztec narratives of the conquest, which also appeared in an excellent Italian edition (1988), and which includes the *Códice Florentino*, the *Anales históricos de Tlatelolco*, and the *Códice Aubin*, in nahuatl; and the *Códice Ramírez*, Diego Múñoz Camargo's *Historia de Tlaxcala*, and Diego Durán's *Historia*, in Spanish.

Wachtel admits that he does not know the reason why Moctezuma should receive "The Whites as gods" (45).

In *El reverso de la conquista* (20), León Portilla indicates some of the "possibilities" that Moctezuma considered, but does not explain the "rationality" of his decisions.

For Paz, see *El laberinto de la soledad* (85): "The arrival of the Spaniards was interpreted by Moctezuma — at least at the beginning — not so much as an external danger but as the internal persecution of a cosmic age." In fact, the "end of the world" was a third possibility, but it was not what Moctezuma considered, "at least at the beginning." In *Posdata* (126-43) Paz discusses the subject in greater detail, but he does not identify the "possibilities" that I will discuss in my essay.

In *Quetzalcóatl y Guadalupe* (219-24), Jacques Lafaye does not clarify the situation at all.

37. I say "most critical" because for Edmundo O'Gorman this was not even mentioned as a working hypothesis; which means, scientifically speaking, that he adopted a "unilateral" Eurocentric position in the name of "objectivity" (but an objectivity constituted on the basis of European "subjectivity"). Here I would

like to take Moctezuma's "subjectivity" seriously, and describe it while taking into account the conditions of possibility of a rigorous hermeneutics.

38. These means were the following: (1) listen to the opinions of the warriors in the tradition of Tlacaélel (who would only act in the second "figure"); (2) ask the opinions of the *tlamatinime*, or philosophers; (3) listen to the counsel of the astrologers, who informed him that Quetzalcóatl would come from the East one *ceacatl* (date that coincided with the arrival of the Spaniards); (4) sound those who deciphered "omens" or presages (all eight of these—which included events related to fire, earth, air, and water, the four fundamental elements for the Aztecs as well as for the pre-Socratics—indicated necessary dire "futures"). See the eight "Presagios funestos" (dire presages), León Portilla 1978: 29ff.

39. The "abnormal" (such as a birth defect in a child) was either eliminated (as in the case of the Spartans) or deified (as in the case of the handicapped and infirm who were placed as gods on Monte Albán, in the Zapotec culture of Mexico). That humans should "appear" on the Great Ocean was the "least probable."

40. This "possibility" was the least dangerous; the reduced number of the arrivals could not be a military danger, even with their techniques of war. Furthermore, it is necessary to eliminate, in the analysis of the strategic rationality of Moctezuma, the possibility of an "invasion." This had no sense yet; it was not a real "possibility," given the empirical data obtained in Moctezuma's concrete "world."

41. I have already mentioned that the Toltecs were to the Aztecs like the Greeks to the Romans. The ancient cultivated people were a model in everything. The Aztec tradition was in fact the *Toltecayotl* (*toltequidad*, like the *romanitas* for the Romans, or the *christianitas* for the Christians, or the *Deutschtum* for the Germans). The historical figure Quetzalcóatl was the priest and wise man *Ce Acatl Topilzin* (ninth century B.C.?), "he who was born on day 1-Cane (*1-Caña*), Our Prince" (see Lehmann 1938). Because he was a solitary young man living close to Tulancingo, he was sought as king of Tula. A great thinker who formulated the ontology of Ometeótl, he was opposed in advance to the cult of Tlacaélel: "It is said that when Quetzalcóatl lived there, the sorcerers tried to deceive him many times, so that he would sacrifice men. But he never wanted to, for he greatly loved his people, who were the Toltecs" (*Anales de Cuauhtitlán*, Códice Chimalpopoca, folio 5; León Portilla 1979: 307-8). It is certain that they expelled Quetzalcóatl unjustly, but he promised to return. The Aztecs, and especially Moctezuma, had many reasons to be afraid: first, because the Aztecs had cruelly subjugated the rest of the Toltec people; second, because the sacrificial myth of Huitzilopochtli was contrary to Quetzalcóatl's way of thinking; third, because, being a deposed king, he could try to take Moctezuma's place (we will see that this is the "rational" conclusion of the emperor, as is "explicit" in the text about Cortés's reception in Mexico). It is interesting that Cortés advised Moctezuma "not to sacrifice men. And the next day [Moctezuma] called his main priest and asked him to pretend for a few days not to sacrifice men in the presence of the Spaniards" (Torquemada, book 4, chap. 40: 173). This was a sign indicating the connection between Cortés and Quetzalcóatl, the wise man of Tula.

42. We can read the following about the "Fifth Sun": "The Sun was also that of our prince in Tula, that is, of Quetzalcóatl" (*Documento de 1558*; León Portilla 1979: 103). In that case, the predictions of "the earth moving, there will be hunger, and from that we will perish" (ibid.) would indicate the end of the "Fifth Sun." This was the most generalized interpretation. Octavio Paz (1976: 85) thinks that this possibility was the first that Moctezuma considered, but that is not correct.

43. Actually, Moctezuma's enemies never completely supported Cortés, because if he was defeated by the Aztecs, they would have something on which to base their acceptance of Aztec domination again.

44. Moctezuma had only one positive possibility, in fact: that the recent arrivals were human beings, and, in this case, he would subsequently be able to destroy them with his warriors faithful to Huitzilopochtli, as Cortés had only a few dozen soldiers. Because this was the weakest possibility, it had to be left to the end, after the lack of fulfillment of the other more important ones had been "rationally" proved.

45. Moctezuma demonstrates the ethos of the *Calmécac*, the temperament of heroes and wise men. This explains his address to Cortés (who did not have any possibility of "interpreting" the immense ethical greatness of the man he faced, and in no way, as merely a good soldier and able politician, had the stature of Moctezuma): "Five, ten days ago, I was worried: I had my gaze fixed on the Realm of the Dead . . . " (quoted above). The *tlamatini* contemplates what was beyond the merely "terrestrial" (*in tlaltícpac*), the transcendent (*topan mictlan*). And there he resolved, thinking like Quetzalcóatl, that "he liked his people very much"; and "he was wondering what was going to happen to the city" (*Informantes de Sahagún*; León Portilla 1979: 35). In abdicating, Moctezuma avoided (at least as far as was in his power) more suffering for his people. He stepped aside and abdicated . . . as Quetzalcóatl had done in Tula. Quetzalcóatl-Cortés should have understood this argument! Moctezuma was the new Quetzalcóatl of his Mexico and sacrificed himself for it.

46. Inverting O'Gorman's profound hypothesis that Columbus "could not discover America," we can now say that Moctezuma "could not discover an invasion" before the arrival of Pánfilo Narváez.

47. The Aztecs saw horses and Spanish soldiers die, they lived together with the Spaniards for many weeks in Mexico, they did not see other extraordinary "signs," and so forth.

48. Clearly an a posteriori, and not an a priori, error.

49. "Modern" man never understands the "reasons *of the Other*" (Dussel 1992; emphasis in the original).

50. Cortés should have left the city of Mexico immediately after his return from the coast with the reinforcements he managed to obtain from the defeated forces of Narváez. However, because he had not understood Moctezuma's "reasons," he believed that he could continue "using" him (apparently Moctezuma had let himself be "used," as he had to continue until the very end to "prove" each one of the "possibilities," which were not "possibilities" for Cortés). The same happened to Alvarado, who thought that he could strengthen his position by showing great aggressivity, not understanding that what had protected the Spaniards in Mexico was not their courage, but the "worldview" (weltan-

schauung) of the *tlamatinime*. When this perspective was discarded, the logic of war had to begin; thus Alvarado inclined the balance against him with his action.

51. Theoretically, he was a little like the Hegel of *The Philosophy of Right*, as well as a theoretician of war like Clausewitz and a politician like Bismarck of the German empire. He never wanted to be king of the Aztec empire, although four kings were his protégés.

52. Only Karl Marx in his "theological metaphors" (see Dussel, 1993), inspired by Judeo-Christian Semitic-biblical thought, shows how "capital," the new Moloch, lives off the life of the oppressed and sucks their blood: the circulation of value is a "circulation of the blood" (*Blutzirkulation, circulación de sangre*).

53. The Spaniards attributed their salvation to the *Virgen de los Remedios*. Therefore, Hidalgo hoisted the Virgin of Guadalupe as a banner of the Americans in 1810, and the Spaniards (*gachupines*) adopted that of the *Virgen de los Remedios*. It was a battle of virgins, a battle of gods, and a battle of classes (see Dussel 1980).

54. The question "Then was it *true*?" is essential: was it *true* that the gods abandoned us, that the empire would be destroyed? This is a strange and profound question that demonstrates the tragedy of the moment. The "Fifth Sun" has come to an end.

55. One should not think that there was little resistance to the invasion. Resistance was heroic and uninterrupted.

Works Cited

Alva Ixtlilxochitl, Fernando de. *Obras históricas*. Ed. Edmundo O'Gorman. Serie de historiadores y cronistas de Indias 4. 2 vols. Mexico City: UNAM, 1985.

Alvarado Tezozómoc, Fernando. *Crónica Mexicáyotl*. Mexico City: UNAM, 1949.

Durán, Diego. *Historia de las Indias de Nueva España e Islas de Tierra Firme*. Vol. 1. Mexico City: Porrúa, 1967.

Dussel, Enrique. *El humanismo semita*. Buenos Aires: Eudeba, 1969.

_____. *Para una ética de la liberación latinoamericana*. Vol. 1. Buenos Aires: Siglo veintiuno, 1973.

_____. *Método para una filosofía de la liberación*. Salamanca: Sígueme, 1974.

_____. "Christian Art of the Oppressed." *Concilium* 132 (1980): 40-52.

_____. "La razón del Otro. La *Interpelación* como acto-de-habla." Paper presented in Mexico during the public *Diálogo* with Karl-Otto Apel, 1992. Published in *Discursethik oder Befreiungsethik*, ed. Raúl Fornel. Aachen: Augustinus, 1992. 96-121.

_____. *Las metáforas teológicas de Marx*. Estella: El Verbo Divino, 1993.

García Icazbalceta, J. "Historia de los Mexicanos por sus pinturas." *Nueva Colección de Documentos para la Historia de México*. Vol. 3. Mexico City: n.p., 1890. 59-92.

Garcilaso de la Vega, the Inca. *Comentarios reales de los Incas*. Lima: Universo, 1967.

Hegel, G. W. F. *The Philosophy of Right*. Trans. T. M. Knox. Oxford: Clarendon Press, 1945.

_____. *Differenz des Ficht' 'chen und Schelling'schen Systems der Philosophie*. Hamburg: Felix Meiner, 1962.

_____. *The Science of Logic*. Trans. A. V. Miller. London: Allen & Unwin, and New York: Humanities Press, 1969.

_____. *Hegel's Logic*. Trans. William Wallace. Oxford: Clarendon Press, 1975.

Lafaye, Jacques. *Quetzalcóatl y Guadalupe. La formación de la conciencia nacional en México*. Mexico City: Fondo de Cultura Económica, 1977.

Lehmann, Walter, "Geschichte der Königreiche von Colhuacan und Mexiko." *Quellenwerke zur alten Geschichte Amerikas*. Stuttgart: L. W. Kohlhammer, 1938.

_____. ed. *Colloquios y Doctrina Christiana (Sterbende Götter und Christliche Heilsbotschaft)*. Stuttgart: L. W. Kohlhammer, 1949.

León Portilla, Miguel. *El reverso de la conquista*. Mexico City: Joaquín Mortiz, 1978.

_____. *La filosofía náhuatl*. Mexico City: UNAM, 1979.

_____. *Los antiguos mexicanos*. Mexico City: Fondo de Cultura Económica, 1990.

Luhmann, Niklas. *Systemlehre*. Frankfurt: Suhrkamp, 1988.

Marcuse, Herbert. *Hegel's Ontologie und die Theorie der Geschichtlichkeit*. Frankfurt: Klostermann, 1968.

Mendieta, Gerónimo de. *Historia Eclesiástica Indiana*. Vol. 1. Mexico City: UNAM, 1945.

O'Gorman, Edmundo. *La invención de América. El universalismo de la cultura del Occidente*. Mexico City: Fondo de Cultura Económica, 1958.

Paz, Octavio. *Posdata*. Mexico City: Siglo veintiuno, 1970.

_____. *El laberinto de la soledad*. Mexico City: Fondo de Cultura Económica, 1976. First published 1950.

Popol Vuh. Mexico City: Fondo de Cultura Económica, 1990.

Ricoeur, Paul. *La symbolique du mal*. Paris: Aubier, 1963.

Sahagún, Bernardino de. *Historia general de las cosas de Nueva España*. Vol. 1. Mexico City: Porrúa, 1975.

Seler, Eduard. *Gesammelte Abhandlungen zur Amerikanischen Sprach- und Altertumskunde*. Vol. 4. Berlin: Ascher und Behrend, 1923.

Todorov, Tzvetan. *La conquête de l'Amérique*. Paris: Seuil, 1982.

_____ and Georges Baudot. *Récits aztèques de la Conquête*. Paris: Seuil, 1983.

Torquemada, Juan de. *Monarquía Indiana*. 4 vols. Mexico City: Porrúa, 1986.

Wachtel, Nathan. *La vision des vaincus. Les Indiens du Pérou devant la Conquête espagnole, 1530-1570*. Paris: Gallimard, 1971.

◆ Chapter 7

On Writing Back: Alternative Historiography in *La Florida del Inca*

José Rabasa

It is well known that Inca Garcilaso de la Vega makes constant reference to his condition of writing as an Indian (see, for instance, Wey-Gómez; González Echevarría; Zamora; Jákfalvi-Leiva; Pupo-Walker). The expression "porque soy indio," which appears in two distinct places in *La Florida del Inca* (1605), was already present in his translation of León Hebreo's *Diálogo de Amor* (1590), and recurs later on in the *Comentarios reales de los Incas* (1609-17).[1] Garcilaso's marginality is at once a "result of" and a "response to" the constitution of European subjectivity and history as universal. In this essay I will take these references to his Indian position as a point of entry for examining, in *La Florida*, the conditions of possibility of the colonial (colonized) subject to constitute himself or herself as an author and develop a discursive alternative to the West.

Rather than taking as a point of departure the European "self" that, as Tzvetan Todorov would put it, discovers the "Other," we ought to trace the simultaneous and inseparable production of both "Europe" and "its Others" (Todorov 3). In the process of traveling to America, the Modern Western episteme not only established itself but subjected indigenous knowledges by confining them to superstition and witchcraft. From this perspective, "otherness" is to be understood as a product of discourse rather than as some form of alterity that would preexist the cognitive self without mediation (see Certeau 225-27 passim). One could further argue that the production of "otherness" is a historiographical a priori, whether in the form of the past (of the dead, of what was, but perhaps still informs the present) or of ethnography (of foreign forms of life, which are, notwithstanding, apprehensible as such). However, the definition of otherness as savagery or barbarism—clearly in a binary opposition with civilization—does not necessarily exclude a will to truth that pursues objective knowledge of the other culture. By objective knowledge, I do not understand neutral or value free, but a systematic objectification that is consistent with a bias—that is, the production of an object of knowledge in the etymological sense of the verb *obicio*, "to throw toward," "to bring or place in view." The attributes of savagery or barbarism would, then, be the result of an excess that overwhelms the operating taxonomy. And yet, excess can also constitute the beginning of a new investigation.

In my view, what is outstanding in Spanish American colonial historiography is not the assimilation of new phenomena to a regime of similarities (which, echoing Foucault, we have insisted in finding), but rather the creation of general concepts that enable the classification of cultural particulars (cf. Foucault 17-44). In colonial historiography, let us say from Gonzalo Fernández de Oviedo to Bernardino de Sahagún, to take two apparent opposites, we can trace an epistemological mutation in which the subject and the object of knowledge have splintered. In the works of these writers we find a reflection on their position as cognitive subjects as well as an elaboration of taxonomies that would enable other subjects to continue their historiographic program. For Oviedo the New World is a "mare magno, in which neither the pen nor the style of one writer can suffice" ("mare magno, en que no puede bastar la pluma ni estilo de uno") (*Historia* 5:417).[2] By implication, writing its history is an infinite task that requires constant revision. Sahagún, however, constitutes a method and research team that enables the production of a text, if not by the informant himself or herself, by Indians turned anthropologists.[3] One might add that in one form or another both writers aspire to establish what we call today disciplines. These historiographical practices, of course, do not exclude the inscription of alien cultures as barbarian—in reference to both behavior and an evolutionary stage. In the case of Sahagún one can trace not only the intention of producing a register of Nahua culture in its own terms, but also the conception of Nahua epistemology as ruled by a web of resemblance: "This work is like a dragnet to bring to light all the words of this language with their exact and metaphorical meanings" ["Es esta obra como vna red barredera para sacar a luz todos los vocablos desta lengua con sus propias y methaphoricas significaçiones" (*Florentine Codex* 13:47)]. Nahua culture follows a different logic that, to a great extent, Sahagún defines as irrational and in an anterior stage to Western rationality: in brief, as superstitious and vulnerable to the influence of the devil. Thus, for Sahagún the Nahuas of the sixteenth century were lying neophytes and, consequently, problematic subjects that continued to practice their rites clandestinely. To override these cultural practices, he envisions his *Historia* as an instrument to aid confessors to draw out the truth, "as they say, with a hook or *manu obstetricante*" ("como dicen con garabato o *manu obstetricante*") (fragment in García Icazbalceta 384). If one couples liars with a "proven" inborn lasciviousness that incapacitates the best converts for priesthood, the result is new Indian Christians that have inherited negative cultural traits (see *Florentine Codex* 13:74-85).

Oviedo also defines the barbarism of the Amerindians on the basis of an excess—in his case, a body of pleasure that leads him to hesitate between an aesthetic representation and moral opprobrium. As Oviedo states in the *Sumario*, Amerindian women are so lascivious, voracious, and vain that they abort to avoid the burden of child care and to prevent "[that] their breasts would droop, breasts of which they are very proud, and do have very good ones" ("[que] se les aflojen las tetas, de las cuales se precian mucho, y las tienen muy buenas") (79). Oviedo complements these external data on the female body and sexuality with observations on the size of the vagina:

> [Después de parir] se cierran de tal manera, que según
> dicen los que a ellas se dan, son tan estrechas, que con
> pena los varones consumen sus apetitos, y las que no
> han parido están que parecen vírgenes. (*Sumario* 79)
>
> [After giving birth], they close up in such a way that,
> according to those who give themselves to them, they
> are so tight that males can barely satisfy their appetites,
> and those who have not given birth seem to be virgins.

Somehow the smallness of the vagina would explain the insatiable desire of Indian women who, according to Oviedo, are incapable of being chaste. Undoubtedly there is much to object to in Oviedo's empiricism, but to say the least we cannot attribute to him an episteme ruled by similitude. These physiognomic observations are much closer to the mug shots that illustrate contemporary handbooks of anthropology than to Renaissance analogies between human and animal bodies.

These examples from Oviedo and Sahagún give us a clue as to the position of the subject of knowledge in colonial historiography. But if there is an opposition between civilization and barbarism, the separation of these terms is not as clear-cut as we would like. In Sahagún, for example, there exists the possibility of training trilingual collegians, as well as his belief that Spaniards in the Indies tend to be degenerate and affected by the constellations (*Florentine Codex* 13:74-85). On the other hand, the conquistadors in Oviedo's *Historia general*, more often than not, are characterized as irresponsible adventurers. Hernando de Soto is reduced to a killer: "This governor was very given to hunting and killing Indians" ("Este gobernador era muy dado a esta montería de matar indios") (2:156). But the moralist Oviedo, who disapproves of Soto's *aperreos* (setting dogs on Indians), tortures, and massacres, knows himself how to set dogs on Indians and burn them at the stake when he deems it appropriate (see, for instance, 3:273).

These passages from Sahagún and Oviedo suggest that the distinction between the colonial subject as colonized and the colonial subject as colonizer is not simply a question of different narrative focalizations that would limit themselves to either defend or condemn the conquest of Amerindian cultures (cf. Adorno; Bhabha; JanMohamed). Obviously these Manichaean oppositions exist. However, less clear-cut expressions present, to my mind, much more interesting forms of counterdiscourse. If in fact all inversions of binary oppositions reiterate the logic that informs them, the reduction of colonial discursive possibilities to positions of colonized and colonizer that mutually represent each other as lacking culture would, in the end, fall into the same trap.

To the lying neophytes of Sahagún and the voracious women of Oviedo, we should add one more fiction: the noble savage of Bartolomé de Las Casas.[4] I highlight the fictive character of Las Casas's noble savage to underscore its utopian function: as a utopian figure the noble savage dismantles the denial of the co-evality of the "Other" that Johannes Fabian has traced at the root of the production of anthropology's object of study (see Marin; Fabian). As I have argued elsewhere ("Utopian"), Las Casas's utopian ethnology manifests the conditions of possibility of anthropology in general and, in particular, reveals the semantic field where the "West" defines "the rest of the world" and positions itself as the universal cultural model. Implicit in the Lascasian critique is the possibility that the "time of the 'Other'" could invade the temporal fortress of the "West" (cf. Fabian 35), which we formulate as "the empire has always been writing back," to paraphrase a recent title (Ashcroft et al.). Las Casas and, as we shall now see, Garcilaso fashion a cultural critique that does not limit itself to an inversion of the binary opposition civilization versus barbarism. The noble savage in their discourse is not the opposite of barbarism, but rather simultaneously includes and denies both terms of the opposition. Moreover, the noble savage as a utopian figure anticipates as well as curtails the corollaries (e.g., the equation of non-Christians with barbarism—or, if all human beings are siblings, being a Christian is not an option) that could be adduced from a Christian universalism that, in the context of sixteenth-century Spain, would inevitably haunt Las Casas's and Garcilaso's discourses.

The limitations of Manichaean inversions become fully apparent when we compare the idealizations of the conquistadors in *La Florida* with the massacres and capture of thousands of slaves, as well as the *aperreos*, mutilations, and tortures that Rodrigo de Ranjel, Soto's secretary, conscientiously documents in his diary, and which Oviedo glosses with moralistic diatribes in his use of Ranjel in the *Historia general* (see 2:153-81). The two other primary sources on Soto's expedition narrate the massacres and tortures with a "bestial" objectivity in Fidalgo de Elvas's *Expedición de Hernando de Soto a la Florida* (1557) or with a laconic detachment in Luis Hernández de Biedma's *Relación* (c. 1544; in Pacheco et al. 3:414-41). Neither author condemns or exalts the Europeans. Garcilaso, however, idealizes both Spaniards and Indians. *La Florida* registers the atrocities, but the Indians themselves condemn the vagrancy, the mutilations, and the massacres that characterize Soto's expedition. Take as an example the last words of a cacique who chases the Spaniards down to the mouth of the Mississippi:

> Ladrones, vagabundos, holgazanes sin honra ni vergüenza, que andáis por esta ribera inquietando los naturales de ella, luego os partid de este río por una de aquellas bocas de este río si no queréis que os mate a todos y queme vuestros navíos. (547)

> Thieves, vagabonds and loiterers who without honor or shame travel along this coast disquieting its inhabitants, depart from this place immediately by one of the two mouths of the river, if you do not want me to destroy you all and burn your ships. (595)

The idealization of both Spaniards and Indians, as well as the continuous questioning of criteria that define nobility and the means of representing European and Indian cultural forms, suggests that Garcilaso is pursuing a deeper truth than a simple inversion of values. Moreover, Garcilaso asks these questions from the point of view of an Indian author.

In *La Florida*, the Inca represents himself and problematizes his authorship as an Indian on two occasions. The first appears in the preface where he begs readers to overlook the faults they might find in his history:

> La cual suplico se reciba en el mismo ánimo que yo la presento, y las faltas que lleva se me perdonen porque soy indio, que a los tales, por ser bárbaros y no enseñados en ciencias y artes, no se permite que, en lo que dijeren o hicieren, los lleven por el rigor de los

> preceptos del arte o ciencia, por no los haber aprendido,
> sino que los admitan como vinieren. (69)
>
> I plead now that this account be received in the same
> spirit as I present it, and that I be pardoned its errors
> because I am an Indian. For since Indians are barbarians
> and uninstructed in the arts and sciences, it seems
> ungenerous to judge their deeds and utterances strictly
> in accordance with the precepts of the arts and sciences,
> which they have not learned, but rather accept them as
> they are. (xlv)

Right after this passage, Garcilaso adds that a favorable reception of his history would encourage "all the Indians, mestizos
and Creoles" ("todos los indios, mestizos y criollos") to carry
out similar enterprises "drawn from their own uncultivated
mental resources" ("sacadas de sus no cultivados ingenios")
(ibid.). Even though in another passage from *La Florida* (which
we will discuss later) Garcilaso specifies how, as a young man,
he and other mestizos and Creoles were not able to receive
an education because of the civil wars that plagued Peru, we
should not limit the definition of Indians as lacking "the precepts
of the arts and sciences" ("los preceptos del arte o ciencia") to a
simple autobiographical fact about his youth. Throughout the prologue Garcilaso elaborates an allegorization of the system that au-
thorizes the writing of history. Rather than reiterating that the condition of being an Indian—and, perhaps, in the last instance an
American—corresponds to a lack of letters, the prologue suggests
a cultural construct that defines being an Indian with an essentialist trait (i.e., lacking blood purity, belonging to another nation) that
would prescribe the incapacity to write history.

If one of the precepts in Renaissance historiography is that
only the wise can write history, we could add that Indians, at
least as Indians, cannot be wise (cf. Mignolo 369). It seems to me
that what is at stake in these historiographical negations is the
possibility of producing an alternative to Western authority. The
resolution of this problematic "porque soy indio" in *La Florida*
gives place to a positive turn in the *Comentarios reales de los Incas*.
There, for example, Garcilaso claims a privileged knowledge of
Quechua:

Para atajar esta corrupción me sea lícito, pues soy indio,
que en esta historia escriba como indio con las mismas
letras que aquellas tales dicciones se deben escribir. (2:5)
In order to forestall this corruption allow me, as I am an
Indian, to write this history as an Indian with the precise
letters that ought to be used for such discourse. (My
translation)

This is not an appeal to linguistic knowledge, as it were, but to a
subjectivity ("que en esta historia escriba como indio") that privileges Garcilaso as knower of correct Quechua phonetics. Let us
now observe, in *La Florida*, how subjectivity, hence marginality,
is deployed as an alternative to the emergent universal European subject that we have traced in Oviedo's and Sahagún's historiography.[5]

Whether Garcilaso invented his sources or whether they truly
existed, all share the common trait of not being histories in the
strict sense of the term. Neither the anonymous informant who
gives him an oral account, nor Alonso de Carmona who supposedly sent Garcilaso his *peregrinaciones* (pilgrimage accounts), nor
Juan Coles who wrote an account at the demand of a Franciscan
provincial, writes history. As Garcilaso puts it, not one of them
"arranged his account in a historical manner" ("puso su relación
en modo historial") (*La Florida* 66; xli). The writings of Coles and
Carmona, though without order, confirm the oral text of his
informant—who, by the way, is the only one Garcilaso characterizes as "a man the son of something" ("hombre noble hi-
jodalgo"). Thus, Garcilaso subverts the hierarchy, as an Indian
writes history and a hidalgo provides the oral account. It is not
on account of a lack of letters that Garcilaso's authority is questioned, but because he is an Indian. The title, *La Florida del Inca*,
underscores the subjectivity of his knowledge, his incapacity as
an Indian to write trustworthy history. Toward the end of *La
Florida*, Garcilaso provides another clue on his usage of subjectivity as a recurrent motif when he explains that he cannot provide an adequate geographic description because the purpose of
Soto's armada "was not to mark off the lands . . . but to search
for gold and silver" ("no era andar demarcando tierras . . . sino
buscar oro y plata") (545; 505). He thus displaces the apparent

colonialist intention, expressed in several places in *La Florida*, of writing a history that would facilitate a new conquest. *La Florida* is far from being a text with any strategic value. Garcilaso certainly has another much more important end in mind: to rescue the image of Amerindians by representing them as magnanimous and able in all realms of culture. In his constant insistence on the nobility of spirit in Indian discourses, Garcilaso provides not only an idealized vision, but his own vindication as an Indian writer of history. An Indian who writes and speaks such discourses cannot but be noble. Indeed, this attribute of nobility goes hand in hand with savage—that is, lacking "artes y ciencias." Such are both Garcilaso's Amerindians and himself. As in the case of Las Casas, the noble savage figure assumes a utopian turn as it dismantles and renders absurd the categories that inform the prescription that Indians cannot write history.

The second instance of "porque soy indio" in *La Florida del Inca* anticipates and counteracts readers that would question the veracity of Garcilaso's courageous and eloquent Amerindians:

> Pues decir que escribo encarecidamente por loar la
> nación porque soy indio, cierto es engaño . . . que antes
> me hallo con falta de palabras para contar y poner en su
> punto las verdades que en la historia se me ofrecen.
> (192-93)
> But to say that I exaggerate my praise of the nation
> because I am an Indian is indeed a falsehood, for . . . I
> lack sufficient words to present in their proper light the
> actual truths that are offered me in this history. (159)

It is precisely in this context that Garcilaso recounts how he lacked schooling as a child and goes on to "certify upon the word of a Christian that we have written the truth in the past, and that with the favor of the Highest Truth" ("certificar en ley de cristiano que escribimos verdad en lo pasado y con el favor de la Suma Verdad") (ibid.). The juxtaposition of these passages, pertaining to his untrustworthy praise of the "nación" and his certification of truth in "ley de cristiano," suggests a paradox that one could very well find in a number of *converso* apologetic texts written against the *estatutos de limpieza de sangre* (statutes of blood purity) (see Shell 312-16). Before Indians or *conversos* could make a true statement they would first have to prove their trust-worthiness. The paradox involves a circular argument and infi-nite regress, but by the same token Garcilaso displays how the writing of history is ultimately plagued by circularity (cf. Rodríguez-Vecchini 618-19).

As is well known, in the course of the sixteenth century *hidal-guía* and *limpieza de sangre* came to be identified with the Spanish character (see Shell 315-16 passim; Caro Baroja 2:267-93 passim). Garcilaso himself alludes to that Germanhood, that ancestral bond that identified nobility with the Goths and, therefore, con-signed the alterity of other nations to the inheritance of negative cultural traits: "The nobility of those Spaniards and of all the people of present-day Spain comes without any question what-soever from those Goths" ("La nobleza de nuestros españoles, la que tiene toda España sin contradicción alguna, viene de aquellos Godos") (*La Florida* 473-74; 505). An ironic streak runs through this certifying passage. One cannot but see it in contra-riety with those places where Garcilaso praises the nobility of the Indians or dismisses critics who would say

> que en otras historias de las Indias Occidentales no se
> hallan cosas hechas ni dichas por los indios como aquí lo
> escribimos . . . y que aquí lo hacemos o por presumir de
> componer, o por loar nuestra nación, que, aunque las
> regiones y tierras estén tan distantes, parece que todas
> son Indias. (192)
>
> that such deeds and speeches of the Indians as I relate
> them here are not to be found in other histories of the
> West Indies . . . and [I may] be accused of having
> written either to fictionalize or to lavish praises upon my
> own nation since all of these lands and regions, though
> far apart, are regarded as the Indies. (157-58)

In *La Florida*, to belong to a "nación" is an attribute that unites all the Indians of America. Garcilaso's constant insistence on the nobility of the Indian nation allows us to read the "porque soy indio" passages as statements on the debate over the *estatutos de limpieza de sangre* that differentiated *viejos cristianos* from *conver-sos*.

In these passages and, in general, throughout *La Florida*, there is a questioning of the category of *limpieza de sangre* and an equally prominent elaboration of the motif of the noble savage. The eloquence of Amerindians not only disproves European prejudices, but from the mouth of his informant Garcilaso tells us that Spaniards who were well read in the classics would compare Indian speeches to the most famous in Roman histories and would assert that "the youths . . . seemed to have been trained in Athens when it flourished in moral letters" ("los mozos . . . parecían haber estudiado en Atenas cuando ella florecía en letras morales") (194; 160). Obviously the comparison with antiquity is not in reference to a common paganism, but to ancient cultures and languages as cultural ideals of the Renaissance.

Garcilaso is fully conscious of how these speech forms (that is, borrowings from classical historiography) efface Indian modes of address, and he does not fail to signal that his translations are not literal but cultural: "It is the style of the Indians to assist each other in their reasoning" ("Es estilo de indios ayudarse unos a otros en los razonamientos") (187; 153). Before quoting the youth who had remained silent while the elders spoke, Garcilaso again characterizes their discourse as "helping each other in their reasoning" ("ayudándose unos a otros en sus razones") (187; 153ff.). Furthermore, he prefaces their speech with "interpreted in Castilian, their words are as follows" ("interpretadas en la castellana, dicen así") (187; 153ff.). He does not give a word-for-word translation, because the speech is cited as if it had been given by one individual rather than produced collectively. The "interpretadas en la castellana" cancels any pretense of a "realist effect" as it distances the reader by insisting on the cultural translation of the Indian speech genre (cf. Barthes; Bakhtin). In this regard Garcilaso's commentary on the Indian style of reasoning is profoundly dialogic; it leads the reader, on the one hand, to imagine alternative forms of reasoning and, on the other, to conceptualize a culture where authorship is collective. Thus Garcilaso defines cultural differences and underscores another subjective dimension of his history. In fact, his function as amanuensis would seem to be imitating the style of "ayudándose unos a otros," while highlighting that his own version in Spanish is a form of minority discourse and an alternative author-ity.

Beyond a vindication of Amerindians, *La Florida* draws a generalized critique of the myth of *limpieza de sangre* and the criteria that define nobility. The short account of the French Protestant corsair who battles for days with a Spanish merchant provides Garcilaso with the means of expanding the critique of blood statutes to the religious wars that plagued Europe in the sixteenth century. Garcilaso first relativizes, if not democratizes, the concept of nobility:

> No se sabe cuál fuese la calidad [del mercader español], mas la nobleza de su condición y la hidalguía que en su conversación, tratos y contratos mostraba decían que derechamente era hidalgo, porque ese lo es que hace hidalguías. (94)
>
> The quality of [the Spanish merchant] is not known, but the nobility of his equipage and the cavalier mien which he displayed in his conversation, manners and business dealings revealed that he was by rights a gentleman, for these are the things which constitute nobility. (32)

Derechamente (by rights) both the French corsair and the Spanish merchant behave like hidalgos. But after narrating the ritualism they keep in the battlefield as well as in the exchange of gifts during the truces, Garcilaso goes on to establish a rule that must be followed with enemies from another religion and nation:

> [Los del puerto que se negaron a ayudar al español] no advertían que el enemigo de nación o de religión, siendo vencedor, no sabe tener respeto a los males que le dejaron de hacer, ni agradecimiento a los bienes recibidos . . . como se ve por muchos ejemplos antiguos y modernos. (99)
>
> [Those in the harbor who refused to help the Spaniard] did not take into consideration the fact that the enemy of a nation or religion, being the victor, knows respect neither for ills withheld nor for good deeds rendered . . . as is proved by examples both ancient and modern. (38)

In my reading, this observation would convey an opinion on the meanness of the Spaniards in the port, rather than lend an argument to intolerance or justify religious wars.

Menéndez de Avilés's 1565 massacre of the French Hugue-
nots in Florida was still a fresh event in the memory of Garcilaso's contemporaries. This massacre gave rise to a series of
accounts—Laudonnière, Ribault, Thevet, Haykluyt, Le Moyne
—that denounced the cruelty of the Spaniards in the context of
the "black legend." Toward the end of *La Florida*, Garcilaso mentions that Menéndez de Avilés brought back to Spain seven Amerindians from Florida. When they went by a village in Córdoba,
Garcilaso's informant ran out to the countryside to meet them
and get news from Florida. Having learned that he had participated in Soto's armada, the Indians answered: "Having left
those provinces as desolate as you did, do you want us to give
you news of them?" ("¿Dejando vosotros esas provincias tan
mal paradas como las dejasteis queréis que os demos nuevas?")
(585; 641). The Amerindians were so mad at him that they took
their bows and threw their arrows into the air, "in order to make
this man realize their desire to shoot arrows at him and the skill
with which they might do so" ("por dar a entender el deseo que
tenían de tirárselas y la destreza con que se las tiraran") (ibid.).
A few years later, one of the caciques, already baptized, returned to Florida to aid a group of Jesuits in the conversion of his
nation. He and his people ended up killing all the Jesuits. The
Amerindians danced with the vestments and ornaments, but
three took a crucifix and "as they gazed upon it, suddenly fell
dead" ("estándolo mirando, se cayeron muertos") (586; 642).
Garcilaso does not tell us who witnessed this divine intervention, but mentions that Father Pedro Ribadeneyra also consigns
it in writing.

One could argue that if the rule about war between nations
and religions is a universal principle, the massacre of the Jesuits
would be justified. I would rather read a discourse on tolerance
in this series of killings and cruelties among different nations,
however. This would not exclude that Garcilaso's novel argumentation on the nobility of Amerindians would also provide a
beautiful vision that could compete with the magnificent water-
colors and engravings of John White, Jacques Le Moyne, and
Théodore de Bry. In this respect, Garcilaso at once fulfills the intended service to the Crown of rescuing Florida from foreign nations, and elaborates an apology of his Indianness.

As an alternative history *La Florida* does not set itself out to invert the civilization versus barbarism binary but to subvert the possibility of constructing such an opposition. The will to truth that informs Sahagún's and Oviedo's historiography gives place in Garcilaso to a display of the rules, motifs, and forms of argument that *authorize* European representations of the New World. In fact, his "porque soy indio" entails a sustained questioning of a privileged European subject of knowledge. Garcilaso's deployment of the noble savage figure as a utopian mode of discourse enables him to reduce to the absurd the prescription that Indians cannot write history. His subjectivity, his position as an Indian, leads him to claim a perspective denied to those who write from the experience of traveling from Europe to America. If Las Casas's noble savage figure draws a critique of the civilization versus barbarism binary, Garcilaso embodies and articulates the subjectivity of *a* "noble savage." *La Florida* is in a profound sense a minor text that capitalizes on marginality and ultimately lends an argument to toleration and particularism—and all in the context of a Christian universalism that embraced all human beings as siblings but on condition that they abdicated their culture (Shell 327-35).

Notes

An earlier version of this paper, "Autoridad y alteridad historiográfica en *La Florida del Inca*," was presented in the panel "Discursos Propiciados por el Encuentro de América y Europa, y la cuestión del *Otro*," organized by Alvaro Félix Bolaños at the 47th International Congress of Americanists. I received useful commentaries from the other members of the panel and from the public. Diana Wilson de Armas provided invaluable editorial suggestions. A fuller version of this essay, " . . . *porque soy indio* . . . : Subjectivity in *La Florida del Inca*," is forthcoming in a special issue of *Poetics Today* on "Semiotics of Culture and Cultural Studies (Literature, History, and Anthropology in/about Latin America)," edited by Walter Mignolo. I want to thank the General Research Board at the University of Maryland for a semester fellowship that made it possible for me to research and write this article.

1. Inca Garcilaso de la Vega (1539-1617) was the illegitimate son of Sebastián Garcilaso de la Vega, one of the first Spanish conquerors of Peru, and Chimpu Ocllo (baptized as Isabel Suárez), a descendant of Inca nobility. Garcilaso's father recognized him in his will as a natural son and left him an inheritance of four thousand pesos so that he could study in Spain. Garcilaso was baptized as Gómez Suárez de Figueroa, but adopted his father's surname when he established himself in Spain. He first went to Spain in 1560, and lived in the village of Mon-

tilla in Andalusia for most of his life. His first work was the translation of the *Dialoghi di amore*, by Jehudah Abarbanel, better known in Spain as León Hebreo. This translation was first published in Madrid in 1590 with the title *La traduzion del Indio de los tres Dialogos de Amor de León Hebreo, hecha de Italiano en Español por Garcilaso Inga de la Vega, natural de la gran Ciudad de Cuzco, cabeza de los Reynos y provincias del Piru*. The other two main works of Garcilaso are *La Florida del Inca* and the *Comentarios reales de los Incas*, which consists of two parts. *La Florida del Inca* first appeared in Lisbon in 1605, with the full title of *La Florida del Ynca. Historia del Adelantado Hernando de Soto, Gouernador y capitan general del Reyno de la Florida, y de otros heroicos caualleros Españoles e Yndios; escrita por el Ynca Garcilasso de la Vega, capitan de su Magestad, natural de la gran ciudad del Cozco, cabeza de Reynos y provincias del Peru*. The first part of the *Comentarios*, which focused on pre-contact Peru, appeared in Lisbon in 1609 as *Primera parte de los Comentarios Reales que tratan del origen de los Yncas, Reyes que fueron del Perú, de su idolatría, leyes y gobierno en paz y en guerra: de sus vidas y conquistas, y de todo lo que fue aquel imperio y su republica, antes que los españoles passaran a el. Escritos por el Ynca Garcilaso de la Vega, . . .* The second part, which focused on the conquest and the subsequent civil wars among the Spaniards, was intended initially to bear the title of *Segunda parte de los Comentarios Reales*, but first appeared posthumously in Córdoba in 1617, under the title *Historia general del Perú. Trata del descubrimiento del; y como lo ganaron los españoles. Las guerras civiles que hubo entre Pizarros y Almagros, sobre la partija de la tierra. Castigo y levantamiento de tiranos: y otros sucesos particulares que en la historia se contienen. Escrita por el Ynca Garcilaso de la Vega, . . .* For a biography of Garcilaso, see Varner. I have modified when I felt necessary John Grier Varner and Jeannette Johnson Varner's translation of *La Florida del Inca*. When two page references are provided consecutively after quotations from this work, the first corresponds to the Spanish edition, and the second to the Varners' English translation.

2. Gonzalo Fernández de Oviedo first came to America in 1514 as supervisor of the smelting of gold in Pedrarias Dávila's expedition to the Darien. With the exception of a few short trips to Spain, Oviedo lived in America until his death in 1557 in Santo Domingo, where he had been the *alcaide* (governor) of the fortress since 1533. Oviedo wrote two main texts on the New World. The first was the *Sumario de la natural historia de las Indias*, a short treatise written for Charles V in 1526. The second is the multivolume *Historia general y natural de las Indias*. There was an edition of the first part of the *Historia general* in 1535 and an expanded version in 1547. The *Historia general* was not published in its entirety until the nineteenth century. The latest internal date in the manuscript of *Historia general* is 1549, at the end of part 3, where the author announces his intention to write a fourth part. Oviedo tried to publish an edition that would include parts 2 and 3, but was not granted authorization (see Gerbi 129-31).

3. Bernardino de Sahagún is the most accomplished ethnographer among the Franciscans in sixteenth-century Mexico. He arrived in New Spain in 1529 and remained there until his death in 1590. Sahagún was an active member of the Colegio de Santa Cruz de Tlatelolco, where the sons of the indigenous elite were trained to read and write Latin, Spanish, and Nahuatl. These trilingual collegians participated in the collection of materials, in the transcription of oral reports into the Roman alphabet, and, in general, in the different tasks involved in

the production of the *Historia general de las cosas de la Nueva España*. The *Florentine Codex* is the most complete version of a series of texts that Sahagún elaborated over the years. With the aid of the collegians, he collected and compared oral reports from elders in different towns. For a discussion of Sahagún's method, the different texts, and the stages in the production of the *Historia*, see Klor de Alva. Recent editions of the *Historia* include a Spanish version of Sahagún by Angel María Garibay K. and an English bilingual edition of the Nahuatl version and the Spanish prologues by Arthur J. O. Anderson and Charles E. Dibble.

4. The noble savage as a utopian figure is particularly true to the anthropological reflections in the *Apologética historia sumaria* (c. 1555-59), and not to the inversion of the conventional roles of sheep (Christians) and wolves (pagans) in the *Brevísima relación de la destrucción de Indias* (1552). In addition to these two works, Las Casas wrote the *Historia de las Indias* (1527-c. 1560). The *Historia* covers the main events in the colonization and conquest of America until 1527. Originally the *Apologética* was to be part of the *Historia*; although some parts of the *Apologética* date back to 1527, the bulk of the text was written between 1555 and 1559. Parts of the *Apologética* were used against Juan Ginés de Sepúlveda in the 1550-51 debates over the inferiority of the American Indian and the legitimacy of their conquest (see Zavala; Losada). Only the *Brevísima* was published during Las Casas's life. Las Casas was born in 1484 and first went to America in 1502. He held an *encomienda* until 1514, when he renounced his claim because of the unjust nature of the institution. His career as a protector of the Indians began in 1515 and lasted until his death in 1560. Las Casas was responsible for two major social experiments, first in Cumaná, in present-day Venezuela (1520-21), and then in Verapaz, Guatemala (1537-50). The *Apologética*, which postdates these events, defines a theoretical and political transition to a later Las Casas who condemns outright the Spanish colonization of the New World and calls for a full restitution of Indian sovereignty (see Rabasa, "Utopian" 273-74). Las Casas was the bishop of Chiapas from 1543 to 1547.

5. If one can argue with Heidegger that only after Descartes's *Meditations* and *Discourse on Method* can we speak in a strict sense of subjectivity and objectivity in epistemology, and consequently of a negative meaning of the term subjectivity, one might add that this epistemic mutation (and the negative meaning of subjectivity) had been in the offing for at least two centuries (see Heidegger 127-29 passim). This mutation, as I have pointed out here, can be observed in passages from New World historiography that reflect on method. In fact, as I have suggested elsewhere ("Columbus"), this mutation can already be traced in Columbus. Normand Dorion, however, has shown not only that Descartes was fond of reading treatises on the art of traveling, but that these texts provided a methodological model beyond the mere adoption of travel tropes (92-102).

Works Cited

Adorno, Rolena. "El sujeto colonial y la construcción cultural de la alteridad." *Revista de Crítica Literaria Latinoamericana* 14, 28 (1988): 55-68.

Ashcroft, Bill, Gareth Griffiths, and Helen Tiffin. *The Empire Writes Back: Theory and Practice in Post-Colonial Literatures*. New York: Routledge, 1989.

Bakhtin, M. M. "The Problem of Speech Genres." *Speech Genres and Other Essays.* Trans. Vern W. McGee. Austin: Univ. of Texas Press. 66-102.

Barthes, Roland. "The Discourse of History." Trans. Peter Wexler. *Structuralism: A Reader.* Ed. Michael Lanek. London: Jonathan Cape, 1970. 145-155.

Bhabha, Homi. "The Other Question: Difference, Discrimination and the Discourse of Colonialism." *Literature, Politics, and Theory.* Ed. Francis Barker et al. London: Methuen, 1986. 148-172.

Caro Baroja, Julio. *Los judíos en la España moderna y contemporánea.* 3 vols. Madrid: Arion, 1961.

Certeau, Michel de. *The Writing of History.* Trans. Tom Conley. New York: Columbia Univ. Press, 1988.

Dorion, Normand. "L'art de voyager. Pour un définition du récit de voyage à l'époque classique." *Poétique* 73 (1988): 83-108.

Durand, José. *El Inca Garcilaso, clásico de América.* Mexico City: Sep Setentas, 1976.

Fabian, Johannes. *Time and the Other: How Anthropology Makes Its Object.* New York: Columbia Univ. Press, 1983.

Fidalgo de Elvas. *Expedición de Hernando de Soto a la Florida.* 1557. Madrid: Austral, 1952.

Foucault, Michel. *The Order of Things: An Archaeology of the Human Sciences.* New York: Vintage, 1973.

García Icazbalceta, Joaquín. *Nueva colección de documentos para la historia de México. Códice Franciscano. Siglo XVI.* Mexico City: Salvador Chavez Hayhoe, 1941.

Garcilaso de la Vega, Inca. *Primera y segunda parte de los Comentarios Reales de los Incas.* 1609-17. Vols. 2-4 of *Obras completas.* 4 vols. Ed. Carmelo Saenz de Santa María. Madrid: Atlas, 1960.

———. *La Florida del Inca.* 1605. Ed. Sylvia L. Hilton. Madrid: Historia 16, 1986.

———. *The Florida of the Inca.* Trans. and ed. John Grier Varner and Jeannette Johnson Varner. Austin: Univ. of Texas Press, 1951.

Gerbi, Antonello. *Nature in the New World: From Christopher Columbus to Gonzalo Fernández de Oviedo.* Trans. Jeremy Moyle. Pittsburgh: Univ. of Pittsburgh Press, 1985.

González Echevarría, Roberto. "The Law and the Letter: Garcilaso's *Comentarios.*" *Myth and Archive: A Theory of Latin American Narrative.* Cambridge: Cambridge Univ. Press, 1990. 43-92.

Heidegger, Martin. "The Age of the World Picture." *The Question Concerning Technology and Other Essays.* Trans. William Lowitt. New York: Garland, 1977. 115-154.

Henige, David. "The Context, Content, and Credibility of *La Florida del Ynca.*" *The Americas* 43 (1986): 1-23.

Jákfalvi-Leiva, Susana. *Traducción, escritura y violencia colonizadora: un estudio de la obra del Inca Garcilaso.* Syracuse, N.Y.: Maxwell School of Citizenship and Public Affairs, 1984.

JanMohamed, Abdul R. *Manichean Aesthetics: The Politics of Literature in Colonial Africa.* Amherst: Univ. of Massachusetts Press, 1983.

Klor de Alva, J. Jorge. "Sahagún and the Birth of Modern Ethnography: Representing, Confessing, and Inscribing the Native Other." *Bernardino de Sahagún: Pioneer Ethnographer of Sixteenth-Century Aztec Mexico.* Ed. J. Jorge Klor de

Alva, H. B. Nicholson, and Eloise Quiñones Keber. Studies on Culture and Society 2. Albany: Institute of Mesoamerican Studies; Austin: Univ. of Texas Press, 1988. 31-52.

Las Casas, Bartolomé de. *Historia de las Indias.* 3 vols. Ed. Agustín Millares Carlo. Mexico City: Fondo de Cultura Económica, 1965.

———. *Apologética historia sumaria.* Ed. Edmundo O'Gorman. Mexico City: UNAM, 1967.

———. *Brevísima relación de la destrucción de Indias.* 1552. Facsimile ed. Manuel Ballesteros Gaibrois. Madrid: Fundación Universitaria Española, 1977.

Losada, Angel. "Observaciones sobre la 'Apología' de Fray Bartolomé de las Casas (respuesta a una consulta)." *Cuadernos Americanos* 212, 3 (1977): 152-162.

Marin, Louis. *Utopics: Spatial Play.* Trans. Robert A. Vollrath. Atlantic Highlands, N.J.: Humanities Press, 1984.

Mignolo, Walter. "El metatexto historiográfico y la historiografía indiana." *Modern Language Notes* 96 (1981): 358-402.

Miró Quesada, Aurelio. *El Inca Garcilaso y otros estudios garcilasistas.* Madrid: Cultura Hispánica, 1971.

Ortega, Julio. "El Inca Garcilaso y el discurso de la cultura." *Revista Iberoamericana* 44 (1978): 507-513.

Oviedo y Valdés, Gonzalo Fernández de. *Historia general y natural de las Indias.* 5 vols. 1535-47. Madrid: Atlas, 1959.

———. *Sumario de la natural historia de las Indias.* 1526. Madrid: Historia 16, 1986.

Pacheco, Joaquín F., Francisco de Cárdenas, and Luis Torres de Mendoza. *Colección de documentos inéditos relativos al descubrimiento, conquista y organización de las antiguas posesiones españolas en América y Oceanía.* 42 vols. Madrid: José María Pérez, 1864-84.

Pupo-Walker, Enrique. *Historia, creación y profecía en los textos del Inca Garcilaso de la Vega.* Madrid: Porrúa Turanzas, 1982.

Rabasa, José. "Columbus and the Scriptural Economy of the Renaissance." *Dispositio* 14, 36-38 (1989): 271-301.

———. "Utopian Ethnology in Las Casas's *Apologética.*" *1492-1992: Re/Discovering Colonial Writing.* Ed. René Jara and Nicholas Spadaccini. Hispanic Issues 4. Minneapolis: Univ. of Minnesota Press, 1989. 263-289.

Rodríguez-Vecchini, Hugo. "*Don Quijote y La Florida del Inca.*" *Revista Iberoamericana* 48 (1982): 587-620.

Sahagún, Bernardino de. *Florentine Codex: General History of the Things of New Spain.* 13 vols. Trans. and ed. Arthur J. O. Anderson and Charles E. Dibble. Santa Fe: School of American Research; Salt Lake City: Univ. of Utah Press, 1950-82.

———. *Historia general de las cosas de la Nueva España.* Ed. Angel María Garibay K. Mexico City: Porrúa, 1956.

Shell, Marc. "Marranos (Pigs), or From Coexistence to Toleration." *Critical Inquiry* 17 (1991): 306-335.

Todorov, Tzvetan. *The Conquest of America: The Question of the Other.* Trans. Richard Howard. New York: Harper, 1984.

Varner, John Grier. *El Inca: The Life and Times of Garcilaso de la Vega.* Austin and London: Univ. of Texas Press, 1968.

Wey-Gómez, Nicolás. "¿Dónde está Garcilaso? La oscilación del sujeto colonial en la formación de un discurso transcultural." *Revista de Crítica Literaria Latinoamericana* 17, 34 (1991): 7-31.

Zamora, Margarita. *Language, Authority, and Indigenous History in the Comentarios reales de los incas.* Cambridge: Cambridge Univ. Press, 1988.

Zavala, Silvio. "Aspectos formales de la controversia entre Sepúlveda y Las Casas en Valladolid, a mediados del siglo XVI." *Cuadernos Americanos* 212, 3 (1977): 138-151.

◆ **Chapter 8**

The Opossum and the Coyote: Ethnic Identity and Ethnohistory in the Sierra Norte de Puebla (Mexico)

Pierre Beaucage

They say that long ago the opossum walked along in splendor. In the new land he said: "Here I shall rule." Then the coyote came along and said: "You? So small and you want to be the king? I am bigger and I shall rule. . . . The opossum answered: "Small as you see me, I shall rule; big and small, I shall rule over you all . . ."
—Nahuat tale from San Miguel Tzinacapan[1]

Ethnic Identity and Culture

The anthropological contribution to the study of ethnic identity or ethnicity is recent and quite heterogeneous. During the past fifteen years, when ethnic identity became the focus of many anthropological studies, one could read or hear the most varied, often contradictory, statements regarding its nature and its place in the dynamics of change. This situation may cause some surprise, because for more than a century anthropologists have assigned themselves culture as their subject matter: a vantage point for the study of "the perception of one's own culture as distinct," if we are to define ethnic identity descriptively.

The specific phenomenon of ethnic identity did not interest nineteenth-century scholars: they believed in "laws of cultural evolution," which meant the development and spread of a few "superior," "active" cultures and the disappearance of the others. Twentieth-century cultural anthropology explicitly rejected such premises, which it considered racist, but usually paid little attention to ethnicity; culture was defined as the material and intellectual apparatus that distinguishes human from animal, and

149

cultures were reified as self-contained wholes. Why, then, analyze at length how one *feels* as an Eskimo or Boshiman? Yet
many field-workers noticed, en passant, that most human
groups had neighbors whom they felt different from and superior to, and that their testimony about themselves was often
loaded with the idea of this difference and superiority.[2] It is the
growing interest in minority studies that brought the question of
identity to the forefront.

Even so, the interest of cultural anthropologists in the subject
was diminished because of the postulate that there was an inevitable, worldwide trend toward "acculturation," which mostly
meant adopting Western ways. Although Herskovits, for example, went to great lengths to explain that even in situations of
outright domination "mutual borrowing and subsequent revision of cultural elements seem to result" (530), he then pro-
ceeded to define any movement tending to consolidate a dominated culture as "counter-acculturation" and considered it as
basically hopeless.[3] Similarly, Wagley and Harris, in the first
comparative study of "minorities in the Americas," claimed that
it was the "ethnocentrism" [read: strong ethnic identity] of Brazilian and Mexican Indians that reduced their "adaptability" to
modern conditions; but this also ensured their very survival:

> These groups are, in a sense, imposing hardships upon
> themselves by insisting on their isolation and by
> resisting the introduction of schools, modern hygiene,
> and progressive forms of agriculture. In Mexico, as in
> Brazil, the State, and to a large extent the majority group
> which controls the State, is actually striving to remove
> barriers to upward mobility against the resistance of the
> Indians themselves. (268)

The acculturation theory was thus the legitimation of a twofold state intervention: education, that is, forced acculturation,
on the one hand, and development, the penetration of capitalism in native areas, on the other. For the natives' own good,
their culture and identity had to be replaced by national ones
(Boege 228ff.).

Even if Marxism was based on a paradigm opposite to that of
cultural anthropology, its theory and policies regarding the na-

tives involved a similar positivistic view of culture and a mechanist theory of modernization. For some Marxist anthropologists, the incomplete development of capitalism explains the "caste" relationships [read: native persistence] in peripheral areas: these are bound to give way to the cultural homogeneity and class relations typical of capitalism. However painful the transition may be for those being so proletarianized, it is an essential step toward social revolution (Pozas; Aguirre Beltrán). Other Marxist scholars were opposed to that view, claiming that the overexploitation of Indians (the rationale of ethnic difference) is necessary for the reproduction of a dependent, backward capitalist society (Bartra; Díaz Polanco; Deverre). Both trends agree that "Indian consciousness [read: ethnic identity] hinders the development of class consciousness," and thus has to be superseded by the latter.

In the 1970s, however, as everyone was forecasting their imminent disappearance, Indians started to rise and speak, forcing anthropologists and politicians to reconsider their view on "acculturation" and "modernization." Organized native movements appeared, and their spokespersons claimed that they looked forward, not backward, and that the real role of the "benevolent state" might be just the opposite of what it claimed to be. At first, these movements appeared so strange to both scholars and traditional political groups that they were considered spurious—even more so because the Indian spokespersons are often acculturated and thus, to quote Labrousse, "reassume an ethnic identity which until now they were trying to hide" (24). Moreover, the "new Indianness" involves reconsideration of traditional Indian cultures: old discourse and rituals are given new meanings, and new forms appear. Beyond the tribe, reservation, *resguardo*, or *comunidad*, new organizational structures emerge, at regional, national, and even international levels.

As a result, the seventies saw the emergence of a different perspective in anthropological studies, which some call "ethnicist" or even "populist" (Díaz Polanco). Its partisans claim that the actual strength of Indian movements is a proof of the vitality of Indian identities, in spite of centuries of domination, culture change, and intents of assimilation. They developed new concepts, such as "cultural persistence" (Castile), "ethnodevelopment" (Bonfil Batalla et al.), and "ethnogenesis" (González; Roosens). The recent "Indian awakening" in the Americas has undoubtedly forced anthropologists not only to include ethnic identity in their object of study but to consider it an active factor in social change. At the same time, the old reification of culture gave way to a new trend that could be called "essentialist." Some scholars now claim that cultures are "superorganic systems" that "persist" for their own sake, quite independently of historical vicissitudes (Castile xx-xxi)—a position that obviously corresponds to the discourse of the new Indian leadership.

What may have been underestimated in some recent studies about revival and development of minority ethnic groups are the material limits that exist to such a process. An ethnic community that has only a few thousand members, living off a subsistence economy in a remote area, has far less margin for maneuver, in the actual world, than one whose population is in the millions, with control over large tracts of land, cities, and some modern state apparatus—even if politically subordinated. Even within one country, and regarding one type of ethnic group (Amerindians, for example), we find that the situation varies greatly from one group to another (Beaucage 1987a; Valdés and Menéndez).

Once the phenomenon of ethnic identity is recognized, it appears that many elements taken for granted in the traditional positivistic view of culture have in fact a strong rhetorical component. For example, in a typical Mesoamerican multiethnic region such as the Sierra Norte de Puebla, in eastern Mexico, one could easily deduct from interviews with the Nahua, the Totonac, and the mestizos that each group constitutes an almost self-contained cultural entity, separated from the others by a world of differences at every level: from food to supernatural belief, from family structure to political organization. A survey of material and social life in the three ethnic groups, however, reveals a continuum.

Thus the first theoretical step in order to apprehend ethnic identity is to distinguish it from the broader category of culture, with which it is so often confused. The *culture* of a given human group can be defined in relatively objective terms: its material relations to the physical world surrounding it (ecology, technology), the relations established among humans regarding the appropriation of resources and social production (economy), those relations that involve power and its regulation (politics), and the symbolic relationships between humans, as well as with the material and supernatural world (cognitive systems, values, beliefs, ideology).[4] *Ethnic identity* or *ethnicity* belongs to this last sphere and designs the symbolic array by which a human group (and individuals belonging to it) defines itself by its culture, which, in turn, means an explicit or implicit relationship/ distinction with (an)other culture(s). For there is no "ethnic phenomenon" without interethnicity, without a relationship (of whatever kind) with the Other. It follows that, in the context of the Americas, *Indianity* or *Indianness*, as an identity, is necessarily a postconquest phenomenon. Before the conquest, there was of course ethnicity, but it opposed one Indian group to the others, without any need or possibility for a term meaning "Amerindian," as distinct from "humankind in general."

Complex relationships relate culture and ethnic identity. Culture provides the raw materials, so to speak, for the elaboration of ethnicity. What distinguishes ethnic identity from all other identities (class, gender, age, and so on) is the use of cultural criteria: language, ways of life, values. But ethnicity does not reflect culture: its content (as it appears in verbal as well as nonverbal communication) reveals a "work on culture," implying selection, valorization, structuring, and often creation. At the same time, the culture of the Other(s) is being redefined, usually following an antithetic pattern. Five hundred years of American history give us multiple "definitions of the Indians" that bear testimony of this "work" and often present more information about those who made the "definitions" and their relationship with the American natives than about the latter (Matos Moctezuma; Jacob). The same can be said about Indian definitions of non-Indians (Whites, Blacks, or mestizos), unfortunately far less known. The result of such "work on culture" is to break the continuum of society at a given point and, through cultural criteria or markers, create an ethnic frontier (Barth). Within this frontier, people will be brought to feel "kith and kin" in opposition to the outside, whatever their differences may be; outside of the frontier are those who are "basically different," whatever points of similarity may exist.

For the criteria or ethnic markers to be efficient, they must be simple, readily grasped, and based as much as possible on external indices; they tend to become stereotypes. The criteria used vary from one group to another, from one period to another. In fact, almost anything can do—"race," religion, dress, language or accent—that is, "virtually anything which has not been explicitly or publicly affirmed by other ethnic groups as ethnic emblems" (Roosens 18). At a given point in history, markers may be changed and the ethnic frontier may be shifted. Up to 1960, French-speaking Canadians identified themselves through "tongue and faith" (*la langue et la foi*); after the Quiet Revolution of the sixties, only language remained, thus making possible the inclusion of French-speaking immigrants from Lebanon and Morocco, as well as nonpracticing *Français de France* (held previously in a kind of limbo!). Members of a given ethnic group may move the barrier from one interethnic relationship to another: the typical North American WASP, for example, sees himself or herself as "White" in opposition to Blacks and Asians; as "English" in opposition to Italian Americans and "Frenchies" of New England; and probably as "Christian" in relation to Jews and Arabs.

Among the criteria most frequently found to define ethnic barriers, and thus ethnic identities, are those of "race," territory, and history (Castile). The ethnic group likes to represent itself as "one large family," and this is reinforced by the fact that the most common form of recruitment is the appropriation of the newborn. This usually implies the idea of a common descent and "racial purity," both being generally contradicted by historical data, where such exist. One also finds norms regarding endogamy and adscription rules (either inclusive or exclusive) for individuals born of mixed unions. When physical traits are used for the adscription of members to a group, they are highly culturalized. However "natural" may seem the "color of the skin," the hair texture, or the phenotype to assign people to a given category, countless studies have shown that these elements are always deeply compounded by considerations of social status: a poor farmer with a light shade of skin is "Indian" or "Negro," a dark-skinned doctor or businessman is "Mulatto" or even "White" (Wagley; Labelle).

The relationship with a given territory is also loaded with symbols. If most ethnic groups identify themselves with a "homeland," the actual situations vary a great deal. Mesoamerican Indians traditionally cease to consider as one of theirs a member who goes to live permanently in the city, for, as the Mazateco Indians state, "we *ha shuta enima* work in the bush" (Boege 19). Other communities with large diasporas identify with the place where most of them—or some of them—still live: Haiti or Armenia, for example. Here again, it is not the fact of actually inhabiting a land that is determinant, but the symbolic link with "the land of the ancestors." The Central American Garifona (or "Black Caribs") still define themselves as "coming from Yurumai" (Saint Vincent Island in the West Indies), without maintaining any hope, or desire, of ever going back there. This relationship, however high in the symbolic sphere, may be strongly affected by very material political events concerning the land itself. The creation of Israel in 1948 permanently modified the ties that existed between Jewish communities all over the world and the Holy Lands of Palestine. In the same order of thinking, after 1960, the Quiet Revolution redrew the ethnic boundaries in Canada: *la nation québécoise* replaced *le peuple canadien-français*, and Quebec was now to be their homeland, which left the *Francophones hors-Québec* in quest of a new place and definition.[5]

If this "ethnic work on culture" is to be efficient in building identity, it must remain largely unconscious. Culture modified as ethnicity has to be considered *the real culture* even if the gap with observable reality is evident to the members of another cultural group and to internal dissidents. This felt authenticity is not hampered by the fact of borrowing from others elements of one's self-definition, such as the "harmonious relationship with Nature," which has become a part of modern self-definitions of Indianness, and *l'entrepreneurship québécois* (said to be part of today's *québécité*).

If we remain at this descriptive stage (where many monographs end), concrete ethnic identities appear as patchworks of different traits, loosely connected, rather arbitrary and fluctuating in time.

Ethnicity, Power, and Social Class

To add even more complexity to the picture, ethnicity often refers, directly or indirectly, to a power structure, a fact that was either ignored or underrated by the positivist students of culture. As we have already seen, ethnic identity necessarily refers to the Other, and few, if any, interethnic relations were ever made in a void of power relations. In class societies, ancient or modern, ethnic relationships coexist with another basic type of social relationship: that based on the control of resources, monopoly of force, and hegemony in the field of ideas. The links between the two orders of phenomena are particularly complex and vary in function of (a) the prevalent class relations (slavery, feudalism, merchant or industrial capitalism); (b) the way according to which the relationship was established and maintained between the groups (conquest, colonial rule, commerce, migration); and (c) the distribution of the members of each ethnic group between the classes, and the dynamics of this distribution (upward or downward mobility). Although ethnic and class barriers may coincide in a given situation, I will argue that the former is irreducible to the latter, contrary to the traditional Marxist assumption. A good part of my later discussion of the Sierra material will deal with ethnic identity in the context of a given class structure, so it is necessary to state more explicitly my position in this respect.

Referring to class and the Amerindians, I would suggest that we now have three different situations. The first is that of *merchant capitalism*, which was already present, if not dominant, in colonial days, and is still to be found in most Indian areas. Merchant capital is mostly interested in the circulation of goods and makes its profit from exchange. The direct producer, whether a hunter, a sharecropper, or a petty farmer, conserves a considerable amount of autonomy, which is necessary for his or her productive efficiency. Acculturation, that is, the adoption of cultural patterns from the dominant group, exists, but it is limited to certain key sectors: some technological and economic change, religion, and so on. The margin of material autonomy left to the dominated group permits cultural resistance, and the dominant group itself is not interested in assimilation, which would mean economic loss if Indians had to stop hunting or tilling the land. This situation first prevailed on the frontiers of the colonial empires in North and South America and, later, in areas where slavery or serfdom were abandoned (as in Brazil and Spanish America after independence). Ethnic barriers are strong and the markers are "racial" or cultural.

When capital moves into *production*, usually agricultural, it needs increased circulation of people as well as goods. Labor is controlled directly by the owner of the means of production and there is a need for cultural homogeneity at the national level (from language to consumption habits). In Spanish America, this trend clearly appeared during the second half of the nineteenth century, with the victory of the Liberals over the Conservative party and the church. The process remained largely contradictory, however. The state, in the hands of either the military or civilian "enlightened despots," tried to substitute "national identity" for ethnic and regional differences (through the school system, military service, and so forth). At the same time, the prevailing pattern of accumulation, export-oriented plantation agriculture, makes for the persistence of a large, ethnically stigmatized, rural labor force. Thus, at the economic level, an ethnic hierarchy is forced upon native workers, while at the political-ideological level, their distinctiveness is denied. For the dominated group in this context, ethnic identity becomes the space from where resistance can be organized against the prevailing political-economic order; the struggle for land is one of the most typical forms of this resistance (see Schryer). In Mexico such a conflictive situation started with the Laws of Reform (1856) and lasted, on a national scale, until the Revolution (1910-17); it is still prevalent in many rural areas of Mexico, as well as in Central America and the Andean countries.

Third, when plantation agriculture gives way to *industrial capital*, pressure for assimilation considerably increases, as does the need for a more qualified and mobile labor force. Capital and state now possess much more sophisticated means of achieving assimilation than before: mass media (especially electronic ones), consumerism, communication networks, and so on. At the same time, there is less need for direct repression of dominated cultures, as long as they do not openly contradict the dominant project. Thus the concrete affirmation of ethnic identity may cover a wide spectrum of demands. Some Indian communities still fight for the "land and liberty" they are being denied, while new ethnic organizations, with a definite place in civil society, are more concerned with preserving and developing native cultural heritage. Such is the current composite situation in Mexico and the Andes.

From the preceding examples, we can see that class structure and class dynamics have a direct impact on the manifestations and transformations of ethnic identity, and that the only way to overcome the puzzling diversity and apparent arbitrariness of the forms it takes is to adopt a historical perspective.

Ethnohistory and Ethnic Identity

The relationship between history and ethnicity is twofold: the ethnic group is, materially, a product of History, but ethnic ideology also re-creates History so as to give consistency and meaning to a concrete situation and political projects (Roosens 17). The latter, which I will call ethnohistory, means both selecting "reference events" as markers of origins and destiny, and erasing "nonsignificant" and troublesome memories (Dolan 17-20). A dominant Europe saw its mission unfolding throughout the centuries, from the Crusades to the *Chemin de fer Congo-Océan*. Subordinated groups seek in History the reasons why they have been deprived of the bright future they obviously deserve—and find the culprits. For Quebec nationalists, it was Louis XV, selling out New France to England, maybe following some wicked advice from Voltaire;[6] for the Pan-Germanists, it was the Machiavellian Cardinal de Richelieu, dividing their fatherland into tiny feudal states, and, later, the Jews; for American Indian activists, it was the European explorers and colonizers to whom they gave such warm hospitality and who then took away their lands (Ryser 28; Wankar 31ff.). Yet History also reveals the secret destiny of the group to Those Who Have Wisdom and thus shows the path for political-ideological action. As a schoolchild I learned that Catholic Quebec had to spread its faith to a Protestant, materialistic North America; North American Indians similarly kept a unique spirituality after the loss of their lands and independence; and Germany preserved racial and linguistic purity, which legitimized its supremacy over a decadent Europe. Far from being just "false consciousness," this ethnohistory is a basic element for the elaboration of ethnic identity and can influence the transformation of society and culture, within certain limits. One evident condition is that the process of selecting and modeling elements of culture into ethnic identity should bypass its individual creators and become part of an ethnic ideology and movement capable of making History.

In the following pages, basing myself on data from the Sierra Norte de Puebla, Mexico, I will first sketch the main cultural and structural features of the region. I will present and try to interpret the categories with which the different ethnic groups classify each other, then proceed to analyze some elements of the discourse on ethnic sameness and difference among the Nahua, and between the Nahua and the mestizos. I will illustrate the relationships between ethnic identity and ethnohistory by giving excerpts from the oral traditions of both groups. This will eliminate, I hope, some of the arbitrariness that appears in the ethnic discourse, as well as shed some light on the maintenance of this ethnic frontier in the lower Sierra, a mountainous area three hundred kilometers east-northeast of Mexico City.[7]

Culture and Ethnic Categories

Traveling in the Sierra, one sees more cultural continuities than frontiers. Mestizo and Indian settlements have much in common, with their irregular rows of stone-walled, tile-roofed houses surrounding the large churches. Now young Indian men wear factory-made clothes instead of the traditional white *calzones* and shirts, and the basic food everywhere is the tortilla, complemented with beans, hot peppers, and a variety of wild and grown vegetables. Yet, a closer look reveals that ethnic differentiation is one of the basic dimensions of social life in the Sierra. On Sunday, the market day, in a large township center such as Cuetzalan, the streets are filled with people from the surrounding hamlets. Most Indian women still wear the traditional dress. They speak Nahuat among themselves, but most will address merchants in Spanish. They frequent only the streets, the marketplace, and the co-op house; they make short stops in the shops to purchase some extra goods or have a drink; and, long before dark, they leave town and return to their villages. Indians and non-Indians have talked and exchanged, in fact in a very ritualized way, but they have not mixed. A closer look at ethnic categories reveals an intricate situation.

Ethnic Categories in the Sierra Norte de Puebla

1. Lower Sierra Nahua

Maseual ["Indian"]
Maseualtajto
["Nahuat speaker"]

Koyot ["foreigner"]
Koyotajto
[Spanish speaker]
Koparito
Xalkoyot
[acculturated]

Totonako (metsxipetstik)
[Totonac ("barefooted")]

Analteko ["from overseas"]
Uejkakayot ["from faraway"]

2. Totonac

["Totonac"]

["non-Totonac"]
Luua'n ["snakes"]
mejikanero ["Nahuat speaker"]

Tutunaku

rason ["mestizo"]

3. High Sierra Nahua and mestizos

Rico ["rich"]
Catrín ["city dweller"]

Koyot ["foreigner, light-skinned"]

Maseual ["Indian, peasant, dark-skinned"]

4. Lower Sierra mestizos

gente de razón
["people of reason," non-Indians]

indios, inditos
["Indians, little Indians"]
Mexicaneros ["Nahuat speakers"]
Naquitos, pioncitos
["little Totonac, little laborers"]

For the natives, the fundamental level of identification is not the ethnic group, but the local community: *sanmigueleño* (from

San Miguel Tzinacapan), *cuetzalteco* (from Cuetzalan), *ecateco* (from Santiago Ecatlan), and so forth. At this level, ethnic belonging is not immediately relevant; for a *sanmigueleño, cuetzalteco* will designate both the mestizos from the township center and the Indians from its nearby villages. If one goes up from the community level, only one term, for the Nahua, refers to their identity: *maseual*, which could be translated as "Indian" because it includes all natives, irrespective of their specific ethnic group. When a distinction is needed between them and their Totonac neighbors (whose material culture is very similar to theirs), Nahua will usually refer to language: they speak *maseualtajtol* ("the Indian speech") and their Indian neighbors speak *totonakotajtol* ("Totonac speech"). At times the Nahua will call the Totonacs by some derogatory terms borrowed from Mexican Spanish, such as *nacos* or *naquitos*, or even by *metsxipetstik* ("barefooted"), definitely insulting.[8]

Maseual is symmetrically opposed to *koyot* (feminine: *xinola*, from Spanish *señora*), which refers in the broadest sense to the foreigner, the mestizo, the city dweller. Such a polysemy does not create much confusion in the lower Sierra, where most non-Indians arrived during the latter part of the nineteenth century and remained in the small towns where they kept (or adopted) an ostensibly urban style of life. So strong is the social meaning of *koyot* that the coyote animal is usually referred to as *koyotekuani* ("coyote-wild-beast") to avoid any possible misunderstanding. When necessary, *koyot* will be broken into *cuetzalteco* (from the neighboring town), *ajkopahua* ("from the highlands"), *uejkakayot* ("from faraway"), and *analteko* ("from overseas"). According to Nutini and Isaac (234, 242), this ethnic opposition between groups identified as *maseualmej/koyomej* extends to the northwestern part of the Sierra.

Although *maseual* and *koyot* are posed as mutually exclusive categories, two terms exist for intermediate situations: *xalkoyot*, which refers to an Indian who adopts the ways and dress of the non-Indians, and *koparitos*, which refers collectively to the highland Indian peddlers, who speak Nahuat but whose dress and ways are seen as halfway between the two cultures.

The Totonac do not seem to have any generic term to designate all Indians; their only specific referent is strictly reserved to their own ethnic group, *tutunaku*. The others, whether Nahuas, mestizos, or foreigners, are all included in the category *luua'n* ("snakes") (Córdoba Olivares 104; Aschman 95), within which they may distinguish a subcategory, *rason* or *liderason* (the mestizos) (Ichon 17).

When comparing the semantic fields for identity-alterity among the two native groups, one is stricken by their noncorrespondence. The Nahua see themselves as *the* Indians, an attitude enhanced by the fact that they know of their wide (if broken) geographical distribution, that toponyms throughout the country are usually Nahuatl, and that their language is called *mejicano*, "Mexican," in popular Spanish. The Sierra Totonac inhabit a relatively small, compact territory; they are the most isolated from the road network, and their rate of bilingualism is much lower. They are almost exclusively farmers and depend for specialized goods and services on highland Nahua artisans (potters, firework-makers) and petty traders as well as on non-Indian middlemen. Thus, it is understandable why the same derogatory term designates the Nahua and the non-Indians, because the Totonacs engage with both in mercantile relations that involve a considerable vulnerability and distrust; the Nahua feel that way only with the mestizos. The nicknames chosen for the dominant Other—the snake and the coyote, dangerous predators—are quite significant in this respect.

The mestizos, the economically and politically dominant group, refer to themselves as *gente de razón* ("people of reason") to the exclusion of the words *ladino* and *mestizo*, which are widespread elsewhere in Mesoamerica. Contrary to the latter terms, *gente de razón* does not refer to a circumscribed ethnic entity; it includes all "educated, civilized people," both Mexican and foreigners. Its only clear-cut frontier is with the Indian groups, labeled in various ways: *inditos* ("little Indians"), *pioncitos* ("little laborers"), *mejicaneros* ("nahuat speakers"), or *naquitos* ("little Totonac"). The general use of the diminutive *-ito* here is meant to express superiority with a good deal of paternalism. The term *indio* ("Indian") without a diminutive is an insult. The word *indígena* ("indigenous, native"), of scholarly origin, has been introduced recently in the Sierra and is now replacing the other Spanish expressions. Brought in by schoolteachers, politicians, and government officials, it implies a more positive connotation for native culture and is now commonly used by natives when they speak Spanish; it is also to be heard from local non-Indians, at least in public events or when conversing with foreigners (in private conversation, the old vocabulary still has its place).

In the lower Sierra reference to social class is also made, to *los del rancho* ("those from the farms") and *los pobres* (the poor), on the one hand, and *los catrines* ("the townspeople, the well-dressed") and *los ricos* (the rich) on the other. Often a strict parallelism exists between class and ethnic categories, although anyone will immediately acknowledge that there are wealthy Indians and poor town-dwelling mestizos.

This brief look at native ethnic categories from the lower Sierra shows that they reflect, as well as contest, the ethnic hierarchy: to condescending terms for those below correspond insulting labels for those above. Far from expressing the acceptance of subordination, these categories contain seeds of rebellion.

It is interesting to note that in the upper Sierra the terms *maseual* and *koyot* do not refer to any discrete social groups, but rather to the ends of a continuum that allows for many intermediate situations. *Maseual* is the most polysemic, meaning "Indian," "peasant," "dark-skinned," and is first opposed to both *rico* (rich) and *catrín* ("city-dweller, well-dressed"); *koyot* is limited to "light-skinned foreigners." The main categories are the social ones. The ethnic categories are few and blurred, which suggest that they have less social relevance than the social ones, which are immediately referred to.

The Discourse on Ethnic Identity: The Markers

There is no clear, general racial difference between Indians and non-Indians in the Sierra.[9] When the Nahua refer to the Indian population, however, they may use the Spanish word *raza*: "Nobody can change the *raza*, the root of our father and mother: Spanish remain such from the day they are born until they grow up and die, and the same with us, who are Indians" (Taller ms.).[10] They may also use the native term *taktson* (literally "stump" or "clump [of grass]"): "*Taktson* is a plant or stem that has its beginning, then it grows and casts its seed. . . . *Taktson* is also a family, because the father had these children, and they shall have more. It is like a root" (Taller ms.). Such an equivalence means that *raza* does not signify belonging to a physically marked collectivity. Rather, it situates an individual within duration, in relation with his forebears as well as descendants.

Beyond the family, united by blood ties, and the local community, defined by neighborhood and a common land base, native discourse will define the broader community, the ethnic group, in terms of selected emblems: dress, language, work, and ritual.

Dress

Dress is the most evident marker of ethnic identity. It distinguishes Indians in general from mestizos, for both Nahua and Totonac share the same form of dress. For men, as in most of Indian Mexico, the standard dress is white cotton breeches (tied at the calves or ankles), a pullover shirt, a black or brown woolen poncho, a straw hat, and sandals. Women's dress consists of a white cotton skirt held up by a wide red woven belt, an embroidered blouse, and a *huipil* or shawl made of light woven gauze in the lower Sierra, of wool in the higher range; in the lower Sierra the dress is necessarily completed by a bright-colored necklace and earrings. Each community can be distinguished by some particular detail of the woman's dress: type of embroidery, color of the necklaces, and so forth. The mestizos' clothing is more varied and reflects social class more than mere ethnicity: poor craftsmen and laborers are dressed in cheap, threadbare, manufactured or locally made pants and shirts, and women wear printed cotton dresses, completed by a manufactured woolen shawl (*rebozo*). Merchants, teachers, and government officers follow urban fashions as closely as they can afford.

What is considered "traditional Indian dress" has changed substantially over time (Johnson; Kandt). Today's male dress has no pre-Columbian origin (except sandals) but is a direct heir to that of Andalusian peasants of the sixteenth century; the hat came from the Philippines; and the poncho was introduced to Mesoamerica from the Andes, at the same time as sheep-breeding spread throughout the region. Contemporary male clothing became standard in the area only toward the end of the nineteenth century. Before that time, men had no shirt and wore short, wide breeches and broader-rimmed hats (woven by Oaxacan Indians). Female dress has remained much nearer the pre-Columbian model (skirt, belt, and *huipil*) although it also has made recent borrowings (such as the embroidered blouse) (Chabot).

For the production of meaning, the essential feature of Indian dress is not its origin, but the difference it creates, to the point that mestizos will frequently say, as a shorthand way to identify someone ethnically: "Es de calzón" ("He wears breeches") or "Es de pantalón" ("He wears pants"). With the natives, this production of difference obviously appears when people migrate. Seasonal workers, who go to Veracruz as farmhands or to Puebla and Mexico City as masons, dress then as mestizos; most resume their Indian dress and identity upon their return. An Indian who adopts the dress and ways of a mestizo out of context is called *xalkoyot* (literally "sandy," fake, "mestizo").

For the past fifteen years, under the influence of schools (which discourage and even forbid children to wear native dress) and increased contacts with the outside, the significance of dress as an ethnic marker has been decreasing, particularly for men. Although it is still very important in the more isolated communities (especially in the Totonac area), in the larger, more urbanized villages, younger men no longer wear breeches or sandals. Similarly, some younger women have replaced the skirt with printed cotton dresses. Ethnic discourse and ideology have taken note of culture change at this level, but react to it by dissociating clothing and identity: "Today, our clothes are changing, they change our clothes, but only our clothes for our race, nobody changes it, and nobody can change it, you know" (Taller ms.).

An interesting difference in gender exists regarding the valorization of native dress. Apart from being "proper to natives," male Indian clothing is considered cheap and comfortable; female dress is expensive and beautiful, and adds much to a woman's charms. Natives will thus resent any attempt by a foreign male to adopt local garb, even if it is more suited to the climate.

Yet they consider it quite natural for a townswoman to wear an Indian skirt and blouse, especially as holiday dress. The case of adopting the male clothing is seen as a derision, but wearing the female dress is considered a (normal) valorization of the ethnic marker.

Language

As can be expected, language reaches a much deeper level than does dress. "We who are Indians (do it) all with the Nahuat language (*maseualtajtol*), it is in the Nahuat way (*maseualkopan*) that we talk to each other" (Taller ms.).

The term *maseualkopan* links language and culture, because it means both "the Nahuat way" and "the Nahuat tongue." The superlative *yekmaseualkopan* adds a further nuance: "the *real* Indian way" (of speaking or doing). The latter term shows that Nahua are conscious of language acculturation, which manifests itself both in vocabulary and sentence structure. For example, some people will say *seguiroua* (from Spanish *seguir*, "to follow") instead of *tojtoka*, or use the Spanish prepositions *de* and *para* to break the complex structures of the Nahuat verbs. But here again, it is not linguistic acculturation, i.e., speaking or not speaking "pure" Nahuat or Totonac, or being unilingual, that determines a person's identity. It is being able to share with others a communication code that non-Indians are not supposed to understand.

In fact, mestizos raised in the Cuetzalan area all have a basic understanding of Nahuat, just as mestizos in Huehuetla understand Totonac. Native etiquette demands that Indians address each other in their common native tongue, and interethnic hierarchy requires Indian men to speak to mestizos in Spanish. Spanish is defined as "the language of public life," and interethnic contacts are usually restricted to commerce, administration, or ritual (both with the Catholic hierarchy and in the highly ritualized relations with non-Indian *compadres*). Mestizos would also like Indian men to address each other in Spanish in their presence, "to show they have nothing to hide." Although the mestizos know enough of the surrounding Indian languages to carry on business, they do not master all their subtleties. Both

Nahua and Totonac often take advantage of that to make fun of them with impunity . . . another way of "setting the frontier."[11] For the non-Indians, only Spanish is a "real language" (*un idioma*), because it has a "grammar" and is the language of government and "educated people"; Indian languages are only "dialects" (*dialectos*) and signs of the "backwardness of the region." It is still common for town-born schoolteachers to forbid the use of any Indian language on the school premises, and only in recent years have some of the teachers shown any interest in learning some Nahuat or Totonac. Recent government policies aimed at implementing bilingual education in the Sierra have met with strong resistance from many teachers and their union.[12]

The contempt shown by local Spanish speakers toward this important ethnic marker, language, may explain the extreme satisfaction with which the natives have met the interest of some foreigners since the midseventies to learn and write their language. The various leaflets and books published in Nahuat and Totonac are shown with pride to visitors: "Our language is nice. We also have words for everything!" They are eager to teach Nahuat or Totonac words to anyone interested, although warning that "a whole lifetime would be necessary to speak it properly"!

The case of language shows that a marker of ethnic identity is never just a marker. In a hierarchical situation, it marks up or down. "Speaking in dialect" was long a stigma, but writing and studying Nahuat and Totonac definitely raised the collective self-image.[13]

Work

We have already seen that the traditional division of labor in the Sierra assigns commerce and administration to mestizos, leaving manual work, particularly farming, to Indians. To the mestizos this division is of course natural, because Indians "lack the training" ("les falta la preparación"). The Indian view of the question has contradictory aspects. On the one hand, the Indians seem to share, to a certain point, the negative view of their destiny. A Nahuat tale, "The Three Brothers," states this clearly:

> There were three brothers . . . well, they lived on the farm as we live on the farm. They talked about how they envied those who earn quick money, while they didn't. They worked hard and they were poor, and they suffered a lot. They did earn a few pennies, but with hardship; they got scratched by thorns, bitten by ants, and the like. While the mestizos, they don't, they know Spanish, they know things, they read, they do a little work but they earn a lot of money. (Pérez 6-7)

On the other hand, one finds a clear valorization of the Indian ability to farm:

> Because the Indian part [of the population] goes to the bush and works well. He hoes and does everything well, the one who grew up in his father's hand. He grows up and becomes the same; he knows a lot, he knows a lot about work. And the one who doesn't know [the mestizo] doesn't succeed. (Taller ms.)

If farm labor is so highly valued, it is because, with the help of the gods, it produces corn, "our subsistence." This is mainly the Indians' task. Therefore, let each ethnic group keep its specialty and things will be fine.[14] The same tale of "The Three Brothers" relates the mischance of Indians who decide to learn in order to become lawyers and get rich. When natives first had access to jobs such as schoolteachers, health promotors, and so forth, some problems developed in their communities, because the new officeholders had to face a mixed attitude of pride and envy; any deviation they made from standard, "proper" Indian behavior was strongly criticized. Their reintegration was usually made possible through their ostentatious (and generous) participation in ritual.

Ritual

Indians identify themselves—and are identified in relation to—a well-developed community structure as well as networks of interpersonal ritual relations revolving around various kinds of godparenthood (*compadrazgo*). In the Sierra, the civil community hierarchy is clearly distinguished from the religious one, although they have multiple points of intersection. The civil structure is less developed, and Indian communities share it with non-Indians; it consists of the elected officials, such as the mayor, the eldermen, the justice of the peace, and so forth. These maintain the (delicate) link between the communities and the state apparatus (Durand 41-120; Arizpe 118-33). The religious structure is more under Indian control and has been vested with ethnic and community identity. Apart from its main patron saint, any community honors a multitude of saints; for example, Sánchez counted forty-seven annual religious celebrations and festivals in the village of San Miguel Tzinacapan, and about fifteen in the neighboring hamlets (191). Each celebration is organized by a *mayordomo* with his aides (*diputados*), and the various ritual dance groups of the major festivals are dressed and fed by a *teniente*. Any adult man is expected to serve at least once during his lifetime in one of the dozens of available offices; the wealthier will be pressed to accept the main *mayordomías* and thus bear the cost of the most expensive festivals (Chamoux 322-49; Ichon 251-54; Sánchez 159-96). Failure to carry out one's obligations, whether as a dancer or a sponsor, is believed to bring personal or collective calamity.

Anyone who has witnessed a religious festival in an Indian village sees that it is a particularly significant manifestation of collective identity. In spite of the presence of the priest and the Catholic ritual of mass, which link it with Catholicism as a whole, the immediate, more conspicuous level of identification is the local community. Villages compete with each other as to whose festival will be more brilliant with regard to the number of dance groups, fireworks, and public attendance. Even more than the village, though, the Indianness itself is thrown into relief, for the basic ritual elements, such as the dances and fireworks, are common to all Indian communities, Nahua and Totonac. In fact, on the patron saint's day, each community plays host to its neighbors, who come in large numbers, and then in turn will send dancers and people to the others' *fiestas*. Mestizo festivals (like that of Cuetzalan) are more like town fairs, with voluntary participation and little religious content; the only "ethnic elements" present are the Indian dances, and they are meant to attract tourism, not to express religious faith.

Outside the public arena is a world of native ritual that belongs to the private, domestic sphere. Aiming at healing natural and supernatural ailments, it centers on the relationship between the magic healer, his or her patient, and the patient's family. The public religion involves mostly Catholic rituals and symbols, but the domestic religion has a primarily pre-Columbian content and deals with the "loss of the soul-companion" (*tonal*), witchcraft, the evil winds, and the evil eye. This is the deepest level of Indian identity, one to which the individual is slowly introduced by his or her elders, as he or she grows, and which may be only partly revealed to foreigners, after years of relationship. The extensive knowledge it involves is considered Indian property, and only Indians can summon the Beings of the Underworld whose aid is needed to cure. As an Indian woman friend once commented, concerning a sick (non-Indian) child: "His mother brought him to the doctor, but it is of no use. He has lost his soul-companion, and doctors don't learn about that in university!"

This brief survey of discourse relating to ethnic identity in the lower Sierra shows that it does divide the cultural continuum at very precise points, these frontiers being generally accepted by both Indians and non-Indians. Culture change affecting the markers will not entail the suppression of the frontier, but rather the redefinition of socially relevant markers. The interethnic border can be crossed, however, in spite of an official discourse to the contrary, as the categories *xalkoyot* (individual transition) and *koparitos* (collective transition) demonstrate. Transfers are always from the Indian to the non-Indian side. The term symbiosis, which has been applied by Siverts to describe interethnic relationships in Mexico, would hardly fit here, for the ethnic division of labor and social production is considered as basically unfair by the Indians (Pérez), and the Indian peasant movements of the 1970s and 1980s were intended to correct the situation.

I propose that the ethnic categories and discourse just described are a means of giving sense to a situation produced by a specific social history. A full demonstration would exceed by far the span of this essay and would necessitate the detailed analysis of the available archival material on regional history (a research still in progress). I will limit myself to some materials taken from oral tradition to illustrate how each of the two main groups, the Nahua Indians and the mestizos, summons the past to explain the present—a process resulting in the constitution of two strong, opposed ethnic identities.

Identity and Ethnohistory: The Nahua

Although there is no formal, centralized apparatus to transmit oral tradition among the Sierra Indians, research undertaken by the Taller de Tradición Oral reveals a huge body of "words from long ago" (*tajtolmej de in uejkaujkayot*) that are passed on, mostly along family lines. For the purpose of this essay I selected four clusters of stories: regarding origins, the French intervention (1862-67), the arrival of the mestizos, and the Revolution (1910-17).

The Nahua from Cuetzalan do not claim to be "born from the land." The oldest stories from their oral tradition tell that they came from the highlands and that Totonac Indians once occupied the area where they now live. Witness to this early history are the pre-Columbian ruins scattered throughout the territory, particularly the spectacular ceremonial center of Yohualichan ("the House of the Night"):

> I saw those men half-naked, as they lived long ago; they had only a loincloth on . . . They dressed the same as those I saw dancing, once, in Mexico, which they call Aztecs: these are our root. Here before, in Yohualichan, there were only Totonac, so they spoke. There is still an underground path that leads from here to Tetelilla [on the Totonac side of the Tozan River]. (Taller I: 4)

> Men who pass by early, going to their fields, can hear the braying of donkeys . . . And the ghost of a woman or something like a priest would be seen at noon and then disappear. At night, you could hear things . . . but as I never went out at night, I heard nothing. (I: 8)

> One night I went watching over my cornfield by the pyramids and I could hear the clap-clap of women

making tortillas. Yet, everybody was asleep in the hamlet
. . . It was the village of Those Who Lived Long Ago
[*uejkaujkayomej*]. (I: 8)

Stories such as these are the cornerstones of native collective
identity. They lay the base of the relationship between the
group and its territory. No explanation is given as to when or
why the Nahua replaced the Totonac: "Our grandfathers and
grandmothers came here . . . " The most important fact is that
the present inhabitants have the proper respect and fear regarding those who lived and, in a way, still live on the land: "I never
went out at night . . . " This is how they spiritually appropriate
the land, while they appropriate it materially by tilling it.

Ethnic identity, however, does not exhaust collective identity.
As I have explained, the basic, daily level is that of the community,
its main symbols being the patron saint and the church, the most
conspicuous building in the village.[15] Another set of native stories
reflects the founding of the community as well as the two main facets of its relationships with the neighboring town of Cuetzalan
(now mestizo, but formerly an Indian community):

First they started to build the church down in Tecolapa
. . . but there is no spring there so they had to go far for
water . . . Some people, maybe the older, or the more
interested, came up here looking for water: it was only
rocks and bush. And they found a large spring and
decided to build the village here. . . . At night you can
see the bats hanging from the rocks of the cave the
water comes from. This is why it was called Tzinacapan
["Spring of the Bats"]. (I: 9)

As for Cuetzalan, the Indians were there and some birds
passed: they were trogons [*kuesaltotot, Trogon mexicanus*].
This is why it is called Cuetzalan, but its real name is
Kuesalan ["Place of the Trogons"]. (I: 2)

They say that at the beginning there was a competition
between Cuetzalan and here [San Miguel Tzinacapan] so
that the first one to finish its church and roof would
become the head of the township. We from San Miguel
finished the walls first, but then we went to the
highlands to bring tiles for the roof. Those from
Cuetzalan started later but when they came to the roof,

they thatched it with *anayo* leaves *[Beilschmedia anay]*: so
they won and became the seat of the municipality. (I: 11)

The preceding text accounts for the present domination of
Cuetzalan, but attributes it to treachery. This sets the structure
that is prevalent as we move from the quasi-mythical "at the beginning" to later periods. The oral tradition is mostly constituted by memories of traumatic events. As can be expected,
there is little about the Spanish conquest (1520), the three centuries of colonial rule, and the Wars of Independence (1810-21),
but there is a lot about the French intervention (1862-67) and the
Revolution (1910-17).

Regarding the conquest and independence, we have the following:

First came the Spaniards but Hidalgo threw them out, he
threw them out. Until now, they never thought of
coming back, but they say that someday they will want
to come back but it will be the same . . . The tale will
remain as it started. . . . Hidalgo threw them out and
won over them. It took him eleven years and eleven
days. I read that in the history book. (I: 11)

In the Sierra, memories of the Spanish conquest and the Wars
of Independence have their roots in the influence of the schools
and the patriotic celebrations such as the fifteenth of September.
What is interesting here is the reinterpretation and reappropriation of the official patriotic discourse, with important differences. The overthrow of the Spaniards is seen as following the
conquest, "after eleven years and eleven days." Hence, "the
Mexican Nation" did not throw the Spanish out, the Indians
did. And logically, Nahua call all Spanish speakers in Mexico today *koyomej* ("foreigners"): they must be descendants of the invaders, whatever their racial traits may be.

As for the nineteenth-century French-Austrian intervention,
and the ill-fated Emperor Maximilian, local tradition is very
much alive, for the area was physically occupied by foreign
troops. Typical stories run as follows:

Then came a man, they say he was an *analteko* ("one
from overseas"). He named himself president. He would
send his people to our villages, to the houses of those

who work the land; and they would take away anything
they found to their offices. This is how the war started.
. . . And we sent them back to the other side of the sea,
we left them on the other side. (II: 1)

After expelling the invaders from the Sierra, natives enrolled in
the rebel army went to fight as far away as Puebla, where they
took part in the famous battle of May 5, 1862.

From the French intervention on, memories of military struggles intertwine with what the Indians see as another kind of invasion: the settlement of many mestizos in the lower Sierra, an
area that had remained almost totally Indian until the middle of
the nineteenth century. Parallels between the two events are
easy to draw, because the regional mestizo elite, like most Mexican Conservatives, took sides with the invaders. The Sierra Lib-
eral leader, Juan Francisco Lucas, was an Indian from Xochia-
pulco, in the high Sierra, and the leader in the lower Sierra was
also an Indian, from Cuetzalan: Francisco Agustín Dieguillo, or
Palagosti. Not only did both events take place at the same time,
but the Indian leader Palagosti later became mayor of Cuetzalan.

Before, there were many Indians in the town of Cuetzalan,
and very few mestizos, not like now. And all houses were
thatched on the whole street. I used to see it when I was
twelve [by 1909-10]. When my father brought me to the
market, we saw only thatched houses. (III: 3)

Palagosti won over the *analtekos*, he pushed them back
where they came from. . . . Juan Francisco Lucas named
Palagosti mayor, yes, an Indian mayor for Cuetzalan so
that he should rule. He would tell the mestizo to do this
and that and he would tell the farmer [i.e., the Indian]
to come and carry a message. . . . Palagosti made the
first town hall and the first church; I still saw that
church. After Palagosti came A. M., who was a mestizo.
First there was an Indian, and then, they were all
mestizos. This is what happened. (III: 1-2)

He [Palagosti] threw the mestizos out of Cuetzalan! But the
man who came after him was a bastard! He let them in
again, for some money, which he spent, and he ended his
life cleaning the park, with his hoe, for the mestizos!*

The two parallel fights of the second half of the nineteenth century did not have the same outcome. The *analtekos* were defeated and "pushed . . . back where they came from"; the mestizos not only remained but saw their power increase. The Indian hero's behavior is not called into question: "He kicked out the mestizos as he had kicked out the invaders" (III: 1).[16] Some informants accuse an unnamed "successor" of betrayal to the Indian cause, but most point to economic factors:

> Then came the Gs. [a well-known mestizo family]. They set up their coffee-processing plant, they brought in big machines. All those mestizos that are not from here came to Cuetzalan. They bought coffee, then, and they hulled it with their hulling-mills. And after the mestizos came, even Indians who had money started to buy their own mills and hull their coffee. But we who are always poor, we can't make ends meet, well we never got any better. And those who always have money, they would deceive us, they would cheat us with their scales when we sold them our coffee. (III: 3)

> The elders tell us that many people, whom they called *ajkopauanij* [highlanders], came to Cuetzalan. They would say: "Lend me your home [i.e., house site] and go work in the fields. I will take care of it. Don't worry. When you come back, it will always be yours." Our brothers believed them . . . Many years passed. When they wanted their homes back, some were good-hearted and gave them back. Others answered: "The house is mine, now. Because the law says if I am here so many years, the property is mine." (III: 4-5)

Oral tradition relating to the second half of the nineteenth century gives some of the crucial "reference events" that shape the Nahua ethnic consciousness up to now: Indians fought for the land against all invaders, whether they were Spanish, French, or mestizos. The mestizos stayed, though, in spite of Palagosti's second battle, and expropriated the Indians from the town of Cuetzalan, the seat of the municipality. Indians withdrew to the villages and hamlets, thus fixing the present-day territorial pattern.

In the case of the Revolution, the situation is at first sight more complex. Indians refer to the partisans of Pancho Villa as the "foreigners," but all handbooks of Mexican history have described them as *the* authentic revolutionaries fighting against landlords and foreign capital!

> The Villistas carried away your mules, your bulls if they caught them, your poncho, and of course your money. They stole the turkeys where you had them. They reached for women and abused them. (IV: 4)

> Salvador Vega was Villista; they were thieves because they robbed things. They raped women, they caught them. We were afraid of them. We had to hide, in the bush, in the mountains. (IV: 8)

> Then those from here went to see General Barrios and told him: "Give us arms!" . . . And after we were armed, we would catch them [the Villistas] wherever we found them and because we knew them, we killed them. This was their end. (IV: 12)

In the Sierra de Puebla, then, some Cuetzalan mestizos took arms under the banner of *Villismo*. Salvador Vega, for example, was the son of a wealthy cane-grower and rum-distiller. The main activity of the Villistas seems to have been rape and plunder in the surrounding villages. Indians allied themselves with another revolutionary caudillo, Rufino Barrios, a follower of Venustiano Carranza, and obtained military supplies that enabled them to fight back successfully. (They were undoubtedly helped by the fact that at the national level, Carranza succeeded in eliminating his opponents and became president.)

Identity and Oral Tradition: The Mestizo Story

Mestizos from Cuetzalan and Zacapoaxtla have their own oral tradition regarding regional history. Rather indifferent to mythical origins (with one exception), they have their own accounts of the French intervention, the impact of their own arrival, the works and deeds of the "first Indian mayor," and the Revolution. The following excerpts come from interviews with two elderly aristocrats, one *cuetzalteca* and one *zacapoaxteco*:

> The name Cuetzalan comes from the fact that in the old

Indian days there were beautiful quetzal birds
[*Pharomachrus mocinno*] around. The Indians used the
feathers for their headdresses, when they danced.*

The French army committed many misdemeanors in the
region. This is why you find so many blue-eyed people in
Xocoyolo: the French soldiers raped many women there.*

Juan Francisco Lucas is an Indian who started a "caste
war" of the Indian race against the *gente de razón* in the
Sierra.*

Palagosti had helped Lucas fight against the French. As a
reward he was named mayor by Lucas and then, he
started to build a town hall. You guess how he made it?
With a thatched roof! Because he did not know any better.*

Regarding the arrival of the mestizos and the spread of cash
cropping, sugarcane, and coffee, the elderly *cuetzalteca* recalls:

My grandfather was a hard worker, a very religious and
good-hearted man. He is the one who brought coffee here.
It was given to him by a priest, in Oaxaca. He worked so
hard on his farm, planting and weeding, at times he did
not even eat. He promised the Virgin of Ocotlán to build
her a sanctuary if he succeeded. He saw the poverty of the
little Indians [*inditos*]. So he started to give them coffee
plants, for free, so that they could work and get some
money. And he would buy their grain. This is how he
slowly became better off. And he kept his promise and
built for Our Lady the Sanctuary of the Little Jars.*

During the Revolution, armed bands of revolutionaries
roamed through the countryside. They took the town of
Zacapoaxtla and used the town hall as a stable for their
horses.*

Cuetzalan remained quiet because of General Rufino
Barrios. He is also the one who made our nice main
square during those years. Some progress-loving mayors
built our beautiful town hall and had the streets paved.
And our new church was built following the model of
Saint Peter's Church in Rome. This is why our town was
called: Cuetzalan del Progreso.*

Conclusion: Ethnic Identity as Process

We have seen how, on a synchronic level, ethnic identities in the lower Sierra can be defined by a set of cultural markers, which appear to be arbitrarily selected from the wide array of cultural traits: language, work, clothing, and ritual, rather than "race" or food. This *apparent* arbitrariness of the markers and the frontier they set has led anthropologists to conclude that the traits selected *are in fact* arbitrary and that the only thing that counts is the setting of a frontier. For the functionalists who follow Barth, the rationale of ethnicity is ultimately ecological-economic: the optimum division of natural resources between human groups. This led them to conclude that mestizo/Indian relationships in Mexico are of a stable, "symbiotic" type, transcending historical events. Marxist anthropologists do take history into account, but the same apparent arbitrariness of ethnic emblems induced most of them to consider ethnic identity as one more form of "false consciousness" whose function is to hide class exploitation (both intra- and interethnic) from the oppressed majority. Whatever their differences may be, both schools thus considered ethnic identity as a *sign* of a hidden, more important reality.

Partisans of the hermeneutics of culture took an entirely different path and stated that ethnic markers and discourse define an *essence*, that is, the sharing of a common set of symbols that characterizes a "persistent people." This essence is given as ahistoric, not affected by social and economic changes, as shown by the already-mentioned metaphor of the "superorganic system."

Neither ecology, class, nor symbol-sharing alone is of much use for the understanding of ethnic identity in the lower Sierra Norte de Puebla. Each group has constructed its pattern of identity in the course of a long process of interaction with the Other. To take only two examples, Indian men adopted their present garb at the beginning of the twentieth century, that is, approximately when mestizos stopped wearing it, and mestizos ostentatiously underplay their sharing of "Indian" beliefs and practices concerning the supernatural. Rather than being an "essence" that would unfold through history, ethnic identity is thus the result of an (unconscious) process of *constructing difference*, a process that includes as a central element the permanent structuring of collective memory along two opposite lines.

Far from symbiotic, the relationships between Indians and mestizos have been marked by permanent tensions and intermittent outbreaks of violence. For more than a century, both groups have competed for land, the basic resource. More recently, lower Sierra Indians eagerly excluded mestizos from the food trade by organizing a regional cooperative along ethnic lines (Martínez Borrego). Would ethnicity then be a mere concealment of class conflict? The dynamics of old and recent struggles do not support this view. The lower Sierra movement succeeded in good part because it united a majority of Indians, the poor and the better-off alike, while a class movement in the upper Sierra collapsed (Beaucage 1987b).

I share Boege's and Schryer's position to the effect that the only operational approach to identity has to integrate economic, political, and ethnocultural dimensions into a historical perspective. Even if a satisfactory account of regional history in the Sierra is still lacking, I hope that the few examples taken from the oral tradition of both groups have shown how ethnic identities were shaped by certain traumatic events that happened during the past 150 years (primarily the French intervention and the Revolution) as well as by structural changes (the arrival of the mestizos in Cuetzalan and the spread of cash cropping). In conclusion, contrary to the high Sierra, where interethnic contact was permanent since the seventeenth century (García Martínez), regular mestizo/Indian relationships in the lower Sierra first occurred in a context of armed confrontation in which the two took opposite sides—first in 1862, and again in 1910. The penetration of cash cropping and the extension of commerce shifted conflict to the economic sphere. Cultural markers and ethnohistory served to define and explain persistent opposition.

There is a common structure in the long narratives recounted by elders from both groups about a violent past: the continuous, all-encompassing conflict between natives and mestizos. The Indians claim and demonstrate through their vision of history that they are the area's legitimate inhabitants and that the mestizos are dishonest intruders. Mestizos use their own version of the same facts to show that they bring progress to a stubborn, ignorant race, only to be paid back with ungratefulness, when not with sorcery.

Both groups are confident about the outcome of this dubious, protracted battle. Mestizos see "progress spreading to the most remote hamlets," although they note with some awe that this is increasing rather than decreasing Indian self-consciousness:

> The "little Indian" [*indito*] is the one that grows his corn and coffee on his farm. He works and comes to the market and creates no problems. The Indian [*indio*] is the one who, half-studied, thinks he is a kind of lawyer [*licenciadillo*] and creates all kinds of trouble!*

While Nahua elders do complain about the loss of some of the old ways, they find that their present situation is relatively much better:

> Our grandfathers were a bit stupid [*xoxitos*]. Today's youngsters are cunning, they carry their machete or their gun in their belt. But then, the old men killed themselves working and didn't even buy a good weapon. This is why the mestizos despised them. They saw them as dogs, in their poor clothes, and they hated them. (II: 2)

History shows that the content of Indian identity in the Sierra has varied according to the contexts, just as that of the opossum, the clever trickster of myths and tales. And does not the myth predict final victory to this opossum over its powerful rivals from the forest?

> Then the coyote said: "This damned one, we will never eat him. It is better to leave him like that or he might eat us. We did everything to him and it was of no use. He is small and we are big but we can't overcome him. We set a trap and did not catch him; we set poisoned eggs and he did not eat them; we called a hunter and he threw himself into the river and escaped. What can we do? Let us leave him alone, it will be better." And this is how they let him in peace, they could not kill him. Here ends the story. (Rodríguez 38)

Notes

This essay is based on a long-term research project carried on in the Sierra Norte de Puebla by the author since 1969. This work has been financed primarily by the Canadian Social Science Research Council. From 1984 on, an intensive study was carried on in the Nahua village of San Miguel Tzinacapan, near Cuetzalan in the lower Sierra, in collaboration with the Taller de Tradición Oral del CEPEC. This group, based in San Miguel Tzinacapan, includes Indians and mestizos and has been devoted for more than ten years to the recollection, transcription, translation, and publication of local oral tradition. Our joint research, still in progress, has dealt mostly with ethnoscience and, since 1988, with ethnohistory. We investigated local archives, both in San Miguel and in Cuetzalan, the township *cabecera*. In Cuetzalan another research team was set up, composed of Mrs. Carolina Ramírez, Mr. Pablo Valderrama, and Mr. Gabriel Jaimez. I want to thank the local authorities, Mr. Agustín Ramiro and Edgardo González, successive mayors of Cuetzalan, as well as Mr. Agustín Alvarez and Mr. Blas González, auxiliary mayors of San Miguel, for their precious cooperation. I am also extremely grateful to Mrs. Ema Flores, keeper of the Cuetzalan archives, and to Lic. Blanca del Raso, director of the history department at the Universidad Autónoma de Puebla, who kindly recommended me to the municipal authorities of Libres so that I could complete the archival research.

1. Rodríguez 20-22. All translations are my own unless otherwise indicated.

2. Ethnocentrism seems to be a universal corollary of ethnic identity and, as such, long preceded the development of capitalism. The Aztecs, for example, referred to two distinct southern groups as *Popoluca* or "stutterers," and to the northern nomadic hunters and gatherers as *Chichimeca* or "sons of dogs." The so-called Eskimo named themselves *inuit*, "the people," and called Southern Indians *inkrelet*, "lice."

3. "It is essentially out of contacts involving dominance of one people over another that counter-acculturative movements arise—those movements wherein a people come to stress the values in aboriginal ways of life, and to move aggressively, either factually or in fantasy, towards the restoration of those ways, even in the face of obvious evidence of their impotence to throw off the powers that restrict them" (Herskovits 531). He then lists as examples, side by side, the Ghost Dance of the Prairie Indians, "the rise of organized labour in various parts of Africa," the Gandhi movement, and the "Vailala Madness" in New Guinea!

4. Such a classification, which obviously owes much to historical materialism, is considered here for its heuristic value, without implying acceptance en bloc of the Marxist philosophy of history.

5. A similarly conflictual redefinition of ethnic identities and boundaries could be observed in Spain after Franco's death, particularly in the eastern provinces of Catalonia, Valencia, and Alicante. For the inhabitants of Barcelona, the largest city, the whole area is one, "because we all speak Catalan." But most *Valenciás* and *Alicantís* stress their differences from the all-too-dominating Barcelonese—from speech to style of life, from cuisine to history (see Beaucage 1990).

6. Didn't Voltaire write "Qui se soucie de quelques arpents de neige?" ("Who cares about a few acres of snow?")?

7. The Sierra Norte de Puebla presents itself as a transition zone between the central highlands, flat and dry, and the warm lowlands of the Gulf coast. Extremely rugged but very fertile because of a ten-month rainy season, the area has constituted one of many "refuge zones" for the Indian population after the

Spanish conquest. Two ethnic groups are found there: the Nahua, whose habitat stretches from the highlands to the lower mountain range, and the Totonac, concentrated in the latter area and in the adjacent lowlands of Veracruz. The Indian population of the Sierra for 1980 was estimated at over 260,000, including about 200,000 Nahua, 60,000 Totonac, and 1,000 Otomi. [My figures are based on the data presented by Valdés and Menéndez, and the *X Censo General de Población y Vivienda, 1980, Estado de Puebla* (Instituto Nacional de Estadística, Geografía e Informática 1983, T 21: 582-600).] I made a correction of +14.7 percent to include children under five years, who are systematically omitted from Mexican figures on Indian population (Beaucage 1987a). Nahua Indians in the Sierra speak two dialectal varieties: Nahuatl to the north (Huauchinango-Xicotepec area) and Nahuat to the south (Zacapoaxtla-Cuetzalan-Teziutlan area). Following actual Mexican usage, I will refer to the people as Nahua, and to the languages as either Nahuatl or Nahuat, respectively. Throughout the area, Indian and mestizo farmers grow corn, beans, squash, and some vegetables and fruit, and keep poultry and pigs for subsistence. In the high Sierra (about 2,000 meters above sea level), this farming is complemented by growing some fruit for sale (avocado pears, apples, plums) and, traditionally, by seasonal labor migration to the coast. In the lower Sierra (500 to 1,000 meters above sea level), coffee is the main cash crop, and the large majority of peasants depend on it to buy corn and satisfy other basic needs. Non-Indians are a minority in most of the Sierra and usually dwell in the small township centers (*cabeceras municipales*) where they live off commerce and trades; the wealthier of them control business and local administration, and own plantations and pastureland in the surrounding countryside. These holdings, although they can be considered small by Mexican standards, contrast with the tiny plots of the peasants, most of whom are Indians. For example, in Cuetzalan in 1970, 45 percent of farmers owned less than one hectare, and another 41 percent had slightly over two hectares. At the other end of the spectrum, six owners had a combined total of 1,500 hectares (Dirección General de Estadística 63, 75). Between one-quarter and one-third of Indian farmers in a given community own no land and work as sharecroppers and farmhands. For a detailed analysis of the social and economic structures of the Sierra, see Arizpe; Beaucage 1973a and b; Chamoux; Durand; Masferrer Kan; Paré.

8. The word *maseual* is related to classic Nahuatl *macehualli*: "retainer" according to Molina (50 v. ff.) and "retainer, commoner, peasant, subject" according to Siméon (216). Etymologically, the word comes from *maseua* ("to merit," i.e., from the gods). At the time of the Spanish conquest, *macehualli* referred to the social class of the free peasants, who were organized in landowning communities under the ruler (*tecuhtli*) and noble (*pilli*). Classes also included merchants (*pochtecatl*), serfs (*mayectli, tlalmaitl*), and slaves (*tlacotli*). After the conquest, the term *maseual* took both an ethnic and a social meaning: "Indian of the lowest condition, . . . servant, day laborer" (Santamaría 673). The derogatory Nahuat term *metsxipetstik* ("barefooted") refers to the fact that until the twentieth century Totonac men went barefoot, while Nahua men always wore sandals. The origin of the actual Nahuat meaning of *koyot* is not clear. In his classic work on Mexican Spanish, Santamaría relates that in colonial days *coyote* referred to the person born from the union of a mestizo man and an Indian woman (225). After independence the word's meaning changed: "About 1828, when anti-

Spanish hatred reached a peak, they [the Spaniards] were injuriously given the nickname of *coyotes*" (308). In rural Mexico today, *coyote* is a very derogatory term that refers to the middleman who buys the farmer's crop. In Indian lore, the rabbit and the coyote form a pair, the deceiver and the deceived respectively; they are often replaced in those roles by the opossum and the jaguar. See López Austin's in-depth study of native animal symbolism.

9. In abstract terms, natives of the lower Sierra will tend to associate a *koyot* with European physical traits (light skin, fair hair, and clear-colored eyes). When asked to classify an individual as belonging to one or the other category, however, no informant ever referred to physical criteria, stressing cultural markers alone: "They speak Nahuat at home," "He wears Indian dress," and so on. Our research therefore contradicts Nutini and Isaac's assertion that in the Sierra de Puebla "Indians accept their position of cultural subordination, attributing it to inescapable somatic factors" (384).

10. Quotations marked with an asterisk are from interviews conducted by myself. The others come from a large corpus of data collected by the Taller de Tradición Oral de San Miguel Tzinacapan in the State of Puebla. Much of this information is presently being published in a book on ethnohistory that has been compiled by the Taller, now in press (referred to as "Taller"). I was allowed to consult the manuscript to which the references are made; the Roman numeral is that of the chapter, followed by the page number. References to parts of the corpus yet unpublished are indicated as "Taller ms."

11. A classic question to check a non-Indian's fluency in Nahuat is ¡*Xinech-taneuj mouelti*! ("Lend me your sister!"); there are also much coarser ones. The linguistic incompetence of foreigners, particularly wealthy gringos who are fooled by clever Indians, is a recurrent theme in oral literature.

12. The Nahua community of San Miguel Tzinacapan has been the center of interesting experiments in alternative teaching, using Nahuat as an instrument of communication at school as well as the first language for reading and writing, from kindergarten to high school (see Toumi; Troianni; Reynoso). A similar approach is now being utilized by the National Institute for Adult Education (INEA) in both Nahua and Totonac areas.

13. In Mexico City, to the saleswoman who asked us, "That strange language you speak, is it English?" my friend Pablo answered angrily: "We speak Nahuat! The language of the Aztecs!"

14. For a detailed analysis of the category "work/labor" among the Nahua of the lower Sierra, see Beaucage 1989.

15. The central place-names, in the village of San Miguel, are given by their position to the church: *tiopantenoj* ("in front of the church"), *tiopanikan* ("behind the church"), *tiopantitan* ("below the church"), and so on (Zamora Islas 30).

16. Our research in the Cuetzalan archives, still in progress, will shed some light on the social history of the lower Sierra, especially regarding this crucial period. For Palagosti's role, as seen from the Zacapoaxtla archives, see Thomson's interesting article.

Works Cited

Aguirre Beltrán, Gonzalo. "Indigenismo en México; confrontación de problemas." *Anuario indigenista* 29 (1970): 280-306. Reprinted in *La quiebra política de la antropología social en México*. Ed. A. Medina and Carlos García Mora. Mexico City: Universidad Nacional Autónoma de México, 1983. 195-212.

Arizpe, Lourdes. *Parentesco y economía en una sociedad nahua*. Mexico City: Instituto Nacional Indigenista, 1973.

Aschman, Peter. *Vocabulario totonaco de la Sierra*. Mexico City: Instituto Lingüístico de Verano/Secretaría de Educación Pública, 1962.

Barth, Fredrik, ed. *Ethnic Groups and Boundaries: The Social Organization of Cultural Difference*. London: Allen & Unwin, 1969.

Bartra, Roger. "El problema indígena y la ideología indigenista." *Revista mexicana de Sociología* 36, 3 (1974): 459-482.

Beaucage, Pierre. "Anthropologie économique des communautés indigènes de la Sierra Norte de Puebla (Mexique). 1. Les villages de basse montagne." *Revue canadienne de sociologie et d'anthropologie* 10, 1 (1973a): 114-133.

_____. "Anthropologie économique des communautés indigènes de la Sierra Norte de Puebla (Mexique). 2. Les villages de haute montagne." *Revue canadienne de sociologie et d'anthropologie* 10, 3 (1973b): 289-307.

_____. "Démographie, culture, politique: la condition indienne au Mexique." *Anthropologie et sociétés* 11, 2 (1987a): 13-31.

_____. "Les identités indiennes: folklore ou facteur de transformation." *Construction/destruction sociale des idées: alternances, récurrences, nouveautés*. Ed. B. Dumas and D. Winslow. Montreal: Cahiers de l'ACSALF, 1987b. 23-42.

_____. "L'effort et la vie: ethnosémantique du travail chez les Garifonas du Honduras et les Maseuals (Nahuats) du Mexique." *Travail, capital et société* 22, 1 (1989): 112-137.

_____. "Fragments de miroirs: l'identité ethnique, parole et travail." *Possibles* 14, 3 (1990): 13-28.

Boege, Eckart. *Los mazatecos ante la nación. Contradicciones de la identidad étnica en el México actual*. Mexico City, Siglo veintiuno, 1988.

Bonfil Batalla, Guillermo, et al. *América latina: etnodesarrollo y etnocidio*. San José, Costa Rica: FLACSO, 1982.

Castile, George P. "Issues in the Analysis of Enduring Cultural Systems." Castile and Kushner. ix-xxii.

_____, and Gilbert Kushner, eds. *Persistent Peoples: Cultural Enclaves in Perspective*. Tucson: Univ. of Arizona Press, 1981.

Chabot, Claire. "Le tissage d'un quechquemitl." *Recherches amérindiennes au Québec* 11, 1 (1981): 56-61.

Chamoux, Marie-Noëlle. *Indiens de la Sierra*. Paris: L'Harmattan, 1981.

Córdoba Olivares, Francisco. *Los totonacos de la región de Huehuetla* (ms.). Mexico City: Instituto Nacional Indigenista, 1966.

Deverre, Christian. *Indiens ou paysans*? Paris: Sycomore, 1980.

Díaz Polanco, Héctor. "La teoría indigenista y la integración." *Indigenismo, modernización y marginalidad: una revisión crítica*. By H. Díaz Polanco et al. Mexico City: Juan Pablos, 1979. 9-46.

Dirección General de Estadística. *Censo Agricola, Ganadero y Ejidal 1970*. Puebla. Mexico City: Secretaría de Industria y Comercio, 1975.

Dolan, Claire. "Introduction: identité, histoire et événement." *Evénement, identité et histoire*. Ed. Claire Dolan. Quebec: Septentrion, 1990. 9-24.

THE OPOSSUM AND THE COYOTE ◆ 185

Durand, Pierre. *Lutte de classes et paysannerie au Mexique*. Montreal: Presses de l'Université de Montréal, 1975.

García Martínez, Bernardo. *Los pueblos de la Sierra. El poder y el espacio entre los indios del norte de Puebla hasta 1700*. Mexico City: El Colegio de México, 1987.

González, Nancie L. *Sojourners of the Caribbean: Ethnogenesis and Ethnohistory of the Garifuna*. Urbana: Univ. of Illinois Press, 1988.

Herskovits, Melville. *Man and His Works: The Science of Cultural Anthropology*. New York: Knopf, 1951.

Ichon, Alain. *La religion des Totonaques de la Sierra*. Paris: Centre national de la recherche scientifique, 1969.

Instituto Nacional de Estadística, Geografía e Informática. *X Censo General de Población y Vivienda, 1980, Estado de Puebla*. Mexico City: Secretaría de Programación y Presupuesto 21, 1, 1983.

Jacob, Annie. *L'Indien des Anglais, l'Indien des Français. Images comparées*. Ms., 1985.

Johnson, I. W. "Quechquemitl y huipil." *Huastecos, totonacos y sus vecinos*. Ed. I. Bernal and E. Dávalos. Mexico City: Sociedad Mexicana de Antropología, 1953. 241-258.

Kandt, Vera. "Artesanía e indumentaria en la región de Cuetzalan en la región de la Sierra Norte de Puebla." *Artes de México* 155 (1972): 75-95.

Labelle, Micheline. *Idéologie de couleur et classes sociales en Haïti*. Montreal: Presses de l'Université de Montréal, 1978.

Labrousse, Alain. *Le réveil indien en Amérique latine*. Paris: Favre, 1985.

López Austin, Alfredo. *Los mitos del tlacuache*. Mexico City: Alianza Editorial Mexicana, 1990.

Martínez Borrego, Estela. *Organización de productores y movimiento campesino*. Mexico City: Siglo veintiuno, 1991.

Masferrer Kan, Elio. "Campesinización y expansión capitalista: los cafecultores de la Sierra Norte de Puebla." *Boletín E.C.A.U.D.Y.* 9, 50-51 (1981): 32-42.

Matos Moctezuma, Eduardo. *Ideas acerca del origen del hombre americano (1570-1916)*. Mexico City: Secretaría de Educación Pública, 1987.

Molina, Fray Alonso de. *Vocabulario en lengua mexicana y castellana . . .* Facsimile of 1571 edition. Mexico City: Porrúa, 1970.

Nutini, Hugo G., and Barry L. Isaac. *Los pueblos de habla nahuatl de la región de Tlaxcala y Puebla*. Mexico City: Instituto Nacional Indigenista, 1974.

Paré, Louise. "Caciquisme et structure du pouvoir dans le Mexique rural." *Revue canadienne de sociologie et d'anthropologie* 10, 1 (1973): 20-43.

Pérez, José de la Cruz. "Eyi iknimej momachtikej koyotajtol/Tres hermanos aprendieron español." *Maseualsanilmej 5, Cuentos indígenas de la región de San Miguel Tzinacapan*. San Miguel Tzinacapan, Cuetzalan, Puebla: Taller de Tradición Oral del CEPEC, 1986. 6-21.

Pozas, Ricardo, and Isabel H. de Pozas. *Los indios en las clases sociales de México*. Mexico City: Siglo veintiuno, 1971.

Reynoso, Alfonso. *Educación, revalorización cultural y etnodesarrollo. Interpretación de una experiencia en tres comunidades indias de México*. Université de Montréal (Anthropology), M.A. thesis, 1988.

Rodríguez, Porfirio. "Takuatsin/El tlacuache." *Maseualsanilmej. 3 Cuentos indígenas de la región de San Miguel Tzinacapan, Pue.* San Miguel Tzinacapan, Cuetzalan, Puebla: Taller de Tradición Oral del CEPEC, 1985. 20-39.

Roosens, Eugeen E. *Creating Ethnicity: The Process of Ethnogenesis.* Newbury Park, Calif.: Sage, 1989.

Ryser, Rudolph C. "Nation-States, Indigenous Nations and the Great Lie." *Pathways to Self-Determination: Canadian Indians and the Canadian State.* Ed. Leroy Little Bear, Menno Boldt, and J. Anthony Long. Toronto: Univ. of Toronto Press, 1984. 27-35.

Sánchez, María Eugenia. *Temps, espace et changement social. Perspectives à partir de la communauté indigène de San Miguel Tzinacapan.* Paris: Centre d'études coopératives/EHESS (M.A. thesis), 1978.

Santamaría, Francisco. *Diccionario de mejicanismos.* Mexico City: Porrúa, 1959.

Schryer, Frans J. *Ethnicity and Class Conflict in Rural Mexico.* Princeton: Princeton Univ. Press, 1990.

Siméon, Rémi. *Dictionnaire de la langue nahuatl ou mexicaine.* Facsimile of the 1885 edition. Graz, Austria: Academische Druck-U. Verlagsanstalt, 1965.

Siverts, Henning. "Ethnic Stability and Boundary Dynamics in Southern Mexico." Barth 1969. 101-116.

Taller de Tradición Oral del CEPEC. *Nikininkakiltiaya toabuelitos . . . /Yo les oía decir a los abuelitos . . . Etnohistoria nahuat de San Miguel Tzinacapan, Pue.* Mexico City: Instituto Nacional de Antropología e Historia, forthcoming.

Thomson, Guy P. C. "Agrarian Conflict in the Municipality of Cuetzalan (Sierra de Puebla): The Rise and Fall of 'Pala' Agustín Dieguillo, 1861-1894." *Hispanic American Historical Review* 71, 2 (1991): 205-258.

Toumi, Sybille. "Las dificultades que surgen al escribir el nahuatl moderno." *Por una educación contra el etnocidio.* By D. Troianni et al. Paris: Association d'ethnolinguistique amérindienne. Chantiers Amérindia, Suppl. 2-9, 1984. 85-93.

Troianni, Duna. "El caso de un rincón de la Sierra indígena de Puebla que se ha convertido en una zona piloto en cuanto a experimentos educativos bilingües-biculturales." *Por una educación contra el etnocidio.* By D. Troianni et al. Paris: Association d'ethnolinguistique amérindienne. Chantiers Amérindia, Suppl. 2-9, 1984. 5-15.

Valdés, María Luz, and Maria Teresa Menéndez. *Dinámica de la población de habla indígena 1900-1980.* Mexico City: Instituto Nacional de Antropología e Historia, 1987.

Wagley, Charles, ed. *Race and Class in Rural Brazil.* Paris: UNESCO, 1952.

_____, and Marvin Harris. *Minorities in the New World: Six Case Studies.* New York: Columbia Univ. Press, 1964.

Wankar (Ramiro Reynaga). *Tawantinsuyu. Cinco siglos de guerra Qheshuaymara contra España.* Mexico City: Nueva Imagen, 1981.

Zamora Islas, Eliseo. *Tzinacapan: toponimia y agricultura.* Paris: Association d'ethnolinguistique amérindienne. Chantiers Amérindia, 1983.

◆ Chapter 9

A Caribbean Social Imaginary: Redoubled Notes on Critical-Fiction against the Gaze of Ulysses

Iris M. Zavala

There is evidence, which still needs refinement, to show that some New World cultures are bookish, that cultural idioms have often included conflictive perceptions, and that tropes have cultural and social meanings. Swans, minotaurs, centaurs, Moloch, Mnemosyne, and a conch have helped redefine a family of concepts—subject, self, nation, liberation, future—in areas of the Caribbean. In fact, the probing of these cultural meanings would lead from the dictionary to an entire encyclopedia of allusion. Compelled toward the oblique by the fear of suture and closure by political circumstances, the still-to-be constructed new worlds have reaccentuated competing models of the social cohesion of ideals in order to assign them new values and projects for the future, which indicates that these societies—and I will refer only to the Caribbean—are bookish or "grammatological" to the root.

The cultural and political reticence or erosive conventionality of imperialist regimes, with their well-established canons of imaginative domesticity, have helped release many energies of symbolic vehemence that redefine the true cartographies of lands whose familial tone had been one of exotism or darkness to metropolitan readers, who wished to be at home in a domesticated space in order to enhance their feverish grandeur. There are several reasons why the Caribbean Other has often been portrayed as the night of deepened doom or the space of madness in the colonial imaginary, under volcanoes or in hearts of darkness, according to imperialist tropes. Strikingly, these fictions look back to the civilizing grandiosities and dreams of unpairing reason that reinforced the violence, mendacities, and savageries of the conquest in the dawn of our modern worlds.

"To the point, please . . . "

Why have imperialist regimes flinched at poems that mark the vulnerability of their authority in the vast geographical space of the Caribbean? ("Hey! Watch it! That's moving far too fast." "Okay! I'll slow down.") One way of answering would be that the extensive and polysemic space of that region, whose mundane discourses have been thoroughly heteroglossic, multiplies its meaning in the energizing field of association and connotation with the myriad openness of the over and undertone. ("Keep 'em rolling!") To sharpen the terms, imperialisms (since Columbus placed the imperial banner of Castile and Leon in Hispaniola five centuries ago) manifest themselves in their difference there (or here, depending on where you are located) through the multiplicity of languages and the various dialects that have claimed linguistic imposition.

I will not try to treat here the large number of propositions concerning imperialism, which the heterogeneity of the Caribbean makes very obvious in both colonial false imaginary identities and patriarchal masteries, and in which gender and sexual constructs are not lacking since the famous letters of Vespucci in 1503-4.[1] At best, one proceeds tentatively. To try to reconstitute the systematic unity of the different forms of imperialism and colonialism in the modern world since 1492, one would have to be able to master the parodic heterogeneity of the different styles. The graphics of the histories of imperialism, colonization, and consolidation of nation-states and national identities have also been written against the custodian of the holiness of purity, with the echo and alloy of Caribbean heteroglossia. Call imperialisms *the gaze of Ulysses.*

Contingent difficulties are the more visible here in languages interwoven with sentiment and allusion, as befits identities that are the heirs of romanticism and Rousseau, with the ecstasies and ebbing sensualities of this culture of tears and feeling. Romanticism was the chief vehicle here for the revolutionary adoption of modernity's requirements in order to emphasize the self's quest for identity. Set against varying backdrops of wars and revolutions of national identity in the romantic age, grandiose scenes of nature and the self, empirical truths of cultural identity, and the complex and difficult relationship between language and experience played an unexpected and uncanny role. In the heart of this romantic self and identity was the whole liberating thrust of the culture of tears. Reaccentuated in the Caribbean, feeling is the very essence of the relationship to the outside in a dialectic of identity and desire. I could venture further and suggest that identities were imagined, poetically experienced, and projected, striving for the partiality of each special point of view.

From an outer edge, these poetically imagined identities also reflect modern colonial barbarism, the widespread silencing of political life, the programmatic degradation of the human person in the colonial atmosphere, and the energies of the inhuman colonial wars. The colonial-determined, uptight atavisms of a self-enclosing decorum have often been discredited in order to provoke outrage. Modern literature has produced a number of remarkable realizations that can hardly be touched on in a brief survey. We need not commit a heresy in order to point out that the Caribbean writers have often been master welders of poetry to politics against imperial paradigms and the empirical actuality of power.

From the interrogations of the first cartographers of identity (Julia de Burgos, Alejo Carpentier, Aimé Césaire, Nicolás Guillén, Frantz Fanon, Luis Palés Matos, Jacques Roumain) to the next generation (Jacques Stephan Alexis, Edouard Glissant, V. S. Naipaul, Derek Walcott, Roberto Fernández Retamar, and the gendered mappings of Michelle Cliff, Nancy Morejón, and myself, among others), the delegitimization of imperialism has been linked to a reconnection of shame and self-determination, and was in some cases relegated to mimicry and ambivalence of language. Inversion has been, I believe, a way of grounding identities: metalepsis is one name Zavala has given to this responsibility.

Apolonia[2] has always insisted that the most serious things are treated here by allowing a necessary play and irony to come to light, against the gravely somber tone of the closed door of authoritarian monadology. ("In hell, she often argues, no one laughs." "But she loves to shock me!") I have still not found hard supportive data to prove her wrong. Laughter bursts out, she often says, adorned with all the violence of refusal. Part 1 of her narrative ends with the description of a state of affairs in which her native audience could not laugh. It was called slavery.

Because this metalepsis marks all possible meanings, the Caribbean dialogical social imaginary has gone deeper to reflect modern barbarism. In the hundred years following the Wars of Independence, which originated in Haiti in 1804, we have moved to a prodigal element of liberatory imagining beyond the long history of allegoric indirection written under the pressure of totalitarian colonial censorship (I am directly referring to Betances, Hostos, Martí, Lola Rodríguez de Tió, and that powerful generation of anticolonial struggle). The "logical terrorists" (to politicize a term used by George Steiner) have reanimated and reaccentuated semantic and grammatical resources in order to project political fantasies against the Manichaean allegories of the colonizers (see JanMohamed). As writing is implied by the successive others, epistemic metaphors are literally folded into different shapes, yet without losing their "aura" in the process.

The organic reaccentuation in intricate twists of mythology and previous poetry, topographical and chronological markers, literacies, the recognition of the unsaid quote or carnivalized pastiche, and the grasp of connoting and condensing, conditions these open-ended texts against the formal enclosure of fixed and sutured identities approved by stale colonial norms. Secondhandedness is the paradigm often used in a reductive domestication to actualize imperialist cultural power. For us, colonialism and subject formation converge implacably.

National identities are indissolubly linked to "narrating" undecidabilities against the inhabited fixed world of colonial fictions. Since the dawn of modernity, the Caribbean colonial and postcolonial culture has fought against the imperial ideology's negation of the possibility of the colonized world and its cultures to create their own destiny. The reductive subaltern passive subject—imaginary and composite—is a product of monological discourse, aiming at a monolithical uniform dependency, essentially unmodifiable. In fact, monology is the political fantasy of the colonialist imaginary. In this emancipatory venture, art has been an important agent in the transmission of culture, patterning the ways by which human beings are supposed to fulfill their roles.

In the general symbolic economy of Caribbean "knowable communities" (redirecting Raymond Williams's coinage) so different from each other in this sea of many lands and languages, the circulation of cultural material has often been unpredictable and highly disturbing. Modernism, for example (and I now limit myself to the Hispanic Caribbean), as a mode of cultural production, reaccentuated and reimagined a joint history even within the powerful constraints created by colonial fragmentation and geographical diversity.[3]

The famous *Letter from Jamaica* written by Simón Bolívar as an exile in Curaçao and Haiti in the 1830s is but part of a legitimizing claim of this community to an Antillean Confederation. This political imaginary took form in 1865 with the confederation of Cuba, Santo Domingo, and Puerto Rico, which expressed a myriad of desires, augmenting the emotional force of a shared community. In 1869 the emancipatory newspaper *La Revolución*, published in New York by the Antillean insurrectionists, wrote:

> What a wonderful spectacle will be offered to the American hemisphere by the republics of Cuba, Puerto Rico, Santo Domingo and Haiti, forming three distinct nationalities, linked in brotherhood by the bonds of democracy and self-preservation and incorporated in one political communion under the beautiful name of "The Federation of the Antilles." (Mathews 81)

A social and historical dimension of symbolic practice has prevented the intellectuals from articulating cultural codes of colonization in the Caribbean. In fact, works traditionally situate themselves at the very edges, to battle against complacency and conformity. Even within the powerful constraints of colonial culture (and I am now directly addressing a Puerto Rican anticolonial imaginary), the writer's political fantasy enables her or him to display the cracks and deep freeze of colonial identities. This imaginary has been refined with each generation since 1898.

This point perhaps explains the bookishness of our imaginaries, the literate and cultural values that are the core of a political imagining. All epistemic metaphors from the cultural anthropophagy of Oswaldo de Andrade, to the metamorphosis of the cannibal of Maximilien Laroche, the baroque of Severo Sarduy, the creolization of Edouard Glissant, the counterpoint of Fernando Ortíz, the *real maravilloso* of Alejo Carpentier, the cultural maroonization of René Depestre, to the dialogical imaginary and the metalepsis I propose, in other words, the primacy of displacing the colonial by the liberatory (or, expressed in other terms, the metaphysical by the semiotic social), have created a constant shift in our remapping of identities. Such entities emerge in the continuum of the struggle for the sign of our histories. In such struggle, metaphoricity and subjectivity have been reconstituted since the contested space of the Caribbean was mapped by the European imperialist epistemologies.

In contrast, the gatekeepers, the wardens, the police, and the space warmongers at whose center the colonial panopticon is situated, have given in to the necessity of arresting the flow, and of suturing the space of contestation. The quality of this dialogical imaginary can only be measured by the critical rigor with which the history of colonialism as a "given" ontology and metaphysics has been thought.

Cultural production has been part of that responsibility, a problem of libidinal economy and strategy forever changing to adapt to the ontic (i.e., the everyday and familiar). The investment against defetishization by the instrumental reason of advanced technologies or the old imperialist pretensions of France, England, Holland, or Spain, or the more modern ones of the United States, have often conducted our political imaginaries against the classical aporia of the canonical mirror metaphor of "imaginary relations" and "imaginary identities."

The dialogical, I do not cease to repeat with Apolonia's intonation, is created by rejoinders and intersecting boundaries of subject positions, changing with every new situation. "Situatedness" is fundamental for the orchestration of our own heteroglossia and the act of "author(iz)ing ourselves." This most powerful Bakhtin-ian metaphor of authoring our own narratives has been the emo-tional-volitive poetical experience of projecting emancipatory iden-tities in our multiple narratives of modernity.[4] What is somehow pursued by writing is subjectivity itself in simultaneity with colo-nial liberation; the coloration of our instruments has been, for this reason, heteroglossic and contesting.[5] Words, phrases, fictions of the self, and cultural exactitudes that were formerly unvoiced now speak out loudly from every page.

No answer has presented itself in simple terms to encourage a belief in transparency, and thus a knowledge built on that illu-sion. The fact that in 1492, the written sign (the supplement of speech) and a language assured the sacred existence of imperi-alism with Columbus's reading a *pregón* (public proclamation) to the aborigines in Hispaniola, meant that all gatekeepers and wardens, whether they exercised political power or not, were constituted at the same time as writing and voice and by the dis-position of graphic power and foreign sounds. That the possi-bility of colonization has always passed through the hands of scribes and foreign idioms and inflections of voice has laid down the terms of many wars. Apolonia excuses herself for contesting Derrida through Gayatri Spivak's inflection but she is quite aware that speech and the speaking voice have been, in the Car-ibbean at least (she intensely dislikes globalizations), potential "thieves of language."

An interesting commentary that Apolonia loves to make to re-calcitrant nonbelievers is on the uses of language. In the Spanish Caribbean, Spanish has become since the Spanish-American War of 1898 a marker to defend the language of identity, well-spring of emotional identification and nearly inseparable from the official language and common language of the streets. In contrast, in the Caribbean that is descended from the northwest European tradition there is invariably a difference between the official and the common languages—French and Creole in Haiti, English and Anglo-Creole or French-Creole in the Common-wealth Caribbean, Dutch and Papiamento or Anglo-Creole in the Dutch colonies. Heteroglossia and polyglossia are part of the Antillean tradition, as Apolonia always points out in her logical paralogics every time she speaks to Ana, who is enclosed in her

Platonic cave by force but knows that the opportunity of escape exists once she is able to identify the point between the real fortress and the imagined one.

"How is it that subjects there can't think themselves as plural?" Apolonia is prone to ask. In this polyphonic universe many island histories resemble that of the Dominican Republic (the first American territory to establish a university, in 1538, anteceding by centuries its Anglo-American neighbor). Before 1492, Santo Domingo was Taino and Caribe; after 1492 and until 1795 it was Spanish; then it became French; then it was Haitian; next it was French again; and soon thereafter it was Spanish once more. By 1821, with the winds of independence, it proclaimed itself part of Bolívar's Federation of Colombia, under the name of The Independent State of Spanish Haiti, a situation that lasted only two months, expiring when the Haitians swarmed across the border and began an occupation that continued for twenty-two years, until 1844. When it was independent again, a caudillo returned the territory to Spain (1861), which misgoverned the island until 1865. Between 1869-70 efforts were made to annex the country to the United States (thwarted mainly by the prejudices of the U.S. Senate); from 1882 to 1889 it was under total control of a tyrant; and from 1905 until 1940, the United States administered Dominican financial and political affairs. The will to action never flickered, however, in spite of the multiplicity of encounters with the Anglo neighbor. Dominican cultural production has not been deaf to the Bakhtinian struggle for the sign to constitute subjectivity and identity: the high sophistry of Juan Bosch's writing and the popular merengue have this point in common. Conservatives call this giving transparency to the invader, thus creating stereotypes and a lack of positive images.

The truth of the matter is that, in a succession of hordes, Spain, England, France, Holland, and the United States have fragmented, muted, divided, subdivided, possessed, and repossessed that sea with many names and geographies and peoples and dreams. Islands have been, historically, the site of struggle, the battling arena of hegemonies, a cacophony of many different discourses uttered by characters whose descriptions change so frequently that it is impossible to assign an origin to the utterances. What is positive is that the islanders know from way back that those cacophonous invaders fortunately are not Cartesian subjects, that is, substantial and enduring, consistent, transparent, and part of the original landscape of the world.

Everything changes into its opposite and back again. Reversal rules; everything is possible in the encounter of evaluative utterances that constitute subjects and identities. No construct is fixed forever and ever. Subjectivity and identities are creative; colonialism unleashes heterogeneity.

(—Oops! eek! accent slippages again and again.
—That is now called hyphenated-Americans.
—No. The hyphen means inclusion.
—Yes?
—Accent slippage is being called Chicano, Hispanic or Spik.
—I don't mind the name. Give substance to my dream.)

"The Antillean mirror that reflects colors of all shades haunts me," is Apolonia's famous anti-Möbius strip. It is not surprising that dialogics helps combat colonialism and capitalism, which materialize in an extremely class- and race-conscious society, and espouse all forms of violence (economic, political, ideological).[6] ("The point is to keep them sweating! Life in the islands is often painted as a paradise, but every paradise has its worm," concludes Apolonia. "What a shame!' " "None of us is like that!" "No," she said, gently.)

Descartes, Euclidean geometries, Ptolemaic panoptics, and even Goethe's chronotope have been unable to silence the voices of difference. Islanders have the knowledge that all these sciences falsify the world and have meticulously inscribed their faces. Many *Odysseys* and Ulysses have brought their arrogant, enlightened, technocratic, bourgeois ideology. According to Derek Walcott, they are

the traitors

who, in elected office, saw the land as views

for hotels and elevated into waiters

the sons of others, while their own learnt something else.

(289)

"Is no woman an island?" Apolonia has been unable to answer that question. She knows, however, and in fact she has
told me many times, that the originality of the dreams there lies
in the double necessity that the imaginary be regarded at the
same time from the viewpoints of the politics of language, the
body, and history. Julia de Burgos (1916-1953) was quite able to
strip the body of its pretensions to an ahistorical truth; the line
"Give me my number" graphically voices the inscriptions of colonialism in her poetry. The birth of modernity in the Caribbean
and in her native island of Puerto Rico brought tragedy because
modernity and progress there in the 1940s appeared with the
manifestation of division. Some called them *pitiyanquis*, that is,
brigands and looters, others' saviors of the country; a Rashomon
of shame and heavenly bliss spins around and around . . .
("Yeah yeah, the pharmakon." "I beg your pardon.")

But let me continue. Questions pertaining to identity and
how to think the subject of the colonial experience take different
strategies. Two imaginaries intersect in simultaneity: one is the
poetical/political fantasy with a context; the other, the creation
of the entropy of the colonial through a politics of style and linguistic contraband. The important thing is that each new plot
provides the reader with imaginative materials that provoke reactions and objections in flux, always circling back to make
words now true now false with the ambivalence and undecid-
ability of uncertainty: we have always been sea-moralists.

What is at issue is the question of how the multiple Caribbean
dialogics should position itself with respect to the competing
ethics and "imaginary identities," and the metaphysical proofs
of intended marginality. The question is whether to accept the
subject position allotted by those imaginary identities, and the
answer specifies how one will identify oneself, what kind of
subjectivity one will take oneself to be. To position oneself
among competing theories and politics of identification, some
claim that a commitment to a concept of community is central,
while others pride the place of the margin and voice the margin
within an "imagined community" that set the stage for the modern nation.[7]

However suggestive other accounts may be, identity is not a
topic, or a trope, but is constituted by a discourse on texts. Both

national identities and nationalism emerged through "grammatology," as some languages are printed and subjects identify themselves as members of the community of readers implied in the symbolic values of the printed form (see During, particularly 43). But speech has its own space, as no human event is developed or resolved within the bounds of a single medium, and Caribbean cultural utterances aimed at opening an understanding of subjective and social identities are also to be found in the heteroglossic multivoiced popular songs.

Subjects have also identified, through popular culture and especially music, those forms of "mass" culture modernist critics are so skeptical about. Heteroglossic and polyphonic Caribbean music introduces "irony" and experience, and offers a sustained rehearsal of dialogy between interrelated cultural universes. Dialogism articulates all series, literary and nonliterary, elitist and "popular," written and oral, literate and nonliterate. From merengue and salsa to calypso, the plena, reggae, and the bolero, the social imaginary takes the symbolic center of social life, in the overthrow of oppressive colonial structures and the ersatz of degraded identities.[8]

Often, these songs constitute "communal utterances" (adapting from Henry Louis Gates) providing a continuity of identity, which may be linked to ethnic pasts. The aforementioned carnivalized music has provided that continuum with slavery and the African past, which can also be felt in the syncopated rhythms. Music and lyrics help construct historical agency within these dynamic narratives, which are often about underground activity that advances and records an unofficial understanding of historical facts. The merengue and the plena (among others) have been such historical agencies.

The polyphonic cultures here capitalize on anti-imperialist fantasies to rescue the reified and fetishized identities. The so-called elitist and the popular are not ships that cross each other in the depth of night. Various forms of music celebrate the imaginary and symbolic victories over oppression, while some popular forms give rise to autobiographical or testimonial "songs of experience," or narratives of the self (the tango, the bolero). The exercise of aesthetic activity is *not* always a matter of class privilege, because culture partakes of the social in intersections (more than in boundaries).[9]

The Caribbean dialogics and social imaginary inaugurated with the discourse of modernity were constructed from the arsenal of poetical idioms (what could be called high modernism) as an integral part of a "culture of feeling" (I adapt Raymond Williams's term in another direction) that cannot be identified with nostalgia. The dialogical social imaginary that gave expression to the narrative of an Antillean joint modernity has helped to articulate a concerted will toward action, which has struggled to redefine the yet to come.

In the long struggle against the Ptolemaic monological consciousness inaugurated by Christopher Columbus in 1492 (see my "Chronotope of the Indies"), the history of such monolithic consciousness has been deconstructed, de-epistemologized, and often dissolved in the hands of Caribbean demystifiers and demaskers.[10] There has been a tradition of opposition historically generated against "mental colonization," against the mimicry of colonized representations and stereotyping, against the bland acceptance of subaltern imaginary identities. ("In short: against worming our ways into the rigged corner of darkness." "She really liked the metaphor.") To be European may mean two sets of things: to be colonial in its worst mimicry of parasitism, or to claim the achievements and authority of Europe as one's own (second-rate-ness of one's own society, dramatized in Puerto Rico with the North American confluence). The thrust is against the bland inhabiting of magical, debilitating worlds of wealth and Europeanness or North Americanness in order to conceal the colonial realities.

An almost obsessive cultural imaginary strives to undo the grotesqueries of the caricatures catering to metropolitan audiences, very often making a series of political, social, and ideological interruptions to remind the reader that representations are not a "given" but produced. The transitory, erotic voyeurism and the identity crisis of those caricatures form a cluster of cultural meanings in filmy gauzes of fetishistic displacement embedding cultural confusion. Because those stories are not convincing, the Caribbean writer's social imaginary must often deal with the gift of wonder and mystery in order to offer a clear vision of the world, and harbor and project a truly postcolonial identity. It is *Samson Agonistes* against the all-pervading gaze of Ulysses.

At other times, the writer's dramatic imagination seeks to offset the complacency of the current self-image (Puerto Rican literature is rich in such a distancing or *Verfremdung*). The reader is cautioned by Apolonia not to treat this effect as a mere artistic device, avoiding the socioeconomic and subjective implication of accepting colonial representation. (This prospect also engages Salman Rushdie and V. S. Naipaul, as different as they are.)

Prototypes are examined; many do not do away with identification, but examine it critically, using a multiplicity of techniques to show that no representation is fixed and final. Michelle Cliff includes the spectator/reader, to show that no one is at the receiving end of a representation [read her *Claiming an Identity They Taught Me to Despise* (1980) and *No Telephone to Heaven* (1987)]. I have been concerned with subject positions straddling multiple realities in order to exercise undecidable univocal authority, and want the readers (both textual and concrete) to decide whose version has maximum significance. I have always been afraid of taking things for granted, of being imprisoned by assumptions. Writing for me is the site of an infinity of mirrored reflections. The concept of mirror and mirage have to be applied; they are not just words but disturbing truths. The colonial is "mirrored," and this gives a kind of security. I have been trying to refine this explicitly.

At this point, of course, Apolonia touches my shoulder to remind me that I am bookish, with a bookishness intended to point out that all versions are conscious and perspectival productions of meaning, and ("Lo! beware of a world dominated by monoglossia that expresses itself in the epistemological mode of norms and authorities." Her theoretical loquacity made me smile. I reach out for her hand. "I, too, have hoped for it, against hope" " . . . but we will walk through hell and high water," she said.)[11]

The point is that in the multiple space of many languages with many inflections, writing is meant to replace a radically new set of problems in social imaginaries that are projects to alter conditions (I do not understand the imaginary as a misrecognition, or as a false representation of the individual). As a process of the productive transformation of other forms of cognition, writing has been, since the inception of the narrative of an emancipatory modernity and independent nation-states in the nineteenth century, a will toward action, a reconnection of shame, a projection of ethics to every new cartographer, and, to balance my story, an embattled fight against colonial performance.

Identities born out of romantic individualism and the romantic search for freedom are aimed at disrupting the multiple imperialist authorized versions. And I have not even touched on gendering the anticolonial for the realization of the conditions of freedom. The point is that nature, women, and art were redemptive spaces outside colonial life as befits the emancipatory thrust of the Caribbean liberationist struggle: the "Our America" Martí coined on the eve of modernity. The displacements toward personal and gendered liberations were connected with the emergence of the new postcolonial. Luisa Capetillo in turn-of-the-century colonial Puerto Rico knew plainly that sexual relations and gendered roles reproduce the conflicts and alliances found in colonial social and economic realities. Her whole work as a socialist and feminist intellectual centered on these problems.

This is now a zone of firm ground: gendering the anticolonial and postcolonial discourses with a liberating imaginary has broken free; no one can any longer write as if that challenge had not been posed. The distance anticolonial and postcolonial women writers have taken here serves to provoke outrage.

Understood as a means of knowing and transforming the social, culture is an arena to be occupied. Questions are raised through texts, often against the myths (racial, patriarchal, colonial) that disperse peoples, along with their histories. The social imaginary is not only a conviction but a changing notion; not simply a cognitive difference, but one based on differences in rhetorical organization, intonation, accentuation, semantics, grammar, and syntax. The uses of language only acquire social meaning and political significance in particular situations (Bakhtinian "situated utterance"). Texts are often driven to frenzy by the spectacle of colonial life or postcolonial communities (Rushdie's shame). She stood at the balcony of her childhood and looked at the Caribbean Sea. In parting, she said: "This imaginary appears as inhabiting the unfixed, the land without memories of the future. And I suppose that fantasy is the prodigal element of freedom." "This has been a high-risk dream, fusing, translating, conjoining from the start." "But, oh well, there has been the uncompromising determination to see it through." "Whose?" "Damn right!" A cognitive imaginary that inverts epistemological imperialisms, cultural dominants, and epistemic violence. The undisguised brutality of instrumental reason in its cacophony of accents, intonations, and masks haunts each geographical space, so spiraling emotional identities should figure no longer in the empty margin or the void of silence. "Venceremos." "La lutte continue." "Kenbe, Pa Laze." "Don't let this universe shrink . . . "

Notes

1. The pressure of sexual and gender constructs that also mark ethnicity in the canonical narratives of the conquest is the topic of my lecture "On the Cannibalistic Discourse of Monology" (currently in press).

2. I am referring to a character in my novel *Nocturna mas no funesta*, also the main character in *El libro de Apolonia o de las islas* (in press).

3. I have written elsewhere of some aspects of the social imaginary and modernism; see *Rubén Darío bajo el signo del cisne* and, more specifically, *Colonialism and Culture*. I fully agree with Edouard Glissant's view of modernism/modernity in *Le discours antillais* (see also Maximilien Laroche, *La découverte de l'Amérique par les Américains* and *L'avènement de la littérature haïtienne*).

4. The interested reader can consult my book on 1898 and the dialogical social imaginary (*Colonialism and Culture*), where I examine modernism in the light of hegemony.

5. I am *hélas* aware that I am only referring to texts, and I cannot provide evidence of how this dialogism took form in popular consent. However, the ulterior development of an Antillean identity against instrumental reason provides a justification for considering it as a form of hegemonic confrontation.

6. I am obviously evoking and reaccentuating Bakhtin's link between Dostoyevski and capitalism (Bakhtin 298).

7. On this debated point, see Anderson, especially chapter 3, and Edwards.

8. Maximilien Laroche (1989) offers a synoptic diagram of Caribbean music by geographical areas. The Haitian merengue comes originally from Mozambique; the North American presence in 1920 brought jazz to Haiti. Some fascinating work has been done on rap, graffiti, and other popular artistic forms

202 ◆ IRIS M. ZAVALA

critical of the establishment (see Kaplan). I offer an appraisal of the polyphonic Caribbean bolero in *El bolero. Historia de un amor*, and in my book on 1898 *(Colonialism and Culture).*

9. The reader will rightly conclude that I am in disagreement with those critics who divorce literature from nonliterature, a debatable problem that also involves Marxist theories, such as Adorno's. In contrast, Bakhtin offers an encompassing understanding of culture in dialogism.

10. I obviously partake with Calvin O. Schrag, who examines the de-epistemologization of monolithic consciousness in another context.

11. I am referring to my two novels, *Chiliagony* and *Nocturna mas no funesta*. See also my article "A Gaze of One's Own: Narrativizing the Caribbean. An Essay on Critical-Fiction."

Works Cited

Anderson, Benedict. *Imagined Communities: Reflections on the Origin and Spread of Nationalism.* London: Verso, 1983.

Bakhtin, Mikhail. *Problems of Dostoievsky's Poetics.* Trans. Caryl Emerson. Manchester: Manchester Univ. Press, 1984.

Cliff, Michelle. *Claiming an Identity They Taught Me to Despise.* Watertown, Mass.: Persephone Press, 1980.

_____. *No Telephone to Heaven.* New York: E. P. Dutton, 1987.

During, Simon. "Postmodernism or Post-Colonialism Today." *Textual Practice* 1, 1 (1987): 32-47.

Edwards, John. *Language, Society and Identity.* Oxford: Basil Blackwell, 1985.

Glissant, Edouard. *Le discours antillais.* Paris: Seuil, 1980.

JanMohamed, Abdul R. "The Economy of the Manichean Allegory: The Function of Racial Difference in Colonialist Literature." *Critical Inquiry* 12 (1985): 55-87.

Kaplan, Ann E., ed. *Postmodernism and Its Discontents: Theories, Practices.* London: Verso, 1988.

Laroche, Maximilien. *L'avènement de la littérature haïtienne.* Quebec: GRELCA, 1987.

_____. *La découverte de l'Amérique par les Américains.* Quebec: GRELCA, 1989.

Mathews, Thomas. "The Project for a Confederation of the Greater Antilles." *Caribbean Historical Review* 5 (1955): 81-95.

Schrag, Calvin O. *Communicative Praxis and the Space of Subjectivity.* Bloomington: Indiana Univ. Press, 1986.

Walcott, Derek. *Omeros.* New York: Farrar Straus Giroux, 1990.

Zavala, Iris. *Chiliagony.* Trans. Susan Pensak. Bloomington, Ind.: Third Woman Press, 1984.

_____. *Nocturna mas no funesta.* Barcelona: Montesinos, 1987.

_____. *Rubén Darío bajo el signo del cisne.* Río Piedras: Universidad de Puerto Rico, 1989.

_____. *El bolero. Historia de un amor.* Madrid: Alianza, 1991.

_____. "On the Cannibalistic Discourse of Monology." Lecture presented at the Fifth International Bakhtin Conference, Manchester, July 1991, and in a more developed version in Spanish as Inaugural Lecture in Warsaw, Poland. Both in press.

———. *Colonialism and Culture: Hispanic Modernisms and the Social Imaginary.* Bloomington: Indiana Univ. Press, 1992.

———. "A Gaze of One's Own: Narrativizing the Caribbean. An Essay on Critical-Fiction." *Feminist Critical Negotiations.* Ed. Alice Parker and Elizabeth Meese. Amsterdam: John Benjamins, 1992. 145-160.

———. "Chronotope of the Indies: Notes on Heterochrony." Forthcoming. Published in French as "Le chronotope des Indes: notes sur l'hétérochronie." *L' "Indien," instance discursive.* Ed. Antonio Gómez-Moriana and Danièle Trottier. Candiac, Quebec: Balzac, 1993. 115-132.

◆ Afterword
Pastiche Identity, and Allegory of Allegory

Alberto Moreiras

Identity has been a pervasive theme in Latin American critical reflection since Independence. In the old days it constituted a basic motif of organicist ideology—Latin Americans, it was argued, should develop an autochthonous culture, whereupon Latin Americans would finally come into their own, and establish their claim to property of the land on a firm foundation. In early postcolonial times identity was the battle cry of bourgeois foundationalism, without which the process of nation building could not properly take place. The more identity the Latin Americans managed to find, understood as the sum of cultural marks of differentiation with respect to metropolitan societies, the less precarious their young social constructions would seem. Given the weak state of civil society in most Latin American post-Independence states, it was important to develop a cohesive ideology that would at the same time orient social and political development and contain the potentially disaggregating tendencies of the vast mestizo and indigenous classes, as well as of the remaining procolonialist sectors within the leading class.

This ideology of cultural/political identity took on a life of its own and in time became a mark of itself. Supposing you were a member of the cultural elite, you could only call yourself an authentic Latin American if you were willing to swear on Latin American identity. But identity was never here, only always ahead, always deferred to some future time when the perpetually unfinished identity projects would finally reach completion.[1] Many discussions concerning Latin American identity today still bear the traces of that essentialist, and essentially Romantic, heritage. Traditional identity-ism is no longer intrinsically linked to criollo anti-imperialist nationalism, but it still fulfills the basic compensatory function of middle-class ideology: it is used as a rhetorical war machine to persuade the generality of the citizens of the overall preferability of the local ruling elite. Identity-ism is still an ideology of containment. It attempts to regulate thought by channeling it into the deadening waters of tradition, understood normatively, not hermeneutically. "A thought of our own, a culture of our own" ("un pensamiento propio, una cultura propia") are never too far from being a thought of the proper, and a culture of propriety.

I would like to center my epilogal contribution to this volume by taking a critical position concerning identity, but one that will at the same time attempt to counter a quasi-automatic recourse to difference, which seems in most discussions to mark the complementary, but not opposed, "other" side of the rhetorical spectrum. As the title of this volume confirms, critical discourse has tended to compensate for the politically dubious overtones of the proidentity theory by emphasizing difference. But difference, in most critical formulations, is not quite understood as resistance to identity; only as its underside. A fallen but very powerful dialectic seems to be operating here, organizing a swampy discursive field within which any substantive positing of identity is constantly undermined by a necessary appeal to identity as difference (i.e., postcolonial identity as difference from the metropolis); and within which any radical appeal to difference is immediately overturned by the necessary co-positing of difference as identity (postcolonial difference as identity against the metropolis).[2]

As you will see, I eventually make my argument hinge upon a partial analysis of Jorge Luis Borges's short story "Tlön, Uqbar, Orbis Tertius." There seem to be obvious reasons to insist upon the fact that a critique of the premises of traditional Latin American identity doctrine is to be found within the Latin American tradition itself. Borges is a substantive part of that tradition. His unfortunate political comments on the side of cruelty and ignominy should be no obstacle to the recognition that in his textual work a momentous confrontation with historical-political issues of first importance takes place.

I will first attempt an analysis of the diverse positions on identity included in this collection. Starting from the assumption that the notion of cultural identity interrogates the possible equation between meaning and being, I will locate three fundamental positions, which I will call modern or symbolic, postmodern or allegorical, and skeptical. The skeptical position will constitute a good transition to the study of yet another position, which I will be calling the postsymbolic, and which I find exemplified in Borges's "Tlön, Uqbar, Orbis Tertius."

I

Imagine a world where identity has been accomplished, where things, individuals, and communities have come to rest within themselves: wouldn't it be the worst of nightmares? It would probably be worse than that, because the very possibility of a nightmare would have been blocked by definition. In that world, the dark horses of repressed desire would no longer have any cause to stir, as desire would have been liberated by and in total self-recognition. The final definition of identity would arrest and bring to a halt any possibility of symbolic expression, precisely because the symbol would have been consummated once and for all. What, however, remains after the symbol is complete, its parts matched in seamless (self-)encounter? Let me risk a hypothesis: on the one hand, the systematic working-through of a totalizing aesthetics, that is, the mere implementation of a comprehensive logical mandate. As implementation of a given identity's mandate to reduce to itself anything beyond itself, it assumes a technical nature.[3] Accomplished identity opens into a temporal horizon where the technological drive to exhaust itself is all there is. But, on the other hand, reflectively, no less systematically, although not dialectically, a counterimpulse arises to the systematic working-itself-through of a totalizing, technological aesthetics of identity. This counterimpulse cannot be understood solely on the basis of a theory of difference. It is not difference, but the material resistance of the real that opposes the systematic work of the identity movement with increasing strength as the system approaches final completion.[4] As Drucilla Cornell puts it, "The very establishment of the system as a system implies a *beyond* to it, precisely by virtue of what it excludes" (1; emphasis in the original). The *beyond* never ceases to expand, in endless and silent work of negation, in the unworking of the identity work, which, at the limit, at the point of maximum resistance, will necessarily precipitate a world conflagration. As we imagine that impossible world, such a conflagration would reduce the very notions of self and community to ashes.

When we propose, for well-intended reasons, the coincidence of a group with itself, we choose to forget that nothing can come closer to collective death than self-coincidence. Communal self-coincidence brings us into the disastrous actuality of the death of politics, because politics is the negotiation of difference. As the recent example of Yugoslavia and the tragic antics of neo-Nazi Germans make abundantly clear, the negotiation of difference by recourse to identity can only organize political abjection.

In an article dealing mainly with potential abuses of the term "post-colonial" in contemporary cultural studies, Ella Shohat points out that the current practice of substituting terms such as "hybridity" and "syncretism" for older, rather monolithic notions of identity carries its own risks: "At times, the anti-essentialist emphasis on hybrid identities comes dangerously close to dismissing all searches for communitarian origins as an archaeological excavation of an idealized, irretrievable past" (109). As Shohat says, some sense of collective identity remains a crucial political necessity for social groups whose communal life has been exposed to serious rupture—let alone for those groups whose very survival may be threatened. Shohat makes a strong case regarding what she calls the "problematic" political agency of "post-colonial hybridity" (110). I recognize the political expediency and even the occasional existential urge for a reified, more or less utopian notion of personal/communal identity; however, the ongoing celebration of hybridity and multiculturalism in the Latin American context can be just as politically paralyzing as it is emotionally comforting. Claims to multicultural identity seem at times to be closer to technological reification than older, more purist notions ever were. My point throughout this essay is not at all to question the force of political resistance or affirmation that identity claims may have. It may be necessary to state explicitly that technological reification in the global scale always already dictates for us a particular identity adscription that we may or may not be in a position to resist actively. *That* technological reification, which is another name for what David Harvey calls capitalism of flexible accumulation, is certainly politically powerful (see Harvey 189-97).

Oppositional identities, or rather, oppositional identity formulations, are often caught up in an ideological, transferential web of interests that in my opinion tends to void beforehand the pretensions of emancipatory counterdiscourse that those formulations customarily adopt. I have no objections to Shohat's assertion that the really significant question for any critical analysis of identity theory is: "Who is mobilizing what in the articulation of the past, developing what identities, identifications and representations, and in the name of what political vision and goals?" (110). The need for a radical identity critique is then, paradoxically, a constitutive part of identity thinking in contemporary times.

Within the mainstream tradition of Latin Americanist criticism, identity has for a long time been taken for granted, in the sense of having been used and abused as a singularly de-ideologized concept. In other words, although identity has long been recognized as a philosopheme, its parallel quality of ideologeme has tended to be dismissed, or even worse, suppressed. Thus reified, identity has often acted as a true schizomachine, truly the last, or the first, of the insidiously destructive mechanisms that constitute the legacy of colonialism. Identity, de-ideologized, is a technical concept that has reached the mantra-like quality of all technicisms. Within mainstream Latin Americanist critical discourse, we now have the technique of identity, to be used and abused upon any and all texts, even if human texts.[5]

The fact that nothing is ever critically proved concerning identity, as identity is not to be proved but only assertively handled, is only more wood for the fire, more grease for the engine. It allows for the perpetuation of the question: the question concerning identity, a sure way to emancipation, the categorical imperative, the pastiche that every postcolonial Latin Americanist critic has for breakfast: "Think so that your way of thinking must be shared by everybody who does not want to occupy a position of infamy: think identity! Repeat identity! Proliferate identity! Don't ever let go!" But the more self-righteous we are on reified identity, the more dangerously deranged we are.

From a battle cry against colonial dependency, identity has come to figure as the primary signifier of another resilient form of dependency: emancipatory ideology. I do not say emancipation, but emancipatory ideology. It may not be the worst kind of ideology, but it is still an obstacle for thought, and it has the peculiar characteristic of being an obstacle against itself. As ideology, it cannot be emancipatory; as a thinking of emancipation, it cannot allow itself to remain within ideology. And yet it does; and the infernal entanglements that it gets itself into, as identity thinking convolutes itself in order to milk out of itself the blatant contradiction that constitutes it, are coresponsible for the condition in which we, as Latin Americanist critics, find ourselves today. The symptom has become the disease.

For emancipatory ideology, there has been only one question: to assert identity. One does not "have" identity by firmly establishing difference, because difference can never be firmly established, but by reducing difference to the imperatives of identity, and most notoriously when the ideologues pretend specifically not to do so. Latin American cultural criticism has come at times dangerously close to being reduced to the question of identity. It has often been suggested that the reasons for that have to do with origins, and that origins determine destiny. In the same breath, then, the emancipatory ideologue argues for and against emancipation. It is the Latin American destiny, we hear, to be forever questing for identity; those are our chains, which are at the same time the mark of our freedom.

Can one break away? Is it possible to think outside emancipatory ideology, and yet think emancipatorily? Without thinking infamy? Can identity, or a critique of identity, still be the way to go? Does it have a positive, usable side? Properly posed, in my opinion, the question reads: Can we have a critical-political thinking on identity that is not a part of the current technologization of politics, and which indeed resists and thinks itself against said technologization?[6]

Identity has always been political. To the extent that identity is always political, an ideology of identity can function, if partially, as a critique of ideology. Identity thinking can conceivably be put to work against all opposed and/or totalizing presumptions of identity. In other words, identity thinking can function homeopathically. A spoonful of identity could possibly arrest identity. Identity could be used as a purely tactical notion. Given today's planetary dominance of transnational capitalism, identity could put a stop to global homogenization, if only in the negative sense of offering itself as pure resistance.

II

The essays in this volume understand themselves as a political intervention in the terrain of culture. They focus directly on the necessity to respond to the overwhelming division of the cultural field between interpreters and interpreted, colonizers and colonized; most of them see themselves as resisting, or attempting to resist, what used to be called first-world cultural imperialism. In this sense, the collection's underlying moment of truth is the realization that Latin American cultural histories withhold differences that global cultural homogenization should not be allowed to suffocate entirely. These differences, which, as historically motivated, can only be understood dynamically, and therefore not essentially, are the negative impulse whence a possible contestation of the globality of Western cultural hegemony can and should arise. The collection tries to engage the task through specific historical analyses of elements of Latin American cultural production that are seen to embody this possibility of resistance. Yet it is obvious that such overall merit stands as purely negative, insofar as it does not depend on a production of real, substantive identity, but on a sort of partial counteridentity arresting global hegemonics. The positive contribution of the collection as such hangs on the individual qualities of the specific articles, as well as on their interrelationship. This is what I will now examine critically and selectively, as I would like to carry the discussion to where I think it is most decisive. I will not engage all of the texts presented in this volume, and of those that I will engage, let me say that I will not necessarily do so at the point in which they seem most, or even least, productive. I would rather focus on some paradigmatic moments, because through them we might attempt to understand the current predicament of Latin Americanist identity theory, and this volume's contribution to it.[7]

I will start with a commentary on Fernando Aínsa's and the first of Enrique Dussel's essays, because I think they are exemplary of a certain kind of Latin Americanist critical discourse. Within their own parameters, they are both in my opinion masterful pieces. I will attempt to critique their ideological underpinnings by pointing out what I consider to be textual inconsistencies. Such inconsistencies are not to be seen as the product of carelessness, but are an intrinsic part of the authors' argumentation. What we could call the essays' ethical tones depend on these inconsistencies, and therefore they are not to be eliminated by mere rhetorical cleansing. In other words, the following critique affects ideological positionings, not rhetorical inadequacies.

Fernando Aínsa begins "The Antinomies of Latin American Discourses of Identity and Their Fictional Representation" with a vague description of Latin America as a continent with "traumatic and fragmentary [historical] experiences, far removed from any gradual and smooth historical evolution." He proceeds to set up and discuss a list of what he calls antinomic constants, which in his opinion polarize cultural alternatives. Latin America would be "without 'intermediate terms,' without moderation or ambiguity." The antinomies that Aínsa points out (civilization and barbarism, country and city, center and periphery, tradition and modernity) "structure a large proportion of contemporary Latin American discourses of identity." His conclusion is that narrative fiction succeeds in the integration of those antinomies even when they do coexist in irresolvable tension, and even when they take the texts that embody them to an impasse in which no set of antinomies seems to be able to take priority. This tense and even paradoxical conciliation of opposites within the literary text finally consecrates what Aínsa considers the "universal vision of what it is to be Latin American." Following Aínsa's logic, it is to be deduced that narrative fiction is the privileged cultural discourse that, by its ability to sustain contradiction without collapsing, can make Latin America "finally feel in charge of its own identity, that is to say, of its long-awaited historical maturity, beyond the antinomies with which the vicissitudes of history are characterized."

I take this position to be in fact the hegemonic position within the Latin Americanist tradition. Aínsa is to a great extent right precisely in view of the historical importance of his ideologemes: a large part of Latin American cultural production, and particularly literary production, has understood itself enmeshed in the antinomies that Aínsa points out. It is also true that most cultural producers who have undertaken conciliatory or integrating tasks regarding those polarities have in many cases failed to accomplish their task despite their best efforts. Likewise, the vindication of precisely such impossibilities of conciliation has been a crucial aspect of Latin American literary ideology.

But Aínsa's logic seems inconsistent on several counts. First, he wavers between a structural and a dialectical presentation, without wanting to take the steps that either one or the other model rigorously requires. Thus, his structuralism is limited and even voided by his constant recourse to historical modifications. But his dialecticism is also voided by the fact that he cannot find mediation between dialectical opposites. Second, in his presentation of fiction as privileged cultural discourse he wavers between a paradigm of revelation and a paradigm of construction, that is, he manages to say at one and the same time, and therefore contradictorily, that literature constructs reality and that literature reveals preexisting reality. Third, his privileging of fiction, and of fiction's defining power vis-à-vis the Latin American cultural predicament, never goes beyond description to a critique of literature as ideology, which leads the reader to confront the sorry conclusion that Latin American cultural authenticity is just the ideological nightmare of irreconcilable antinomies he describes.

At the symptomatic point where Aínsa must admit that in many of the texts he describes the structural polarities would open into blatant contradictions, he eludes the charge that his analysis might be overtly reductive by accusing those texts themselves of being simplistic. There is never a consideration of the possibility that alternative accounts of the antinomies Aínsa identifies, that is, accounts coming from indigenous communities, for example, would immediately inaugurate a possibility of understanding the ideological functioning of those apparently stable polarities that Aínsa's parameters could simply not comprehend.

Aínsa's essay can be taken as an example of a long-standing literary-critical ideology that, by erasing internal contradictions within its own discourse, as well as all thought of the possibility of an opening to perspectives that this ideology is trying to repress, presents itself as able to mediate the antinomies in the literary-aesthetic imaginary. Pretending to privilege literature by praising its way of assuming both sides of a given polarity, Aínsa is in fact privileging the ability of the hegemonic literary critic to mediate those polarities through an act of reading that is understood to be identity-producing. Aínsa's sleight of hand is clear enough: only literary criticism, that is, the literary critic, can reveal the structure that enables Latin Americans to transcend "the vicissitudes of history" and to reach the teleological end of history in historical maturity. By thus secretly privileging literary-critical discourse as the final purveyor of identity, Aínsa is more obviously concerned with critical power than with a historical situation that, in his hands, becomes food for critical processing. Aínsa's optimistic vision of critical mediation is consubstantial with his suggestion that identity is what critics can give, thereby revealing what some had always suspected: the ideology of cultural identity is, at least partially, a weapon in the cultural elite's quest for power.

Dussel's first essay in this volume, although coming from a more agonizing reflection on the universality of thinking as well as from what I believe to be a very different political position, shares some characteristics with Aínsa's contribution. In "Leopoldo Zea's Project of a Philosophy of Latin American History," Dussel sharply establishes the presence of four different directions in Leopoldo Zea's work, with the intention of focusing upon the fourth: the "definition of a problematic horizon" that would attempt to follow a "path of universality" within a Latin American philosophy of history. Dussel gives us a clear and precise definition when he locates this aspect of Zea's work in the tradition of historical hermeneutics. I think Dussel is quite right when he affirms that Zea's programmatic intentions, for many years contested and rejected by dominant trends such as historical positivism, analytical philosophy, and Marxism, are in fact very close to positions taken by many influential Euro-North American philosophers today, and can thus be accepted with ease by the Western (hegemonic) philosophical community.

Dussel takes issue with Zea, however, by rejecting the possibility that a Latin American philosophy of history in Zea's sense can come to be accepted as philosophy "in the restricted sense," that is, what he would call normalized philosophy within the hegemonic philosophical tradition. For Dussel, Zea's hermeneutics refers to a preontological, Lebenswelt, everyday understanding "from which the work of philosophy itself 'in a restricted sense' can start." It is at this critical point that the discussion becomes in my opinion rather Byzantine, and that Dussel opens himself to criticism. Dussel argues in favor of his own (and Salazar Bondy's) previously held position in order to reaffirm, against Zea, that Latin America does not yet have a philosophy that Latin Americans can claim *as their own*. It therefore remains necessary, according to Dussel, for Latin American philosophers "to construct a Latin American philosophy orchestrated with the language and the discursivity of the hegemonic philosophical community." The reason is the following: it is the Latin American philosophers' mission to force the hegemonic community not to go on ignoring the work of Latin American philosophers.

It seems to me that discussions as to whether or not philosophy can be possessed by this or that social group on the one hand prematurely reduce philosophy to the status of ideology, and, on the other hand, dependent as they are on some reformulation of Diltheyan historicism, are singularly outdated from the perspective of what Dussel calls the "hegemonic philosophical community." Isn't Dussel's insistence on and will to integration within the hegemonic philosophical community itself a symptomatic remnant of a barely suppressed colonial mentality, held against all conscious expectations? Why is it ever so important to "make it" at the metropolitan level? When, in a note to his concluding remarks, Dussel formulates his own programmatic project of a "philosophy of liberation," and equates its fundamental philosophical categories with categories that attempt to resist oppression and undo exclusion, he seems blind to the fact that, by definition, an antihegemonic philosophy cannot be at the same time hegemonic. Is it possible to claim oppression and exclusion as fundamental philosophical categories with a view to be included as something other than the oppressed and the excluded within the hegemonic philosophical community? If there is a way out of this double bind, Dussel is not telling us.

I think Dussel's book *Filosofía de la liberación* is one of the best philosophical productions ever to come out of Latin America. His second contribution to this volume is also proof that his present work holds extreme promise and interest. The point is that in the essay under review Dussel's programmatic impulse gets out of hand, into what I earlier called a systematics of technological expansion, the goal of which is nothing but the colonization of the real. If the guiding principle of Latin American philosophy must be, as Dussel thinks, to achieve something like universal recognition, and if that will to universal recognition is not to give up its Latin Americanness, then I think Dussel's project reveals a close dependency on a metaphysics of the will, based upon the notion that the very identity of the philosophical subject is a product of the reduction to itself of all that resists it. I believe the same could be said of Fernando Aínsa's quasi-structural/dialectical objectification of the literary.

Three of the essays in the collection are radically concerned with the status of identity theory in postmodernity: those by Amaryll Chanady, Françoise Perus, and Zilá Bernd. Each one tries to think through the predicament succinctly formulated by Fredric Jameson in his much-maligned article "Third-World Literature in the Era of Multinational Capitalism": "One cannot acknowledge the justice of the general poststructuralist assault on the so-called 'centered subject,' the old unified ego of bourgeois individualism, and then resuscitate this same ideological mirage of psychic unification on the collective level in the form of a doctrine of collective identity" (78).

Jameson's reflection attempts to pull out of this impasse by appealing to the notion of allegory. What is at stake in Jameson's article is precisely a dismantling of the philosophically naive identity doctrines projected upon postcolonial texts while preserving these texts' force as embodiments of oppositional discourse—in other words, as resistance literature. In Jameson's formulation: "All third-world texts are necessarily . . . allegorical, and in a very specific way: they are to be read as what I will call *national allegories*, even when, or perhaps I should say, particularly when their forms develop out of predominantly western machineries of representation, such as the novel" (69; emphasis in the original). He continues: "Third-world texts, even those which are seemingly private and invested with a properly libidinal dynamic, necessarily project a political dimension in the form of national allegory: the story of the private individual destiny is always an allegory of the embattled situation of the public third-world culture and society" (69).

Jameson's article has been accused of unwittingly proposing a paternalistic, that is, ultimately colonial vision of third-world literature by virtue of being reductive in its sweeping determination of that literature as *necessarily* national-allegorical. In my opinion, however, Jameson is being more synthetic than reductive. The real difference between third-world and first-world texts is not that the former are national-allegorical and the latter are not, but that the former are self-conscious about it, and the latter are not:

> Such allegorical structures . . . are not so much absent
> from first-world cultural texts as they are *unconscious*,
> and therefore they must be deciphered by interpretative
> mechanisms that necessarily entail a whole social and
> historical critique of our current first-world situation. The
> point here is that, in distinction to the unconscious
> allegories of our own cultural texts, third-world national
> allegories are conscious and overt: they imply a radically

different and objective relationship of politics to libidinal dynamics. (79-80; emphasis in the original)

Now, it is precisely because third-world literary texts are overtly concerned with a definition of community that it remains quite difficult for the third-world critic to remain unconcerned by identity theory. First-world critics can assume the unconscious crypt transmitted to them by the more or less traditional lack of overt political reference to community construction, and can generally afford to ignore it should they wish to. Jameson's argument in his article is that, far from attempting to erase elements in the third-world texts that are not exhaustively contained by the national allegory idea, first-world critics should concern themselves with learning about their own historical determinations from the third-world text. In other words, it could be said that the third-world text is not just a national allegory, but also embodies an allegory of the first world. "A study of third-world culture necessarily entails a new view of ourselves, from the outside, insofar as we ourselves are (perhaps without fully knowing it) constitutive forces at work on the remains of older cultures in our general world capitalist system" (68).[8] Although Chanady, Perus, and Bernd do not directly engage with Jameson's article, I believe that some of its ideas will prove helpful to understand their position in the Latin American identity debate.

In "Latin American Imagined Communities and the Postmodern Challenge," Chanady focuses on Homi Bhabha's ideas on dissemiNation and on his critique of Benedict Anderson's notion of "imagined communities" in order to set up the two opposite but parallel limits within which her own reflection is to be framed. Identity has been, she says, problematized as a legitimate concept in postmodern times. This delegitimation erodes the basis of identity as the ground for national or subcontinental "imagined communities." But the overthrow of identity also implies the difficulty of difference. Her solution is an appeal to a notion of plural hybridization, which she presents as a heterology. With it, Latin American culture resists all politics of identity based on what would be a rather simplistic differentiation with respect to a colonizing other. But, just as drastically, it also resists any and all politics of "pure miscegenation," understood as the exclusive defense of mestizaje, because the championing of mestizaje necessarily threatens nonintegrated, therefore marginalized, groups (i.e., indigenous groups, for instance, but by extension also immigrant groups, and so on). What Chanady calls the "radical questioning of the very concept of distinction between identity and alterity" is the basis of her attack on monolithic identity ideologies and of her defense of radical cultural plurality and hybridity.

Chanady's leading essay actively frames the rest. Reading it back from the perspective of the essays that follow it, Chanady's enframing has precise allegorical effects, in the following sense: Chanady's proposal for cultural hybridity within the radical questioning of the identity/alterity distinction forcefully expresses her desire to go *beyond* any positive formulation to be found in the collected texts, which are brought together in a volume on cultural identity/alterity. Those texts are allegorized in advance by Chanady's postmodern challenge, which relativizes all internal positionings in the collection by setting a limit to the validity of any stable positioning. In this sense, Chanady's introduction redescribes the postmodern along the lines suggested by the already-quoted Drucilla Cornell: "the 'postmodern' should be understood as an allegory" representing "an ethical insistence on the limit to 'positive' descriptions of the principles of modernity" (11), subjective identity being of course a classical one since René Descartes. It seems to me that this is the basis of Chanady's obvious sympathy for deconstructive positions such as that of Bhabha.

A rearticulation of Jameson's position on national allegory with Cornell's definition of the postmodern allegory might help critical reflection pull out of the impasse detected by Jameson, when he mentions the difficulty of rejecting bourgeois individualism while attempting to keep some notion of collective identity. This rearticulating move is explicit in Chanady's essay from its first lines. Blanca de Arancibia's warning against thinking identity as closure or nostalgia, reaffirmed by Chanady, organizes one of the introduction's most important dimensions, which is also brilliantly developed along different lines by both Perus and Bernd in their own essays.

Perus's "Modernity, Postmodernity, and Novelistic Form in Latin America" is basically concerned with fictional discourse and with the way the figurative nature of our apprehension of the real through the novel is of essential importance to detect and understand cultural/historical determinations of a given society. Everything in Perus's text hinges upon a definition of postmodernity as a crisis within modernity; that is, postmodernity is "modernity's turning upon itself" once the defining notions of modernity run their course and become exhausted. Perus examines aspects of the Latin American narrative tradition from the assumption that postcolonial Latin America, taking off from an epistemological problematic proper to itself *as* postcolonial Latin America, must figuratively, that is, allegorically question the epistemic notions of modernity, and that it has been doing so since long before that questioning became explicit under the name of postmodernity. Perus's reflection is not limited to the tiresome issue of whether or not there is a real postmodernity in Latin America, or of whether or not the Latin Americans are postmoderns avant la lettre. Her crucial contribution has to do with the following consideration, which is of course of global interest: "whether postmodernity does not run the risk of relegating political discourse, and politics itself, to pure fiction (in the traditional sense of the term), thus returning to a magical-mythical conception of language."

The reason why postcolonial Latin America's figurative self-representation is, like it or not, a critique of modernity is that modern Western civilization "constructed an image of itself that affirmed its destiny to become universalized as civilization by antonomasia, exclusion, or abasement of what remained outside its orbit, or resisted absorption." For Latin American foundational texts, such as Sarmiento's *Facundo*, which were being written with a fierce anticolonialist spirit, but also following metropolitan Enlightened models, the universalizing drive of European modernity became a double bind that made Latin Americans constitute themselves as split and unstable, even at the level of the subject of enunciation. Because the subject is unstable, it cannot assume the teleological, rational linearity of European Enlightened historiography and sociopolitical discourse, but it cannot turn its back on them either. Postcolonial Latin

American discourse has the characteristics of what Perus calls "peripheral transition":

> By "peripheral transition" I mean the constitution or reconstitution of national culture and literature around a double dialogue, tense and conflicting, and between spheres of culture: "universal" culture on the one hand (or, that of the various metropolises, past and present, that can in no way be considered homogeneous), and "autochthonous" culture, mainly oral and popular, although not homogeneous either, on the other.

This dialogic conflict makes it impossible for Latin American narrative to represent that which it aims to represent: the historical/progressive time of the center, transplanted. Transplantation proves more complex than bargained for.

Historically, the way Latin American narrative attempts to solve the conflict takes the shape of a reformulation of progressive time in terms of a return to the origin, implying therefore the negation or reversal of progressive time. As "return to the origin" tries to eliminate cultural disjunction, it will come face to face with myth, as Perus describes:

> Latin American fiction tends above all to reactivate, apply to its own context, and confront with its own traditions, the mythological beliefs and practices that enlightened rationalism claims to have left behind, and the myths that this same rationalism created in order to distinguish itself from its origins or to represent its own periphery.

Narration then leads to a "conjunction of diverse historical and mythical temporalities, which the narrator structures around a zone of contact with a present whose becoming always remains uncertain." It is in precisely this sense that Perus can say that "the pre-Hispanic cultural heritage . . . establishes the basis for a questioning of modern Western civilization."

For Perus, identity is always a suppressed possibility, and that is why its search takes violent and erratic forms. However, by dismantling all critical recourse to essentializing, or fictionalizing, Latin American cultural conflicts, Perus can effectively read the narrative tradition from a historical/political perspective that is as Latin American-specific as it is also of global import. Thus, Perus proves that it is not the postmodern, as she understands it, that will fictionalize politics. On the contrary, modernity, by presenting itself as the myth of the termination of myths, was responsible for a technologizing conception of language whose magico-mythical horizon was all the more powerful for being hidden from view under the disguise of Enlightened universality. The implication is, naturally, that identity doctrines, by being fully contained within the positivity of modernity, do not escape the teleological linearity of symbolic, that is, nonallegoric, fulfillment.

Zilá Bernd begins her essay, "The Construction and Deconstruction of Identity in Brazilian Literature," by stating that the main preoccupation of emergent and peripheral literature "frequently is to provide an explicit or implicit definition of its communities in its narrative." Although Bernd's formulation is clearly more cautious than Jameson's, it does carry a family resemblance. The main difference revolves around Bernd's use of the word "definition." If Bernd were to mean by it that peripheral literatures implement a representation of their communities in the classical sense, i.e., representation as the pull for maximum concordance between meaning and being, then her position would be quite different from Jameson's. But, in fact, she does not mean that. In Bernd's usage, definition equals mimetic translation. By arguing in favor of what I interpret as a translative adjustment between peripheral literatures and their communities, Bernd is opening her text to a reading in the allegorical key.

Both Jameson and Bernd may have a common source in *Le discours antillais* by Edouard Glissant, from whom Bernd also takes the basic frame for her critical development. According to Glissant, literature has a "desacralizing" function, which is demystifying and deconstructive, *and* a "sacralizing" function, "which reassembles the community around its myths, its beliefs, its imaginary, and its ideology" (quoted by Bernd).

For Bernd, literature's sacralizing function in terms of foundational myths leads to discursive homogenization and therefore to a system of exclusion or misrepresentation of that which resists being homogenized. In the Brazilian case, from origins

222 ◆ ALBERTO MOREIRAS

through the romantic period, sacralization took the summary form of "textualization of American space as mythical and marvelous; the conception of time based on a nostalgic attitude toward the past; and the construction of an exclusive discourse, based on a misrepresentation of the Indian."

But in sacralization the desacralizing function lies only half-dormant. As specific sacralizing ideologemes come to exhaustion, their desacralizing negative, always working them over in secrecy, comes gradually to light. The always-specific sacralizing/desacralizing tension within the literary work ends up by changing signs. In Brazil, this happens with the advent of Brazilian *modernismo*, which "initiated the process of destabilizing a homogenizing perspective that had become consolidated." Within the desacralization, however, a new sacralization also lurks.

Bernd thinks that the Brazilian process of democratization, after 1980, is accompanied by a new period that self-consciously embraces or attempts a synthesis of the sacralizing/desacralizing poles. "Contemporary Brazilian literature sees the emergence of texts that associate the recuperation of myths with their constant demythologization, and the rediscovery of collective memory with its continuous rewriting, implying an incessant questioning of oneself." Bernd concludes by associating this synthetic stage to marvelous realism.

Bernd's dialectic model does not therefore culminate in an apotheosis of self-recognition. Meaning and being are held apart by the impossibility of stasis between sacralization and desacralization. In the synthetic mode, which is always to some extent involved, community definition poses itself as its own undermining. The translative endeavor that rules over the interplay of homogenization and heterogenization within a given community's cultural production, as a translation of itself, preempts the possibility of a fixation of identity. But it does so not in recourse to difference. The incessant work of community translation in "continuous rewriting" is in fact simultaneously the radical unworking of identity *and* of difference. What remains is nothing like the original, but, precisely, its allegorical subversion.

I started my critique of the essays in this collection by referring to what we could now call the technological approach to identity, which I found exemplified in Aínsa and Dussel. According to this approach, cultural identity exhausts the determination of a community's being, and therefore it remains a task that must be systematically carried out into completion if that community is to achieve historical maturity in universal recognition. This is the approach that I would like to call "modern," meaning that it is radically caught up within the parameters of modernity.

The postmodern approach, exemplified by Chanady, Perus, and Bernd, follows the notion that identity can only be understood in the allegorical mode, which is to say that identity has no end as it continuously opens itself up to its own undoing. Within this frame, identity has no substantive determination, for it only indicates the set of mechanisms and countermechanisms by which a given cultural community represents itself historically and politically. In other words, identity does not here primarily fulfill an epistemological function, but an ethical function in the critical sense.

Another approach is also to be found within this volume. I want to call it skeptical, because its practitioners seem to be committed to the notion that identity is nothing but a discursive position. For José Rabasa and Pierre Beaucage, if I understand correctly, identity has both epistemological and ethical functions, but only derivatively. Mainly, it is a cultural work, within the historical possibilities of a given social discourse, whose ultimate nature is not structural, but merely superstructural.

In "On Writing Back: Alternative Historiography in *La Florida del Inca*," Rabasa wants to examine "the conditions of possibility of the colonial (colonized) subject to constitute himself or herself as an author and develop a discursive alternative to the West." He briefly but decisively focuses on Fernández de Oviedo and Sahagún to show how their historiography helped establish a disciplinary field within which the parameters of the writing of colonial history were first developed as discursive construction. Within this discursive construction, Rabasa shows that ideological polarities such as that between the colonized and the colonizer, or civilization and barbarism, were actually only the extreme ideological simplification of a much more complex disciplinary web. He then presents Las Casas's and Inca Garcilaso's representations of the noble savage as a case in point: "The noble savage in their discourse is not the opposite of barbarism, but rather simultaneously includes and denies both terms of the opposition." For both of those historiographers something more than a mere inversion of values was at stake. Because Garcilaso wrote from the perspective of an Indian author, his discourse will go so far as to "dismantle and render absurd the categories that inform the prescription that Indians cannot write history." Garcilaso's is then an alternative history made possible by the disciplinary web that it does not so much subvert as expand. Alternative practices within a given disciplinary field, Rabasa seems to be saying, exist only because the disciplinary field does not just operate according to a polarized logic of exclusion: within it, cultural particulars can develop that, even if tendentially they might threaten the stability of the constituted field, in practice they do not. Rabasa's essay documents the presence of alternative colonial history as made possible by the fact that a particular perspectival dominance is always being enacted within the field. Thus, alternative history does not develop against the field, only against one or another of its particulars. It actually contributes to the field's sedimentation.

I am not quite sure whether Rabasa would accept my interpretation of his position as involving a radical critique of the emancipatory possibilities of alternative identities. Granted, oppositional subject-effects are produced by nontraditional historiography. Those subject-effects, however, by contributing to the stability of the discursive field, make hegemonic positions within it all the more dominant. Alternative identities, in that sense, would have a merely compensatory virtue. They would be comforting to the individual able to express them, and to the community able to recognize itself in them. But their epistemological or ethical value would be limited to that of providing internal critiques of representational excesses within the hegemonic discourse. If this position could actually be read in Rabasa's essay, he does not explicitly develop it.

Beaucage's "The Opossum and the Coyote: Ethnic Identity and Ethnohistory in the Sierra Norte de Puebla (Mexico)" begins by tracing the history of the identity question for ethnographic and ethnohistorical studies, and continues by establishing some theoretical propositions that will frame the results of his field investigation. He distinguishes ethnic identity from culture, providing an important definition:

> *Ethnic identity* or *ethnicity* . . . designs the symbolic array
> by which a human group . . . defines itself by its
> culture, which, in turn, means an explicit or implicit
> relationship/distinction with (an)other culture(s). For
> there is no "ethnic phenomenon" without interethnicity,
> without a relationship (of whatever kind) with the
> Other. It follows that, in the context of the Americas,
> *Indianity* or *Indianness*, as an identity, is necessarily a
> postconquest phenomenon. (Beaucage's emphasis)

Ethnicity is then not culture, but a "work on culture" whose result is "to break the continuum of society at a given point" in order to create ethnic frontiers through specific assignments of identity and difference. Another important corollary of Beaucage's explanation is that ethnic markers must be simple in order to be effective, and therefore they "tend to become stereotypes." Of decisive importance for a theory of identity developed from critical reflection on literary and philosophical production is the following: "If this 'ethnic work on culture' is to be efficient in building identity, it must remain largely unconscious. Culture modified as ethnicity has to be considered *the real culture* even if the gap with observable reality is evident to the members of another cultural group and to internal dissidents" (Beaucage's emphasis).

The next step in Beaucage's careful argumentation is to state that only a historical perspective can help us understand construction of ethnic identity, not only because the ethnic group is "materially, a product of History" but also because "ethnic ideology also re-creates History so as to give consistency and meaning to a concrete situation and political projects." Beaucage's position is in counterdistinction to the functionalists and the Marxists for whom identity is only "a[n] [ideological] *sign* of a hidden, more important reality," and thus false consciousness, and to the partisans of an essentialist cultural hermeneutics, for whom ethnic identity is only superficially affected by social and economic changes. For Beaucage ethnic identity is "the result of an (unconscious) process of *constructing difference*" (his emphasis) and can only be properly studied through the integration of "economic, political, and ethnocultural dimensions into a historical perspective."

Beaucage's account is of critical importance, in my opinion, and not least for its vitriolic corollary that identity must be unconscious in order to be effective, which would seem to dismantle some of the political pretensions of collections such as this one. Critical analyses, in effect, void identity markers instead of giving them ground, and do reveal them, from the point of view of the critic, as ultimately arbitrary although historically conditioned constructions that, once perceived as such, cannot be kept except in bad faith. Thus, critical discourse develops a theoretical dimension within which identity must renounce both epistemological and ethical pretensions. Although unconscious identity is still perceived by Beaucage as an important cultural marker, it can have no proper emancipatory value, because its virtue depends on uncritical preservation.

Only one objection: when Beaucage is talking about the religious structure of the Sierra Norte indigenous groups, he concedes that "this is the deepest level of Indian identity, one to which the individual is slowly introduced by his or her elders, as he or she grows, and which may be only partly revealed to foreigners, after years of relationship." I would suggest that this single insight has the potential to throw Beaucage's theory of ethnic identity as historical construction into serious difficulties. If indeed domestic religion is the deepest level of Indian identity, and if this deepest level may be a secret kept from the foreigner, then it seems to me that the foreigner does not have a ground to claim explication of identity from an external, historical perspective. If religious ritual is the deepest level, it is because religious ritual is conceivably understood as the essence of ethnic identity. But this essence is necessarily left out of account by outsiders, necessarily out of reach of outsiders, whether they are intent on explaining it as a mere historical construct or willing to believe that it hides a secret whose brilliance, as Borges would say, could well arrest our thought or destroy our world.

III

I now turn to Borges, as I promised. If all third-world texts are necessarily allegorical, "Tlön, Uqbar, Orbis Tertius" will be too. In this case, however, the national allegory runs into its own impossibility. "Tlön, Uqbar, Orbis Tertius" allegorizes the national allegory. That it also resists modernity by delimiting its mythological presuppositions goes without saying. Borges inaugurates in this short story what I would call a postsymbolic approach to identity. We will see that Borges's beyond-the-symbolic does not fall into allegorical procedures, but questions them from the point of view of the void that the allegory always tries to hide—or to shelter—within itself. Borges does not argue for hybridity against identity, or for difference against mere plurality, and he is equally far from multiculturalism. He does not even concern himself, in my opinion, with skepticism. His melancholy construction moves toward an intensely libidinal perception of history, any history, as symptomatic of the rare but always pending disease of disaster. Whether or not his position is nihilistic, I will not try to decide. Theodor Adorno said, "What would happiness be that was not measured by the immeasurable grief at what is" (Adorno 200; quoted by Cornell 17). Borges's position may well hide a utopian impulse. Its analysis seems fitting as conclusion to a collection of essays that, insofar as I can see, have all assumed a recognition of the end of utopia. As the last of my epilogue, this analysis is also meant to reframe the volume's introduction, and therefore, inevitably, everything in between. To Shohat's advice that, before every analysis of identity, it would be well to ask who is asking what questions, and in the name of what political visions and goals, let me now add that a critical understanding of identity must find its intellectual weapons wherever it can. Borges's critique remains, in my opinion, extraordinarily powerful, and certainly not to be canceled by ad hominem argumentation.

The narrator of "Tlön," Borges, pretends that his reaction to the invasion of our world by Tlön is just to go on quietly with his "undecisive" translation of Thomas Browne's *Urn Burial*—a study on epitaphs. But in fact his reaction is to write "Tlön," which is primarily to translate the Tlönian disjunction of his/our world, as epitaphs translate death and in so doing articulate a kind of survival. Borges responds, in and with his act of translation, to Tlön's universal, totalizing writing, to Tlön's "hypermnesiac interiority" (Derrida, *Ulysse* 104), which is, at the time of the narrator's writing, in the process of self-constitution. Let me assume, if only for the sake of argument, but following the Jamesonian idea that postmodern writing is the allegorical representation of the unrepresentable movement of transnational capitalism, that the relationship between Tlön and our world is a figure of the relationship obtaining between local societies and the global system. Even within this figure—a markedly allegorical figure, a representation of the unrepresentable— the implications of the narrator's performative are far from easily thinkable. To translate a universal translation machine . . . from what side or what fissure can one contemplate such a task? And what is the status of the paradoxical confirmation "Borges" gives to the power of Tlön at the same time that he announces his unconditional opposition to it?

"Tlön," the text, as countersignature and abyssal legitimation of Tlön's world, is not only an epitaph or postscriptum, but also a prologue to the immense labor of translation in progress. As you may remember, Tlön's translation of our world will mean the universal instauration of "Tlön's (conjectural) 'primitive tongue' [idioma primitivo]" (424). With it, "French, English, and mere Spanish will disappear from the planet. The world will be Tlön" (424; my translations of Borges throughout). The multiplicity of languages, of tongues, of idioms, will yield to an only tongue, which will inevitably retrace, translate, but inversely, the process narrated in the biblical story of the Tower of Babel.

According to the biblical book of Genesis, when there was only one language in all the earth, Shem's children, who had left their place of origin, decided to settle down and build a city and a tower whose summit would touch the heavens. They wanted, the text says, "to make a name for themselves," to make themselves unique within the common indistinctiveness, and thus to abandon their errancy, and not to be scattered across the earth. But God, offended, "confuses their tongues." He proclaims His name in the city, Babel, meaning "confusion," and He condemns the Shemites to disseminate across the face of all the earth (cf. Derrida, "Tours" 209-18).

God's war, by the act of giving His name to the Shemites, takes away their name (the name they wanted to make for themselves) and substitutes an idiom, or multiple idioms, for it. God's name is at once for and against dissemination. God's war is a terrible act of paternal love. With his Babelic name, Confusion, God provides untranslatability. But, in so doing, he also gives the possibility of translation. The untranslatable, that is, the properly idiomatic that refuses to let itself be made common possession, is the necessary and perhaps sufficient condition for the task of the translator.

Like the Babelic project, Tlön's creation is a political act. The politics implied are strictly antipaternal, atheist, antitheological. Tlön is nothing in principle but resistance to the Babelic loss of the name, to the Babelic gain of the idiom. From its origins in Idealist circles of Enlightened England, the society whose strange goal is to create an autonomous world goes underground until its resurgence two centuries later in Memphis, Tennessee. Its project is a transcendental project. It seeks the immanentization of transcendence. It wants to create God's kingdom on earth. It is a cosmopolitan project that, upon its resurgence, becomes a curiously American project. It emerges in Memphis, Tennessee, a nominal translation of the site of the pyramids, the pharaonic eskathon, the tomb of logos, and therefore the center of Transcendental signification. In Memphis, a millionaire called Buckley sponsors the publication of a so-called Tlön Encyclopedia.[9] Mr. Buckley, the narrator says, "wants to demonstrate to the nonexistent God that mortal men are able to build a world" (421). Notice the strange structure of that appeal, the hole in the center of the sentence. Did Buckley know that the conception of a world by mortals was also for essential reasons the destruction of the world? The narrator knows it, as his melancholy depends on that knowledge. But Buckley—is he a lucid, active nihilist, or a merely reactive one?

Buckley cuts a melancholy figure too, in perpetual confrontation with a nonexistent God, but a God who makes Himself felt nevertheless, perhaps because of His nonexistence, because of that non-, that deprivation whose gift is the ineludible necessity of a new alliance in the symbolic order, but this time a radically post-Babelic one. It is yet again not just possible but imperative "to make a name for oneself." Following the imperative, Buckley, whether he knows it or not, lucid or blind, also follows the principles of mournful introjection. Buckley's new world has the status of a fetish. Buckley is the prototype of the melancholy artist, whom Julia Kristeva introduces in *The Black Sun*: "The artist consumed by melancholy is at the same time the most relentless in his struggle against the symbolic abdication that blankets him" (9).

The project of creating a new world in open challenge to the essential colonizing power, a paternal God who is perhaps already dead, but whose law posthumously imposes the need for gifts and sacrifice: that project obeys the laws of mourning, the psychic requirement to project onto the symbolic order, as defensive introjection, the decisive loss of the primary object. Borges is staging nothing less than the basic paradigm for the Latin American quest for identity, for all identity quests, in fact, as the postcolonial quest is only a particular case of a universal historical compulsion.

But the primary object is not the paternal object. The loss of God, which in my opinion counts here as the loss of metropolitan "love" and of its sheltering cloak, is a substitute loss, a loss of a second order. How is "Tlön" a reference to primary object loss? The lucidity of "Tlön" is precisely not to posit a symbolic identity as the substitute for another symbolic identity. "Tlön" is postulating a postsymbolic identity, which is, as such, based in an idiomatic, idiotic, post-Babelic acquisition, but not in the acquisition of a new proper name, which could not but function as the sign of a renewed symbolic alliance at the point in which such alliances are no longer possible.

In "Sign and Symbol in Hegel's *Aesthetics*," Paul de Man defines the Hegelian symbol as "the mediation between the mind and the physical world of which art manifestly partakes" (763). Through this mediation, art has the function of conciliating consciousness and world. Consciousness shows itself to be "organic," that is, unifiable with phenomenal reality in and through symbolic processes. The Kantian distinction between experience and representation comes to meet its cancelation in the Hegelian aesthetic symbol. For Hegel, art's function is utopian and messianic, in the sense that in art spirit and nature respond to each other, that is, find their correspondence. The coincidence of meaning and being is thus made ultimately possible. This is the radical way in which the symbol comes to displace allegory as the privileged trope of aesthetic representation. With "Tlön," though, the thought of a correspondence between spirit and nature, between experience and representation, between meaning and being, is destroyed, at least in its traditional sense.

The new conception of the world that "Tlön" announces as about to replace that which is still ours is antitheological, because it is based on the loss of God's name, even if that name is Babel, Confusion. Tlön loses Babel, loses all names, all substantive, proper names where God could have ciphered the law of the humans' eternal confusion: "There are no substantives in Tlön's conjectural *Ursprache*" (414). This is a crucial datum: it is because Tlön refuses all substantivation that Tlön must postulate a world that is necessarily to be understood antirepresentationally and antisymbolically. Tlön then appears as a radical attempt at approaching, i.e., creating, a pre-objectual world, which is what Kristeva calls "la Chose": "Let me posit the 'Thing' as the real that does not lend itself to signification, the center of attraction and repulsion, seat of the sexuality from which the object of desire will become separated" (13). It is because the object of desire in this world is the world itself, rather than any intraworldly object, that is, any object in the proper sense, that for Tlön's inhabitants, as Borges says, "the world . . . is not a concourse of objects in space; it is a heterogeneous series of independent acts" (414). In Borges's sentence, heterogeneity posits the primary real, which is unsignifiable and therefore unorganizable.

Borges's text, like mom's body, the thing in itself, or the death of a loved one, takes us to a region of thought where reason suffers paralysis and becomes catastrophic. It requires to be thought, but it makes itself unthinkable. It requires to be thought on the very basis of its unthinkability. The conflict is absolute and unsymbolizable. Borges's text inhabits an aberrant mourning, a scandal, a disaster of a magnitude similar to the one that takes the Peruvian José María Arguedas to inscribe the final period of his writing upon his forehead, with a revolver; similar to the one that takes Rigoberta Menchú to the painful decision of not having children; to the one that takes Luisa Valenzuela to hand her signature over to the brujo López Rega in *Cola de lagartija*; or to the one that takes Alejandra Vidal, in Ernesto Sábato's *Sobre héroes y tumbas*, to throw gasoline around her bedroom and burn herself up next to her mad father's corpse.

The site of these disasters is the site of the necessity to postulate a project. To posit heterogeneity is to homogenize it; to project the unrepresentable is to represent it. To allegorize is then to authorize. To realize this, and to keep enough lucidity to inhabit its light, to be able to write it in its forced and forceful duplicity, makes the Borgesian text active not reactive, historical not antihistorical, melancholy and joyful, nihilistic but also preparatory. Everything depends on the distance that Borges takes concerning Buckley's project at the same moment in which he repeats it, and precisely through repeating it, that is, through writing it. In that distance we have an absolute critique of identity.

The fundamental act of "Tlön" is narrating the Tlönian project. The narrator says, "There are no substantives in Tlön's conjectural *Ursprache*" (414). But to mention this *Ursprache*, to conjecture it, to posit it is already to substantivize the lack of proper names. In the same way, and certainly not casually, we learn that, within Tlön's language, "the fact that nobody believes in the substantive paradoxically makes their number interminable" (415). In other words, if every idiomatic act creates its own object, as happens by definition in Tlön, then every idiomatic act constructs a new proper name. A totally constructed language, that is, a language that has purposefully abandoned all moorings in the referential real, is the most totalizing, substantive act the human imagination can conceivably think, and do. Idealism then becomes the most terrible of materialisms, because it drives itself to its own absolute negation.

The loss of the common names of things in the Babelic fall is the loss of symbolic capacity. Afterward, meaning and being no longer coincide. Post-Babelic times are idiomatic times, which is to say, asymbolic times, because the capacity to produce the symbol has been destroyed by confusion. When the asymbolic knows itself, and makes itself an explicit project of world formation, the asymbolic actively becomes antisymbolic. Borges radically exploits Tlön's antisymbolic strength, which is the antisymbolic strength of all idealisms. All idealisms, one can say, lack substantives. In 1940, the ominous war year in which the short story is dated, Borges situates the realization of the paradoxically antisymbolic strength of all totalitarian systems, a force that necessarily breaks through the possible unity of spirit and nature, abandoning the pre-objectual world, the real, for its own self-generative capacity.

Borges perceives and resists that, but not in an anachronic or reactionary return to the symbolic. He does it through the mere constatation, and its complex translation into writing, of the fact that the antisymbolic as such is, at the limit, at the point of totalization, the most violent substantivization of the lack of the substantive. The so-called *hrönir*, the Tlönian objects that are starting to make their appearance and insidiously colonize our world, are the sinister proofs of the destructive return of the substantive.

"Tlön, Uqbar, Orbis Tertius," as an artwork postulating the antisymbolic, as giving name to Tlön's heterotopic project, would also be one of those *hrönir*, except that in "Tlön" it is said that everything depends on surviving them, on translating them, on resisting their damaging substantivation. Because "Tlön" translates the absolute machine of universal translation, "Tlön" postulates its own posthumous, postsymbolic character.

The resistance to Tlön in the Borgesian writing, although it does allegorize the need for postcolonial resistance to the metropolitan symbolic, is primarily a resistance to any postulation in the symbolic order, including, then, eminently, any postulation concerning cultural identity. This postsymbolic writing, because it would rather embrace the loss of the primary object, is a depressive, melancholy writing. The measure of its lucidity is given in the way in which it can maintain itself as writing. If all writing is a symbol, if all writing is a failed symbol that must construct itself as allegory, then postsymbolic writing lives in self-mourning. It survives in an undecisive labor of translation whose precariousness, however, shelters the uncompromising joy of knowing itself faithful to itself, following its own law. Its survival attests to a difficult possibility: national allegories, cultural searches for social identity, may not be the ultimate destiny of postcolonial, Latin American writing.

Borges's rigorous theoretical investigation of the cultural identity problematic is among the absent, and among the most incisively critical, in a volume that has also failed to concern itself with at least two other major positions on the subject. I can only mention them now: José María Arguedas's final word in *El zorro de arriba y el zorro de abajo*, and the ongoing theorization undertaken under the misleadingly unified name of liberation theology. I suspect that analysis would show them, in spite of appearances, to be closer to the Borgesian postsymbolic than to the other positions brilliantly represented in this collection.

Let me end with a nagging doubt, much more than an afterthought, but a thought that I have had to keep at bay lest I could not write the essay you have just read: identity is Europe's thought, Europe's most proper thought. Can we think postcolonial identity without occidentalizing, and thus recolonializing, the subject of inquiry? What is identity for the Quechua language? How does a speaker of Yucatec Maya relate to identity thinking? In the endless circulation of signs and concepts that organizes the possibility of cultural production today we are still not hybrid enough, not multicultural enough. Our hegemony, the one that lives through us, is the one that dictates hybridity and multiculturalism, any and all thoughts of counterhegemonic plurality as a means to keep the night of the world in place. The task of critical thinking has barely started.[10]

Notes

1. The Introduction to *On Edge: The Crisis of Contemporary Latin American Culture*, George Yúdice et al., editors, states: "The master discourses of the nation and hispanicity [have] fallen on hard times and no longer [project] the new horizon for the Latin American masses" (xiii). In his own contribution to the volume Yúdice writes: "There have been many different projects for cultural hegemony in the twenty-odd Latin American nations, but they all have one feature in common: its yet-unattained status" (10). Yúdice refuses to talk in terms of identity, and chooses the less-ambiguous term "democratization." I think Yúdice's choice is an admirably effective way of cutting through the sedimented layers of ideology attaching to identity discourse in order to get to the bottom line, which

is simply sociopolitical emancipation, and the ways of furthering it through work in the cultural sphere. For Yúdice, the way to accomplish that is by establishing what he calls rearticulatory practices with alternative traditions — whether those traditions come from Latin American history or from metropolitan developments is not in any case the main issue. That rearticulation, which in Latin America necessarily implies a critique of modernity in the interest of democratization, will follow what Yúdice, adopting a term from Silviano Santiago, calls pastiche. My title for the present essay is meant as recognition of my indebtedness to Yúdice's essay, and to the constellation of critics he mentions, such as Silviano Santiago, Nelly Richard, Néstor García Canclini, and Ticio Escobar.

2. Even extremely clever investigations of the field, such as María Luisa Puga's novel *Pánico o peligro*, fall prey to its demonic predeterminations. Thus, the end of Puga's book does not just represent a conventional, flat ending, but is, rigorously enough, the necessary distillation of Susana's radical quest within the parameters she has made available to herself. A lifelong search for personal identity in dialogic difference terminates in the poignant reaffirmation of a logical impasse: my difference is your identity, your identity is my difference, but please let's not make it antagonic. My point is that the identity/difference dialectic is secretly a totalizing monology. To be sure, Puga understands that, which is what makes her novel one of the best contemporary interventions in the debate.

3. Readers who are already familiar with it will recognize in my appeal to technology a reference to the work of Martin Heidegger in "The Question Concerning Technology." Although I cannot now comment on it, let me refer to the best explication I know of the Heideggerian concept of technology, Zimmerman's *Heidegger's Confrontation with Modernity*.

4. On these issues, see Clark and Cornell, and their discussions of the anti-Hegelian trend in contemporary philosophy, from Heidegger, Adorno, and Blanchot to Levinas and Derrida. See also the forthcoming collection of essays by Paul de Man, *Aesthetic Ideology*.

5. The question of the conflicting values of identity as a philosophical or as an ideological concept is of course quite complicated. In some metropolitan accounts, identity is the foremost concept of Western philosophy. For others, identity is the foremost concept of Western metaphysics. In the latter interpretation, identity presupposes the active forgetting of the difference between being and beings. For the former, there is no such difference; or rather, such a difference is a pseudoproblem, because identity has already dealt with it effectively by postulating that the sum of beings equals being. If we grant that metaphysics is a philosophical ideology, then the truly critical project concerning identity is to disentangle it from its privileged position, in order to show that identity is not beyond ideology, but, on the contrary, that its ascent as an ideological sign marks the beginning of the historical enterprise of concealment undertaken by the Greeks, and partially assumed by Judeo-Christian culture, and that it is therefore the very logos of ideology. There is no naive use of the concept of identity, because identity is not the bottom line of all there is to think — at least not for any thinking that wants to present itself as critical thinking.

6. This essay certainly does not mean to condemn, but only to critique, the important Latin American tradition of identity thinking. This is the tradition that

has managed to keep alive, in philosophical terms, the crucial point that being from Latin America should have a decisive effect on how one thinks. All thinking is of course historically and socially rooted. From Andrés Bello and José Martí through José Carlos Mariátegui, Pedro Henríquez Ureña, Alfonso Reyes, and Samuel Ramos to Leopoldo Zea, Angel Rama, Antonio Cornejo Polar, and Enrique Dussel, to name just a few contributors, Latin American identity thinking has been a stimulating source of intellectual energy and a repository of anticolonialist suspicion. Let me also recognize a personal debt by mentioning José Luis Gómez Martínez's book *Bolivia: Un pueblo en busca de su identidad* and Djelal Kadir's radically different *Questing Fictions*. Another personal debt, one of the more radical recent interventions in the identity debate, is Carlos Alonso's *The Spanish American Regional Novel: Modernity and Autochthony*.

7. I will not directly engage the essays by Arancibia and Zavala, or the second contribution by Enrique Dussel. My reasons for not doing so can be summarized in the following sense: I have not found a way to make them fit into my own narrative. I have not purposefully wanted to avoid them or to silence the recognition of their contribution.

8. The article initiating the controversy on Jameson's position is Aijaz Ahmad, "Jameson's Rhetoric of Otherness and the 'National Allegory.' " See Madhava Prasad, "On the Question of a Theory of (Third World) Literature" for an update of the issues and a bibliographical summary. See also, as directly relevant to the Latin American case and an excellent reflection on the Jamesonian predicament, Santiago Colás, "The Third World in Jameson's *Postmodernism or the Cultural Logic of Late Capitalism*." Yúdice, "Postmodernity and Transnational Capitalism in Latin America," also critiques Jameson.

9. Buckley has a homonymous character in Joyce's *Finnegans Wake*: an Irish soldier quite concerned with Irish nationalism, who will or will not shoot a certain Russian general. The correspondence between the two Buckleys should, I think, be studied, not just because both are pharmakic, sacrificial figures (with a goat in their name, and the law therein inscribed); also because in both *Finnegans Wake* and "Tlön" Buckley barely conceals a reference to Bishop Berkeley, the Idealist philosopher, whose function in *Finnegans Wake* as co(de)-constructor, together with Saint Patrick, of some motifs of Irish national identity is well known to Joyceans. On top of that, *Finnegans Wake* places the conversation between the pidgin fella Bilkilly-Belkelly-Balkally and the patfella Same Patholick under the mood of anxious melancholy. See *Finnegans Wake* 611, passim.

10. Three recent books must be cited here, as they are important enough to redirect the totality of the identity debate from a radical historiographic perspective: Gruzinski's *La colonización de lo imaginario*, Lienhard's *La voz y su huella*, and Mignolo's *The Darker Side of the European Renaissance*.

Works Cited

Adorno, Theodor. *Minima Moralia: Reflections from Damaged Life*. Trans. E. F. N. Jephcott. London: New Left, 1974.

Ahmad, Aijaz. "Jameson's Rhetoric of Otherness and the 'National Allegory.' " *Social Text* 17 (Fall 1987): 3-25.

Alonso, Carlos. *The Spanish American Regional Novel: Modernity and Autochthony*. Cambridge: Cambridge Univ. Press, 1990.

Arguedas, José María. *El zorro de arriba y el zorro de abajo*. Ed. Eva-Marie Fell. Madrid: Archivos, 1990 [1971].

Borges, Jorge Luis. "Tlön, Uqbar, Orbis Tertius." *Prosa completa*. Vol. 1. Barcelona: Bruguera, 1980. 409-424.

Burgos, Elizabeth, ed. *Me llamo Rigoberta Menchú y así me nació la conciencia*. Mexico City: Siglo veintiuno, 1985.

Clark, Timothy. *Derrida, Heidegger, Blanchot: Sources of Derrida's Notion and Practice of Literature*. Cambridge: Cambridge Univ. Press, 1992.

Colás, Santiago. "The Third World in Jameson's *Postmodernism or the Cultural Logic of Late Capitalism*." *Social Text* 31-32 (1992): 258-270.

Cornell, Drucilla. *The Philosophy of the Limit*. New York: Routledge, 1992.

de Man, Paul. "Sign and Symbol in Hegel's *Aesthetics*." *Critical Inquiry* 8, 4 (1982): 761-775.

———. *Aesthetic Ideology*. Ed. Andrej Warminzky. Minneapolis: Univ. of Minnesota Press, forthcoming.

Derrida, Jacques. "Des Tours de Babel." In *Difference in Translation*. Ed. Joseph F. Graham. Ithaca: Cornell Univ. Press, 1985. 165-207; 209-248.

———. *Ulysse gramophone. Deux mots pour Joyce*. Paris: Galilée, 1987.

Dussel, Enrique. *Filosofía de la liberación*. Bogotá: Universidad de Santo Tomás, 1980.

Glissant, Edouard. *Le discours antillais*. Paris: Seuil, 1981.

Gómez Martínez, José Luis. *Bolivia: Un pueblo en busca de su identidad*. La Paz: Los amigos del libro, 1988.

Gruzinski, Serge. *La colonización de lo imaginario. Sociedades indígenas y occidentalización en el México español. Siglos XVI-XVIII*. Trans. Jorge Ferreiro. Mexico City: Fondo de Cultura Económica, 1991.

Harvey, David. *The Condition of Postmodernity: An Enquiry into the Origins of Cultural Change*. Oxford: Basil Blackwell, 1989.

Heidegger, Martin. "The Question Concerning Technology." In *The Question Concerning Technology and Other Essays*. Trans. William Lovitt. New York: Harper, 1977.

Jameson, Fredric. "Third-World Literature in the Era of Multinational Capitalism." *Social Text* 15 (Fall 1986): 65-88.

Joyce, James. *Finnegans Wake*. New York: Viking, 1984.

Kadir, Djelal. *Questing Fictions: Latin America's Family Romance*. Minneapolis: Univ. of Minnesota Press, 1986.

Kristeva, Julia. *The Black Sun: Depression and Melancholia*. Trans. Leon Roudiez. New York: Columbia Univ. Press, 1989.

Lienhard, Martin. *La voz y su huella. Escritura y conflicto étnico-cultural en América Latina 1492-1988*. Revised ed. Lima: Horizonte, 1992.

Mignolo, Walter. *The Darker Side of the European Renaissance: Literacy, Coloniality, and Colonization*. Ann Arbor: Univ. of Michigan Press, forthcoming.

Prasad, Madhava. "On the Question of a Theory of (Third World) Literature." *Social Text* 31-32 (1992): 57-83.

Puga, María Luisa. *Pánico o peligro*. Mexico City: Siglo veintiuno, 1984.

Sábato, Ernesto. *Sobre héroes y tumbas*. Barcelona: Bruguera, 1982 [1961].

Shohat, Ella. "Notes on the 'Post-Colonial.' " *Social Text* 31-32 (1992): 99-113.

Valenzuela, Luisa. *Cola de lagartija*. Buenos Aires: Bruguera, 1983.

Yúdice, George. "Postmodernity and Transnational Capitalism in Latin America." In *On Edge*. Ed. Yúdice et al. 1-28.

———, Jean Franco, and Juan Flores, eds. *On Edge: The Crisis of Contemporary Latin American Culture*. Minneapolis: Univ. of Minnesota Press, 1992.

Zimmerman, Michael E. *Heidegger's Confrontation with Modernity: Technology, Politics, Art*. Bloomington: Indiana Univ. Press, 1990.

◆ Contributors

Fernando Aínsa. Writer and critic working at UNESCO in Paris. His numerous books on Latin American literature include *Las trampas de Onetti* (1970), *Tiempo reconquistado. Siete ensayos sobre literatura uruguaya* (1977), *Los buscadores de la utopía* (1977), *Identidad cultural de Iberoamérica en su narrativa* (1986), and *Necesidad de la utopía* (1990). He has also published two novels, *Con cierto asombro* (1968) and *Con acento extranjero* (1985); two collections of short stories, *Las palomas de Rodrigo* and *Los naufragios de Malinow* (both in 1988); and a book of aphorisms, *D'ici, de là-bas. Jeux de distance* (1986).

Blanca de Arancibia. Professor of French literature at the Universidad Nacional de Cuyo, Mendoza (Argentina). She has co-edited *Teorías y prácticas críticas* (1992), edits the *Boletín del Centro de Estudios de Literatura Francesa*, and has published numerous articles, including "Un continente de dioses sepultados: Abel Posse y la ficción metahistórica" (in *Pensamiento Latinoamericano*, 1991); "Le mythe du Minotaure chez Yourcenar, Borges et Cortázar" (in *Marguerite Yourcenar et l'art; l'art de Marguerite Yourcenar*, 1989); and "Le récit fictif, relève de l'histoire" (in *Mythologies de l'écriture et figures de l'altérité*, forthcoming).

Pierre Beaucage. Professor of anthropology at the Université de Montréal, Canada. He has written several articles on identity construction among the Amerindians of Latin America. His publications include "Démographie, culture, politique: la condition indienne au Mexique" (*Anthropologie et sociétés*, 1987); "Les identités indiennes: folklore ou facteur de transformation" (*Construction/destruction sociale des idées: alternances, récurrences, nouveautés*, 1987); "L'effort et la vie: ethnosémantique du travail chez les Garifonas du Honduras et les Maseuals (Nahuats) du Mexique" (*Travail, capital et société*, 1989).

Zilá Bernd. Professor of French and Brazilian literature at the Universidade Federal do Rio Grande do Sul, Brazil. Among her many articles and books, mainly on negritude and Afro-Brazilian literature, are *A Questão da Negritude* (1984), *Negritude e Literatura na América Latina* (1987), *Antologia de Poesia Negra Brasileira—Cem Anos de Consciência Negra no Brasil* (1988), *O que é Negritude* (1988), *Vozes do Quebec* (1991; coedited with Joseph Mélançon), and *Literatura e Identidade Nacional* (1992).

Amaryll Chanady. Associate professor of comparative literature at the Université de Montréal, Canada. She has written primarily on the fantastic and magical realism, metafiction, discourses of identity, and marginalization. Her publications include *Magical Realism and the Fantastic: Resolved versus Unresolved Antinomy* (1985); "La thématisation de la marginalisation discursive dans le néo-indigénisme équatorien" (*Parole exclusive, parole exclue*, 1990); and "Latin American Discourses of Identity and the Appropriation of the Amerindian Other" (*Sociocriticism*, 1990).

Enrique Dussel. Professor of philosophy at the Universidad Autónoma Metropolitana, Mexico. He is the author of more than thirty books and numerous articles on Latin American history, the philosophy of history, the philosophy of liberation, and the history of ideas. Among his published works are *El episcopado hispanoamericano, institución misionera en defensa del indio (1504-1620)*, 9 vols. (1969-71); *Para una ética de la liberación latinoamericana*, 2 vols. (1973); *La producción teórica de Marx* (1985); *El último*

Marx (1863-1882) y la liberación latinoamericana (1990); and *1492: El encubrimiento del Otro* (1993).

Alberto Moreiras. Assistant professor of Latin American literature at Duke University. He has written *La escritura política de José Hierro* (1987) and *Interpretación y diferencia* (1992), as well as articles on Jorge Luis Borges, José Lezama Lima, Latin American culture, and literary theory.

Françoise Perus. Professor of Latin American literature at the Instituto de Investigaciones Sociales, Mexico. She has published numerous books and articles, especially on the sociology of literature. Her publications include: *Literatura y sociedad en América Latina: el modernismo* (1976) and *Historia y crítica literaria. El realismo social y la crisis de la dominación oligárquica* (1982). She is currently completing two books, *De selvas y selváticos (ensayos de poética histórica)* and *Historia y literatura*.

José Rabasa. Associate professor of Spanish at the University of Maryland, College Park. He has published articles on colonial discourse in Mercator's *Atlas*, Cortés's representation of Tenochtitlan, and the scriptural economy in Columbus's writing. His publications include: "Utopian Ethnology in Las Casas's *Apologética*" (*1492-1992: Re/Discovering Colonial Writing*, Hispanic Issues 4, 1989) and *Inventing America: Spanish Historiography and the Formation of Eurocentrism* (1993). He is currently completing a book on sixteenth-century Florida and New Mexico, *Writing Violence on the Northern Frontier*.

Iris M. Zavala. Professor of Spanish and literary theory at Rijksuniversiteit, Utrecht. She is the author of over twenty books on Unamuno, Valle-Inclán, Darío, modernism and postmodernism, literary theory, utopian socialism, ideology, romanticism, the nineteenth century, and eighteenth-century narrative. Among her titles are *La posmodernidad y M. Bajtín: Una poética dialógica* (1991), *El bolero. Historia de un amor* (1991), and *Colonialism and Culture: Hispanic Modernisms and the Social Imaginary* (1992). She has also published four books of poetry and three novels, the latest of which is *El libro de Apolonia o de las islas*.

◆ **Index**

Compiled by Gwendolyn Barnes-Karol